Zoutpansberg

D1540000

T R A N S V A A L

• Pretoria

• Johannesburg

SWAZILAND

• Lourenço Marques

ORANGE FREE STATE

Modder

• Bloemfontein

BASUTOLAND

Drakensberg

N A T A L

• Port Natal (Durban)

...erg

...ND

HOPE

Gt. Kei

Grahamstown Great Fish R.

...age

• Port Elizabeth

UNION OF SOUTH AFRICA

AND

ADJACENT TERRITORIES

0   50   100   200

MILES

Helen Gorman

ECONOMIC INFLUENCES ON THE SOUTH AFRICAN FRONTIER 1652-1836

Publications of the Institute

CURRENT SERIES

STUDIES ON FOOD, AGRICULTURE, AND WORLD WAR II
STUDIES IN COMMODITY ECONOMICS AND AGRICULTURAL POLICY
STUDIES IN TROPICAL DEVELOPMENT

MISCELLANEOUS PUBLICATIONS

DISCONTINUED SERIES

COMMODITY POLICY STUDIES   GRAIN ECONOMICS SERIES
FATS AND OILS STUDIES   WHEAT STUDIES
WAR-PEACE PAMPHLETS

A Publication of the
FOOD RESEARCH INSTITUTE
STANFORD UNIVERSITY

MISCELLANEOUS PUBLICATION 12

ECONOMIC INFLUENCES ON THE SOUTH AFRICAN FRONTIER 1652-1836

By

S. DANIEL NEUMARK

Stanford University Press

STANFORD, CALIFORNIA

FOOD RESEARCH INSTITUTE

Established at Stanford University, Stanford, California, in 1921, jointly by Carnegie Corporation of New York and the Trustees of the Leland Stanford Junior University, for research in the production, distribution, and consumption of food.

STANFORD UNIVERSITY PRESS, STANFORD, CALIFORNIA

LONDON: OXFORD UNIVERSITY PRESS

© 1957 BY THE BOARD OF TRUSTEES OF THE LELAND STANFORD JUNIOR UNIVERSITY
PRINTED AND BOUND IN THE UNITED STATES OF AMERICA BY STANFORD UNIVERSITY PRESS

Library of Congress Catalog Card Number: 56-7273

DIRECTOR'S PREFACE

The strong upsurge of interest of economists in the economics of development puts a premium on studies that lay bare the pertinent and specific circumstances under which a phase of definite economic expansion has occurred and that can demonstrate and make better understood the interplay of generating causes for such dynamics. This applies particularly to analyses of historical examples of early development in remote colonial parts of the world for which reliable quantitative data happen to be available to an extent sufficient to cover the area as well as the entire period in question.

The present book is the result of such a study. It deals with the development of the frontier economy of the Cape Colony from the middle of the seventeenth to the early part of the nineteenth century. Mr. Neumark taught economics in the Witwatersrand University of Johannesburg for ten years. With a thorough European training and background in agricultural economics he studied the history of agriculture in South Africa. He began to write his manuscript while still living in the Union of South Africa. Later, research assignments that took him to Korea and Indonesia delayed the completion of the book, but by observation and comparison of developments in other agricultural areas he has widened the perspective of the book.

The empirical approach of tracing the various phases of the expansion of the frontier economy through the demand, prices, and production of such commodities as sheep's and goat's meat, butter, soap, sheep's tail fat, tallow, and hides fits into the traditional work of the Food Research Institute. Its result is a new and plausible economic explanation of a substantial part of the extraordinary movement of the frontier, including the Great Trek. The commodity approach adds new vistas to the extensive literature on the colonial history of the Cape. The author presents weighty evidence in support of his hypothesis that even the most distant parts of the frontier were closely tied to the market of the great port of Capetown, and thereby to the military and commercial maritime traffic and the Far Eastern trade of Europe long before the cutting of the isthmus of Suez.

It is gratefully acknowledged that this publication was made possible by funds granted by Carnegie Corporation of New York. The Corporation is not, however, the author, owner, publisher, or proprietor of this publication, and is not to be understood as approving by virtue of its grant any of the statements made or views expressed therein.

KARL BRANDT
Associate Director

STANFORD, CALIFORNIA
September 1956

FOREWORD AND ACKNOWLEDGMENTS

The main work on this study was almost completed some years ago when I was lecturer in economics at the University of the Witwatersrand in Johannesburg. Subsequent perusal of the literature dealing with the early economic development in other parts of the world convinced me, however, that the South African experience, and the American one for that matter, is not entirely unique, but has much in common with that of South America and Australasia. An attempt is therefore made in the concluding chapter to place the frontier expansion in South Africa in a more universal frame by comparison with other new countries.

Following the introduction (chapter 1), chapter 2 provides some historical background for the reader who is unfamiliar with South African history. Chapter 3 deals critically with standard points of view and explanations of frontier expansion.

The central point of our thesis is that the frontier economy of the Cape was to a considerable extent a market-bound exchange economy. The comparative advantages of arable and pastoral farming in relation to the market demand at the Cape for arable and pastoral products are examined in chapter 4. Chapter 5 examines the nature of the demand for meat and slaughter stock at the Cape in relation to Dutch and foreign shipping. In chapter 6 an estimate is made of the amount of meat, in terms of live animals, required by ships putting into Table Bay. An attempt is also made to demonstrate the connection between the number of ships calling at the Cape and the extent of the expansion into the interior. Chapter 7 deals with the nature of the demand for other animal products such as butter, sheep's tail fat, ostrich feathers, ivory, etc.

In chapter 8 we examine the structure of the frontier economy as determined by natural conditions, market demand for frontier products, and transport conditions. Particular attention is drawn to the importance of soap production in the frontier economy. Chapter 9 examines the cattle trade with native tribes and its relation to the expansion movement.

Chapters 10 and 11 deal with the frontier economy in relation to the Cape market during the period 1793–1826, while in chapter 12 the development of a new center of trade and communication in the east is analyzed. Chapter 13 examines the role played by the itinerant trader (the smous) in the expansion movement, and, finally, chapter 14 deals with the frontier economy during the period 1826–36 leading up to the Great Trek.

I should like to thank Professor J. S. Marais of the University of the Witwatersrand, Professor C. W. de Kiewiet, formerly of Cornell University and now president of the University of Rochester, and Professor Carter Goodrich of Columbia University for constructive criticism of the early draft of the manuscript. Professor S. H. Frankel of Nuffield College, Oxford, Professor A. J. H. van der Walt of Pretoria, and Professor W. O. Brown, director of the Africa Research and Studies Program, Boston University, were also kind enough to read the early draft of the manuscript.

My colleagues in the Food Research Institute read the revised draft and made valuable suggestions, and I am particularly indebted to Professors Merrill K. Bennett and Karl Brandt for their valuable editorial guidance, encouragement, and advice. Finally, acknowledgment is due to Mr. P. Stanley King and Helen Gorman for their kind assistance with the maps.

S. Daniel Neumark

Stanford, California
October 15, 1955

CONTENTS

WEIGHTS AND MEASURES, CURRENCY UNITS, EX-CHANGE RATES, AND STATISTICAL NOTES

WEIGHTS

muid = 3.1 bu.

leaguer = 153.7 U.S. gallons

tun = 252 wine gallons

morgen = 2.12 acres

CURRENCY UNITS FROM EARLY EIGHTEENTH CENTURY AT CAPE OF GOOD HOPE

rix-dollar

1 rix-dollar = 8 schillings or 48 stuivers

schilling [skilling]

1 schilling = 6 stuivers

stuiver [stiver]

duyte [doit]

RATE OF EXCHANGE FOR THE RIX-DOLLAR, IN CAPETOWN, SPECIFIED YEARS 1795–1825*

(United Kingdom shillings and pence per Rix-dollar)

Year	Rate		Year	Rate	
	s.	d.		s.	d.
1795.............	4	0	1820.............	1	9.00
1805.............	3	4.00	1821.............	1	8.00
1816.............	2	1.00	1822.............	1	5.25
1817.............	1	9.25	1823.............	1	6.75
1818.............	1	9.00	1824.............	1	5.50
1819.............	1	10.25	1825.............	1	6.00

* Data for 1795 from G. M. Theal, *History of South Africa Since 1795* (5th ed., London, 1927), I, p. 2; for 1805, *ibid.*, p. 176; for 1816–24 from G. M. Theal, *Records of the Cape Colony*, 36 vols. (Govt. of the Cape Colony, 1897–1905), XIX, p. 389.

STATISTICAL NOTES

Dots (. . .) in tabulations and tables mean that no data are available.

Dash (—) in tabulations and tables means zero (0) or insignificant quantities or values.

To denote 12-month periods that include spans of time in two calendar years, the slash has been used, e.g., 1832/33. The dash is used to designate a span of two or more calendar years.

xiii

ECONOMIC INFLUENCES ON THE SOUTH AFRICAN FRONTIER 1652-1836

CHAPTER 1

INTRODUCTION

The present study deals with the economic factors behind the expansion movement in the early history of South Africa. In particular, it attempts to bring into clear relief some of the economic forces of the historical process leading to the frontier expansion of the Cape of Good Hope during the eighteenth century and subsequently to the population movement of the mid-1830's, known in the history of South Africa as the Great Trek. It is not denied, of course, that the trek movement, and particularly the Great Trek, was also stimulated by noneconomic factors. But with these we are not concerned here.

It is, indeed, surprising how often magic words have been employed to turn the realistic frontiersmen of America and South Africa into legendary beings whose actions were to be determined by equally legendary causes. "Love of wilderness freedom" and "the thirst for travel and exploration" have long been regarded as chief contributory causes of frontier expansion, while "fear of being cramped by the view of his neighbor's campfire" is still considered one of the main causes which drove the Cape farmer to penetrate the mountains that shut him off from the Karroo, thus suggesting seclusion, if not misanthropy, as yet another cause of the trek movement. This confusion of mythology with history is hardly conducive to a clear under-standing of historical events.

There is no occasion to quarrel with those who try to explain a certain event by marshaling a great number of possible causes. But to find out just *what* factors were involved in the expansion movement is only a first step. The next important step, surely, is to attempt to answer the question *how* certain factors have affected frontier expansion. Schumpeter expressed the same idea somewhat differently when he said that "analysis of the *modus operandi* of a factor is frequently the best and sometimes the only method for establishing the significance of a given candidate for the role of factor and for forming a rational opinion regarding its comparative weight" (*1*, p. 5).

The general assumption that the colonists at the American and South African frontiers were entirely self-sufficient seems to have led to false lines of reasoning and false conclusions. Admittedly, the self-sufficiency of the frontier households everywhere was a matter of degree. In fact, even today there is a certain element of "self-sufficiency" in the economy of any up-to-date farm household. However, with regard to frontier expansion, what has to be stressed is not so much the extent of self-sufficiency as the significance of the exchange with the outside world. For if the trade of the frontier settlers, no matter how small, was sufficient to enable them to obtain from the outside world such articles as guns, gunpowder, iron for their wagons, and such little luxuries as tea, sugar, and clothes, it also made their "self-sufficient" economy possible on or beyond the frontier. Even if the frontiersmen were 99 per cent self-sufficient, it was the 1 per cent that tipped the scale, for it constituted the minimum factor in the frontiersman's economy.

The essential economic causes of the whole trek movement must be sought not only in the conditions prevailing at the frontier, but also in the economic development of the colony as a whole. It is therefore necessary to investigate the basic character of the frontier economy not as an independent, primitive, and *self-sufficient* economy—as it has, too often erroneously, been represented—but as an exchange economy maintaining close economic ties with the outside world.

Noneconomic factors are sometimes assigned an important role in the expansion of frontiers. The quest for knowledge and exploration has undeniably been a motivating force of great importance in the case of some individuals. However, the quest for knowledge and exploration is perhaps one of the rare human traits confined to the chosen few. Diaz and Columbus certainly belonged to these few, though this can hardly be said of their crews. Again, love of adventure is supposed to be a widespread human trait, and some historians claim that it has played an important part in frontier expansion. However, it is not always clear what is intended to be conveyed by "love of adventure."

It is one thing to say that a spirit of enterprise is required if people are to try their luck in a new country, often against great odds; it is quite another thing to imply that frontiersmen went into the wilds out of sheer love of adventure. Every frontier is supposed to have had its adventurers. The Brazilian *Bandeiras*, those military companies who went into the interior of Brazil to plunder and enslave Indians, might be thought of as the nearest approximation to adventurers plain and simple. Yet even they kept a very sharp eye on the pecuniary side of their "romantic" exploits. As to the frontiersmen, they had to be enterprising pioneers; but they did not necessarily have to be adventurers.

Whatever role noneconomic factors are supposed to have played in the expansion movement of the Cape Colony, the predominance of economic motivation can hardly be in doubt. It is also clear that the dynamics of the expansion movement did not simply spring from the fact that self-sufficient households reproduced and multiplied themselves at the frontier. Nor was it so much self-sufficiency that attracted new settlers to the wilderness. In fact, it was the prospect of other and greater opportunities than subsistence farming that constituted the main attraction.

CITATIONS

1 Joseph A. Schumpeter, "Theoretical Problems of Economic Growth," *The Tasks of Economic History*, Supp. VII, *Journal of Economic History*, 1947.

CHAPTER 2

HISTORICAL BACKGROUND[1]

The Cape of Good Hope was discovered in 1488 by the Portuguese navigator Bartholomeu Diaz, when he was rounding the subcontinent of Africa in search of a sea route to India. At that time the spices, silks, and other riches of the East could reach Europe only by overland route to the Levant or by the Red Sea to Alexandria and thence by sea to Venice, which was the richest city of Europe. The discovery of the ocean route to India was a hard blow to the lucrative commerce of Venice, and in 1504 the Council of Ten was seriously considering the idea of suggesting to the Sultan of Egypt the cutting of a Suez canal. However, it was not until the 1850's that any effective action was taken to cut the canal, this time by France, and it was not until 1869 that the Suez Canal was opened. In the meantime, the discovery of the long-sought route to the East round the tip of Africa brought great wealth to Portugal, before control of the Oriental trade passed successively to other Atlantic maritime powers — the Dutch, the French, and the British.

In 1497 Vasco da Gama doubled the Cape and discovered the coast of Natal, which he passed on Christmas Day. In 1503 a fleet commanded by Antonio de Saldanha entered Table Bay, but it was the Dutch sea captain Joris van Spilbergen who, almost a century later, gave it its present name, while the name Saldanha Bay was given by mistake to a bay some sixty miles farther north.

By 1620 the Cape of Good Hope had become an ordinary port of call for Portuguese as well as for other ships sailing to the East, but it was the Dutch who first occupied it in 1652. In that year three ships of the Dutch East India Company, under Commander Jan van Riebeeck, arrived in Table Bay with the first European settlers. Van Riebeeck's instructions were to build a

[1] In this brief historical review, I drew heavily on two works of E. A. Walker, *A History of South Africa* and *Historical Atlas of South Africa*.

6

fort, to plant a garden, and "to keep on good terms with the natives for the sake of the cattle-trade" (*1*, p. 31).

The Dutch East India Company, with headquarters at Batavia, in Java, was a powerful monopolistic chartered company. It was administered by a board of directors, the Council of Seventeen, in Amsterdam. The directors were nominally responsible to the States-General. Under the Seventeen stood the Governor-General; the governors and commanders of the various settlements were subject to these officials. The Cape, one of these settlements, was to serve the Company's ships as a halfway house to India and as a provisioning station for fresh meat, vegetables, and fruit to save the lives of passengers and crews of the passing ships who might otherwise die of scurvy. Also, "Captains could put off their sick to recover in the pleasant Mediterranean climate of the Cape, take on fresh hands and still earn their bonus of £50 by making the run from the Texel to Batavia within six months" (*1*, p. 31). The Dutch East India Company had, at first, no intention of colonizing South Africa; but circumstances turned the provisioning station into a settlement and the settlement into an expanding colony.

For the first five years farming was carried on by Company employees under strict control. When official farming proved a failure, a number of Company officials were made "free burghers" and given small holdings on which to farm. However, they were forbidden to grow tobacco, in which the Company had a monopoly, or to trade with the Hottentots. The market was limited at first, since "Ships were few and far between, perhaps twenty-five Company's vessels and a stray Englishman or Frenchman, say 5000 souls annually, each stopping for ten days or so" (*1*, p. 40). By the beginning of the eighteenth century the class of "free burghers" had increased in number and influence and become more and more independent of the authority of the Company officials.

Trouble with the Hottentots and fear of the French, who in 1666 and 1670 made some attempts to establish a footing at Saldanha Bay on the north, prompted the Company to encourage settlement at the Cape. However, it was only under the energetic administration of Simon van der Stel (1679–99) that the first real effort was made to attract Dutch and German settlers. Servants of the Company, too, found agriculture and stock farming at the Cape attractive enough to ask to be discharged from the Company's service. But the most important event was the arrival of about two hundred Huguenots in 1688 and 1689 when the free burgher population was only about six hundred. Some of these French refugees were skilled in making wine and brandy. They were also good farmers. The settlers were given farms in full ownership as large as they could cultivate, and stock farming was encouraged by permission to use unoccupied land for grazing. Even so immigration was slow, and fifty years after the first settlement "no part of the Colony, except the land of Wavern (Tulbagh) and the Company's port at Saldanha Bay, was more than fifty miles in a straight line from the Castle"[2] (*2, p. 7*). The real expansion of the colony did not begin before the early part of the eighteenth century. (See Map 1, below.)

MAP 1*

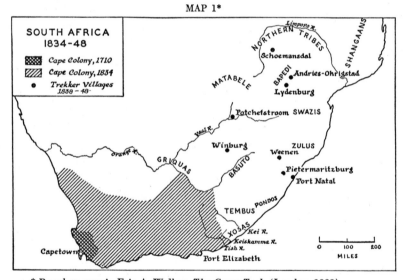

SOUTH AFRICA
1834-48

Cape Colony, 1710
Cape Colony, 1834
● Trekker Villages
1838 – 48

* Based on map in Eric A. Walker, *The Great Trek* (London, 1938).

Simon and his son, Willem Adrien van der Stel (1699–1707) tried to encourage a number of industries such as indigo, olives, rice, and sugar, but they failed, one after another. Willem Adrien's experiments with wool were equally disappointing. The

---

[2] The Castle was at once the fort defending Capetown and the seat of the government. It was founded in 1666 and finished in 1676.

farmers were satisfied with the fat-tailed, hairy sheep, for there was always a market for mutton at Capetown. The great Cape wool industry was still far off; and even as late as 1803, when Jacob de Mist had introduced Spanish rams into the Cape, the farmers still continued to cling to their fat-tailed sheep. Nevertheless, the colony owed much to the energy of the van der Stels. Under Simon the new village of Stellenbosch was established; local government was introduced, and distant parts of the coast and of the interior were explored.

The Governor of the Cape Colony, the Council of Policy, and two free burghers formed the High Court. In 1689 another ruling official was added, the Fiscal, who was appointed to watch the finances and who was responsible only to the Council of Seventeen. He also acted as public prosecutor. In 1682 a Petty Court of two officials and two burghers was set up in Capetown to relieve the High Court from hearing minor civil suits. At the same time a court of Heemraaden, composed of four burghers, was established at the newly founded Stellenbosch to settle local disputes and to act as a district council in matters pertaining to local government. For example, they had to see that the roads were kept in good repair and that taxes were paid. The chairman of the Court of Heemraaden was the landdrost, a salaried official posted near the frontier to look after the Company's interests, whose duties were both judicial and administrative. Each district was divided into wards under officials called the field cornets. This foundation of local government survived the Company's rule in the Cape by many years. The law of the colony was Roman-Dutch.

In the early part of the eighteenth century the colonists were already differentiated into three groups: "the townsmen of De Kaap; the grain and wine farmers of the Berg river valley beyond the natural barrier of the sandy Cape Flats; the cattle-farmers who were already far away behind the mountains of Africa" (1, p. 69).

The townsmen consisted of Company officials, free burghers, and slaves. There were shopkeepers, butchers, and fishmongers, all kinds of tradesmen such as carpenters, builders, and brickmakers, and market gardeners. But the keeping of a boarding-house at Capetown offered perhaps the greatest attraction, for catering for the crews and passengers of the passing ships, apart from being lucrative in itself, also afforded opportunities for smuggling. The situation of the grain and wine farmers as well as of the stock farmers will be the subject of later chapters.

The population grew slowly but steadily. The free burgher population increased from 168 in 1672 to 1,308 in 1700, while in 1740 there were about 4,000 free burghers and 1,500 Company officials, including carpenters, masons, gardeners, etc. Slaves made their first appearance in the Cape in 1657, as the Hottentots could not be persuaded to work in the fields. But West African slaves, mainly Angolese, did not prove a success as agricultural laborers, and most of the slaves were imported from India, Java, Ceylon, Mozambique, and Madagascar. In the first half of the eighteenth century slaves were also imported from the Gold Coast. The African slaves were the cheapest and they did the rough work in the fields, while the Malays did most of the skilled work. On the whole, the slaves were well treated. The slaves were more numerous in the western districts of the Cape, whereas in the eastern districts stock farmers relied more on Hottentot labor. Miscegenation took place between slaves and Hottentots and whites and gave rise to the Cape colored population.

The number of slaves in the service of the free burghers rose from 310 in 1687 to 1,298 in 1708, to 5,787 in 1756, and 16,767 in 1793. Owing to the disproportionate number of female to male slaves, the natural increase was relatively small at first. For example, in 1687 there were 230 male slaves, as compared with 44 female, while in 1708 there were 981 male slaves as against 166 female. From about 1756 the slaves outnumbered the free burghers, in which year the free burgher population was only 5,123. In 1793 the free burgher population was 13,830 as against 16,767 slaves, while in 1795 the total number of slaves (including those in the service of the Company) amounted to about 18,000 as compared with 15,000 free burghers. In 1807 the importation of slaves ceased with the abolition of the slave trade, and in 1834, the year when the slaves were emancipated in the Cape, there were 39,000 slaves as against 65,000 Europeans.

At the time of the first settlement of the Cape, the southwest corner of Africa was inhabited by Bushmen and Hottentots. The Hottentots were pastoral people, and with them a trade in cattle and sheep was carried on. The number of Hottentots was estimated at from 13,000 to 15,000 souls, including women and children. Some of the Hottentot tribes were not always willing to part with their cattle and sheep. This inevitably led to cattle raiding on the part of the colonists and cattle stealing on the part of the Hottentots, followed by reprisals. On the whole, however, the Hottentots offered feeble resistance, and their numbers were decimated by smallpox in 1713 and 1755. Gradually their tribal organization broke down and they began to hire themselves to the colonists, mainly as shepherds and herdsmen.

The little Bushmen were hunters with bows and poisoned arrows. They resented the coming of strangers into their hunting grounds and stole cattle and sheep from both Hottentots and whites. In the 1770's they constituted a serious menace to the colonists, and as late as 1797 they were still strong enough to drive the colonists out of the Tarka district. But their resistance was broken after 1810, though hunting parties, which killed adult Bushmen and captured their children, still went on in later years. Many of the Bushmen withdrew to the semidesert lands of the northwest, where their descendants live now in a reserve under the protection of the government of the Union of South Africa.

The so-called Kaffirs belonged to the Xosa tribe of the Bantu-speaking people. They were cattle farmers who also practiced some agriculture. The Bantus were more virile than the Hottentots, and, what is more, they had highly disciplined warriors organized in regiments. The first contact of the Dutch colonists with the Bantus was at the beginning of the eighteenth century in the course of an expedition to barter cattle and ivory. In subsequent years, traders and hunters were known to have made expeditions into Kaffirland, as the country east of the Fish River was called. In the 1750's the Xosa were settled on the east bank of the Fish River, and from about the last quarter of the century white and black were facing each other across the Fish, eager to barter cattle with each other. Inevitable quarrels ensued over terms of barter, cattle thefts, and grazing rights, the quarrels often leading to disastrous wars. The first Kaffir war broke out in 1779; the second ten years later, in 1789; and the third in 1799. These wars continued right into the second half of the nineteenth century, with ruinous consequences to both Boer and Bantu.

The colony was divided into four districts—the Cape, Stellenbosch, Swellendam, and Graaff Reinet. The district of Swellendam was established in 1745 when it was separated from the jurisdiction of the district of Stellenbosch. The district of Graaff Reinet was established in 1786, and it was this large district that was the center of both Bushman trouble and Kaffir wars.

Toward the middle of the eighteenth century the power of the Dutch East India Company was waning and in 1794 it was declared bankrupt. There was dissatisfaction in the Cape with the native policy of the government and the depreciation of the paper currency,[3] and the colony was in an administrative chaos. The States-General of the Netherlands appointed a commission to inquire into the affairs of the colony, but it was of little avail. When in 1795 the French revolutionary armies invaded Holland and turned it into the Batavian Republic, allied with France, the Prince of Orange, who had fled to England, authorized Britain to occupy the Cape on behalf of the States-General.

The Cape was occupied by the British from 1795 to 1803. During that period the British maintained a considerable armed force at Capetown, and more than £1,500,000 was spent in the colony by the British authorities, much to the benefit of agriculture and commerce. But there was also unrest among the colonists. The district of Swellendam submitted to the British, but the burghers of Graaff Reinet did not surrender until a military expedition had been sent against them. There was also serious trouble with the Bantus and Hottentots (the third, and most disastrous, Kaffir war), and many farms in the frontier districts were laid waste.

When the British evacuated Capetown in 1803, the Cape was handed back to the government of the Netherlands, known as the Batavian Republic at that time. The Dutch East India Company had come to an end and the Cape was now under the control of the Council for the Asiatic Possessions. Jacob de Mist, a member of this council, was sent to the Cape as Commissioner-General. De Mist ruled the Cape according to enlightened principles then

[3] During the years 1793–95 the depreciation varied from 20 to 50 per cent.

current in Holland. Important reforms were introduced under his administration and special attention was given to the improvement of agriculture and stock farming, including the promotion of wool growing. The importation of slaves was checked, and an attempt was made to re-establish friendly relations between the colonists and the Bantus. In less than three years de Mist and Governor Jan Willem Janssens laid the foundation of a most promising colonial system. But their reforms were not destined to be carried out, for when hostilities with Napoleon broke out again, Britain reoccupied the Cape in 1806, this time with no intention of returning it.[4] At the Congress of Vienna in 1814 the Dutch government ceded the Cape and the American possession of Demerara (now British Guiana) to Britain against the payment of £6,000,000. At the same time Britain returned to Holland most of the Dutch possessions in the East Indies which the British had seized in 1811 and administered during the Napoleonic Wars.

In contrast to de Mist's enlightened and liberal rule, the methods of government during the second British occupation were autocratic, though a conservative regard was shown for the old institutions of the colony. On the other hand, trade restrictions were abolished, and during the first fifteen years a profitable market was provided by the large naval and military expenditure.

One of the reforms introduced in 1811 was the institution of circuit courts whereby two members of the Supreme Court went round the colony twice yearly on a circuit. The circuit court was also to report to the Governor on the condition of the country and its inhabitants. The missionaries at Bethelsdorp, who championed the grievances of the Hottentots, lodged charges of cruelty against seventy or eighty leading families on the frontier. Many of these charges were exaggerated and the proceedings of this Black Circuit led to much bitterness between colonists and missionaries, especially those at Bethelsdorp.

Then came the passing of the famous Fiftieth Ordinance in 1828. Hottentots, Bushmen, and "all free persons of colour lawfully residing within the colony" were put on the same level as white settlers in the eyes of the law. This ordinance was largely

---

[4] The Union of South Africa came into being in 1910.

inspired by Dr. John Philip of the London Missionary Society. Needless to say, the ordinance was heartily disliked by the colonists and especially by the frontier farmers.

On the eastern frontier, the Zuurveld, as the present districts of Albany and Bathurst were called (see Map 2, opposite p. 18, and Map 5, opposite p. 146), was the main center of trouble. The Zuurveld was claimed by both the colonists and the Xosas. The colonial authorities decided to expel the Xosas and to settle the area with farmers. But the plan to settle colonists in the Zuurveld on comparatively small farms, to be held on payment of annual quitrents, was not a success. On the other hand, unemployment in Britain after the Napoleonic Wars pointed to emigration, and British immigrants seemed the obvious settlers for the Zuurveld. The British Parliament voted £50,000 for that purpose, and between 1820 and 1821 nearly 5,000 British settlers arrived, including many who paid their own way. This was an important event in the history of South Africa. The majority of the new arrivals were given grants of 100 acres each in the Zuurveld.

In 1834 slavery was abolished throughout the British Empire. The compensation money—£1,235,000—voted by the British Parliament to the Cape was far below the value of the slaves. Moreover, the compensation money would be paid out only in London. Claims were sold to speculators at a loss, and many slave owners were ruined. In the same year there was an invasion of 12,000 Kaffirs into the eastern areas. Within a week 50 farmers were killed, 800 houses were destroyed, and large numbers of cattle, sheep, and horses were carried off. The invaders were driven back beyond the Kei River, and the territory between the Kieskamma and the Kei (see Map 2) was annexed as the Province of Queen Adelaide.[5] However, Lord Glenelg, the Secretary for the colonies, who was a philanthropist, was opposed to the annexation of Queen Adelaide, and before the end of 1836 the province was abandoned. This caused great resentment among the frontier farmers, and Glenelg's policy is considered one of the causes of the northward migration of the Boers (Dutch farm-

---

[5] In 1847 this territory was renamed "British Kaffraria."

ers) in 1836, which is known as the Great Trek. Between 1836 and 1846 about 10,000 people, including women and children, left their homes in the Cape Colony. The *Voortrekkers* (pioneers) intended to establish an independent republican state beyond the reach of the British government.

CITATIONS

1 E. A. Walker, *A History of South Africa* (2d ed., London, 1940).

2 E. A. Walker, *Historical Atlas of South Africa* (Oxford University Press, 1922).

CHAPTER 3

EXPLANATIONS OF FRONTIER EXPANSION
IN SOUTH AFRICA

Although some expansion of van Riebeeck's settlement had taken place up to about 1708, the real expansion movement, the so-called period of dispersion, began only from that year onward. Continuing for a period of about 140 years, the expansion movement ended shortly before the middle of the nineteenth century. In its last phase, from 1834 to 1848, frontier expansion, culminating in what is known in South African history as the Great Trek, was more of a bursting of the frontiers of the colony than the usual earlier expansion. (See Map 1, p. 8.) In 1834 the Cape Colony covered an area of some 120,000 square miles (*1*, p. 16); within thirteen years the white population had expanded into new territories about three times as large. This was the Great Trek, or Great Migration, which was also characterized by an organized exodus of the Boers of the eastern districts of the colony into Natal, the Orange Free State, and the Transvaal.

From the very first the interests of the colonists conflicted with the set policy of the Company. The colonists and local officials desired to embark on a lucrative cattle trade with the Hottentots; the Company was determined to reserve to itself the cattle barter with the natives. The colonists set up cattle farms in the interior; the Company set its face against the expansion of the colony's limit. At the root of this long struggle was the fact that the market for Cape grain and wine was precarious, while Capetown's demand for meat seemed insatiable. The Company "launched *placaaten* forbidding barter or trekking beyond the frontiers" (*2*, p. 63). However, from the days of van Riebeeck such prohibitions were systematically disregarded by the colonists, as is shown by the fact that between 1658 and 1680, for instance, such a *placaat* had to be reissued sixteen times (*2*, pp. 47–48). The drive into the interior of Africa was irresistible.

16

Early in the eighteenth century the Company decided to discontinue the grant of freehold farms. Instead, farmers could obtain "loan farms" (*leenings plaatsen*)—great cattle ranches of 6,000 acres and upward—in return for an annual rent. These farms were held on loan from the Company (hence "loan farm"), first for six months and then for a year at a time. Although legally the Company could revoke the grant at the end of the year, in practice it rarely did so (*2*, p. 95).

How has the expansion movement been interpreted in South Africa? Some writers consider that the "loan farm" system was not only a factor in encouraging cattle farming, but also was responsible for the expansion of the colony. The idea that the loan farm system encouraged dispersion comes probably from John Barrow, the secretary to Earl Macartney, the first British Governor of the Cape, 1797–98. Writing in the beginning of the nineteenth century, John Barrow says: "*Whether the government had any design of dispersing the people by such an absurd system*, under the idea of keeping them more easily in subjection, I can't pretend to say, but it thought proper to encourage the continuance of the system, which is in full force to this moment" (*3*, p. 85; my italics).

The idea that the ban on the issue of freehold land and the introduction of the loan farm system encouraged cattle farming or that these were responsible for the dispersion of the colonists is wholly misleading. In the first place, as pointed out by van der Walt, the movement into the interior had little to do with the restrictions imposed on the issue of freehold land in the arable districts of the colony. The movement, in fact, continued even after the ban on the issue of freehold farms had been lifted and when the southwestern areas of the Cape had proved very suitable to arable farming and closer settlement (*4*, pp. 37–38). But, as will be shown in the following chapter, the real reason why farmers preferred holding large cattle ranches on loan rather than becoming owners of small freehold farms was due largely to the fact that cattle ranching was more lucrative than arable farming. The importance attached to the loan farm system as having been the cause of dispersion is therefore misplaced. Indeed, in introducing the loan farm system the Company merely lent legal sanction to a dispersion which had started earlier, at the same time using the loan farm system as a source of revenue.

It has also been said that insecurity of tenure and the risk that the Company might take back the loan farms deterred the graziers from making improvements (2, p. 95), thus retarding the agricultural, as distinct from the pastoral, development of the colony. However, as shown by van der Walt (4, pp. 52, 55), as early as the 1740's the graziers had already felt sufficiently secure in their right to use the loan farms occupied by them. Second, the loan farm system, far from being the cause of retardation of agriculture, was in part the effect of its slow development in the eighteenth century (4, p. 56).

Yet van der Walt is inclined to blame the loan farm system, if not the farmers, for wastefulness, for encouraging nomadism, for being the cause of the dispersal of the colonists over wide areas, and for having seriously impeded the more intensive development of the colony (4, pp. 58–59).

Nicht nur das verschwenderische Verteilen des Bodens zwang die Kolonisten, sich fortwährend landeinwärts zu zerstreuen, sondern die Leichtigkeit, mit der sie Plätze tauschen konnten, die Bereitwilligkeit, mit der die Kompanie stets neue Ordonnanzen verlieh, liess auch die Neigung des Herumwanderns sich entwickeln.

Das unverständige und fortwährende Verleihen von Ordonnanzen beförderte nicht nur die Zerstreuung der Kolonisten sehr, sondern war, da sie die Unternehmungs- und Arbeitslust lähmte, auch der intensiveren Entwickelung der Kolonie schädlich.

It is difficult to see on what grounds greater intensification, i.e., a greater application of capital and labor per unit of land, could be economically justified, seeing that labor and capital were the scarce factors of production and land was abundant. A more stringent policy in giving out loan farms, even if it could have retarded the occupation of new farms, could not have made arable farming more profitable. At any rate, there was no virtue in farming more intensively if the returns on the expended capital and labor were inadequate.[1] It was not out of human weakness that the colonists obeyed the economic principle demanding an extensive use of the abundant factor, land, relative to the scarce factors, capital and labor.

---

[1] This critical observation is made here with all due respect to Professor van der Walt's pioneering work [*Die Ausdehnung der Kolonie am Kap der Guten Hoffnung (1700–1779)*, Berlin, 1928] in the social and economic interpretation of the expansion movement of the Cape.

Let us now consider the interpretation of the Great Trek. Many economic, political, and social reasons have been advanced; and while considerable attention has been devoted to the exposition of the political and social causes, the economic causes have been mentioned only in a summary manner.

Theal, in his monumental *History of South Africa*, referred to two theories which had been current about the Great Trek for a considerable time. One is that the Trek was merely "a continuation of what was going on since the beginning of the eighteenth century." The second is "that the movement was due to an objection by the Dutch colonists to the freedom of the slaves" (5, pp. 90–91). Writers like Cloete, Wilmot, Chase, Moffat, and Livingstone held that the abolition of slavery was one of the chief economic causes of the Great Trek. Theal, however, rejected both theories as incorrect: the first, on the ground that the Trek, unlike the gradual migration of earlier years, had been a sudden migration; the second, on the ground that the frontier farmers had possessed very few slaves. Yet, in rejecting these two theories, Theal did not advance any definite theory of his own. On the other hand, Cory has demonstrated that in 1834 the frontier farmers did take their slaves over the border of the colony (6, p. 461). Cory, too, in fact, regards the taking of the slaves over the border as one of the causes of the Great Trek. He says (6, p. 460):

With a view to retaining their slaves we find the farmers deliberately leaving the Colony in order to be beyond the reach of the British Government and taking their slaves with them. This was in fact the beginning of the Great Trek which assumed such colossal proportions two years later.

However, Cory maintains that before 1836 the migration of the Boers "had been more connected with the object of finding better grazing for their cattle than that of discontent with the Government," but from about the middle of 1836, "the desire of being quit of British rule and the determination to get beyond its pale took definite form, and that great national self-expatriation known as the great Boer Trek began in real earnest" (7, p. 259). In other words, in 1836 the movement assumed a political character, the underlying causes of which, according to Cory, were the fifteen grievances enumerated by Colonel Somerset in his letter to the Governor of the Cape Colony at the end of 1835 (7, pp. 260–63). The most important of these grievances were as follows:

1. Native depredations.

2. Inadequate protection.

3. Disallowance of self-defense.

4. Allowance by government of criminals to escape unpunished.

5. Imprisonment of respectable farmers on the evidence of their servants.

6. Farmers being taxed in connection with registering claims for slave compensation, while unable to obtain compensation money.

7. Farmers being "summoned from their homes upon the most frivolous complaints from their servants and apprentices, without consideration of the circumstances or of the difficulties to which their absence exposes them."

8. Insecure tenure of their lands: four-fifths of the landholders being without their title deeds.

9. Want of gunpowder.

Undoubtedly, these grievances involving the security of life and property were very serious, although it must also be remembered that not all who joined the Great Trek had come from areas affected by native depredations (*8*, pp. 290–91).

In recent years the tendency has been to take account of the political grievances leading to the Great Trek as well as of its economic motives, with particular emphasis on the availability of free land beyond the frontier as a causative economic factor of expansion.

Walker, who divides the Trek into two distinct periods—the first lasting from 1835 to 1840, the second beginning in 1843 and ending in 1848—simply states that "the first Trek was a more or less organised exodus from the Cape Colony inspired partly by *economic* and partly by sentimental motives" (*1*, p. 4; my italics).

Agar-Hamilton is more specific. He believes that the chief cause of the Trek was the abundance of fertile land beyond the frontier (*9*, pp. 4–8). "This phenomenon dictated the whole history of the Trek, for it was only the circumstance that land was available for settlement that led the emigrant farmers to turn their backs upon the Colony" (*9*, p. 4). Agar-Hamilton also observes that "the Great Trek was only a phase in the age-long process." However, his statement of the problem tells us very little about the forces behind the "age-long process" or about the Great Trek in particular.

The importance of good land beyond the border of the colony is also stressed by De Kiewiet. The trek movement "was stimulated by the knowledge that plenty of good land lay beyond the official boundary. But it was pricked also by a deep sense of grievance" (*10*, p. 54). And, as far as free land is concerned, "the Great Trek was but the acceleration on a large scale of the movement of expansion that had been going on for a century" (*10*, p. 53).

So much for the explanations of the Great Trek. It may be observed that the hypothesis of available free land beyond the border has been accepted, not only as the economic explanation of the Great Trek, but also of the "age-long process" before the Great Trek.

It is necessary therefore to examine the "free land hypothesis" more closely. To say that frontier expansion was due to the availability of fertile land which was either free or cheap is to tell very little beyond the obvious. What is necessary to explain is not why good land in a wilderness could be occupied at all, but why people wanted to take up land in such a place. Obviously what needs explanation is not the demand for land in terms of "love of wilderness freedom." What we really want to know is the nature of the demand for the products of the land, i.e., were the products of the new land raised solely for the purpose of satisfying the needs of isolated and self-contained households, or were they also raised for purposes of exchange. For only if we understand the nature of the frontier economy can we attempt to explain why, for economic reasons at least, people wanted to settle in the wilderness. It would also help to explain why in certain regions and in certain periods expansion was more rapid than in others. Unfortunately, the "free land" hypothesis provides no answer to this question.

The need for new land is presented as one of the chief economic reasons for trekking. If anything, this can mean only a scarcity of land, or of good land, at point of exodus, relative either to the human population or to the animal population. But there is not much evidence to prove that there was actually pressure of human or animal population on the land. The wide credulity that has been lent to the picturesque notion of a farmer being cramped "by the view of his neighbor's campfire" is certainly no proof of overcrowding or pressure on the land.

The land question is considered to have entered upon one of its acute stages in the early 1830's (*1*, pp. 82–84; *2*, pp. 187–88). In addition to drought and locusts, which afflicted the frontier districts at that time, cattle farmers found it less easy to get new land. "The Kaffirs barred the way eastward, and even when Cole offered free grants of land at Kat River, orders came from Downing Street that only British and Hottentots were eligible." As to Crown lands, they were no longer granted freely but sold at auction, which, as Walker explains, meant, from the point of view of the Boers, "that they and their sons would have to pay for what they had learned to look on as the birthright of the Afrikanders" (*2*, p. 187). However, the fact remains that Crown lands were still to be had—this reform did not take effect until the 1840's (*11*, p. 371)—and the pressure of population, if any, could be eased by obtaining the usual 6,000 acres. Moreover, it does not follow that for purely economic reasons the older farmers or even their landless sons would necessarily prefer land which could be had for the taking beyond the borders of the colony to land in the colony for which they would have to pay. In fact, it is not quite clear whether the payment for Crown lands is considered to belong to the category of sentimental or of economic factors. Granted that the farmers might very well have objected to the payment, yet, from an economic point of view, it does not necessarily follow that the advantages offered by Crown lands within the boundaries were not worth the payment. It might still have been more economical to pay a price for land within the colony than to take up "no-price land" beyond the boundaries. To insist that the payment for Crown lands was the deciding factor is to ignore entirely the locational advantages of land within the colony. Indeed, the deciding factor is not the absolute cost of the land but the use to which land can be put in a certain locality. The question is therefore: did the free land beyond the frontiers of the colony offer equal advantages to the graziers or not? Considerations of proximity to, or distance from, the market might suggest that land beyond the border of the colony was less desirable than similar land within the colony, so that the mere fact that a payment had to be made for Crown land could not in itself have decided the issue.

Taxation is sometimes advanced as another possible economic factor in the trek movement. The wilds beyond the frontier offered not only free land but also exemption from taxation. However, as in the case of free land, the decisive factor for a prospective emigrant is not so much the question whether there is or is not taxation, but whether he can on the whole make a better living in his new abode. This crucial question cannot be answered by mere reference to taxation or even to the fact that plenty of fertile land could be had for the taking. This is particularly true with reference to those colonists who had already occupied land within the boundaries of the colony, though it must be conceded that both the payment for land and taxation were probably important considerations in the case of poor, landless men—not necessarily from the frontier districts alone—who wished to become graziers. For such people the land across the border and the avoidance of taxation were certainly incentives to trek. In fact, such people were trekking continually, despite the Governor's refusal to grant them permission to settle beyond the boundaries of the colony. However, men like Louis Trichard and his party, as well as all the other leaders of the Great Trek, certainly did not belong to the category of poor and landless graziers.

It would, therefore, be wholly incorrect to argue that the older and more settled colonists trekked because of the knowledge that outside the colony fertile land was plentiful and free, for land was not the only thing that mattered. The idea that the only things the frontier farmers needed or desired were more land and more cattle not only oversimplifies the issue, but also leads to entirely wrong conclusions and to a misinterpretation of the whole economic development of the colony from its early days. Indeed, such an idea could only arise from a lack of appreciation of the fact that farmers also needed markets and that their need for land and cattle was chiefly determined by the possibilities of exchanging the produce of their land and livestock for articles which could not be produced on the farm. In other words, the price that had to be paid for Crown lands could explain why poor and landless farmers would be compelled to seek free land beyond the boundaries of the colony, but it could hardly explain why old settled frontier farmers should have wished to trek. Yet hardly anyone would contend that, from a purely economic point of view, the Great Trek was chiefly a movement of poor and landless men in search of free land. Nor could it be explained why the poor and landless who had taken part in the Trek should have come from the eastern frontier districts, and not from the older and more settled areas of the colony where land hunger was obviously more acute than in the frontier areas.

In this connection, the question whether the frontier colonists were entirely self-sufficient is of crucial importance. For if they were self-sufficient and outside the exchange economy of the colony, the question of proximity to or distance from a market would be of little economic consequence. Under such conditions the locational factor need not enter into consideration and, consequently, payment exacted for Crown lands within the colony would drive the colonists beyond the boundaries. But the assumption that the frontier farmers were self-sufficient, an idea so dear to many popular writers, is, as will be shown later, devoid of historical basis.

The observation is sometimes made that in some respects the pastoral economy of the frontier Boers was similar to that of the Bantu tribes. Both Boer and Bantu were preoccupied with cattle breeding and the search for pastures. From this it has been concluded that the economy of the frontier Boers had been both primitive and self-sufficient. Such a conclusion is both incorrect and misleading. As to the Boers, it must be pointed out that they had never severed their economic intercourse with the outside world, and the cattle and sheep they bred were mostly intended for the market. It is true that the frontier farmers seldom raised cash crops, but it must not be overlooked that they always bred "cash livestock."

Even the Bantus were not so completely self-sufficient as they are commonly supposed to have been, for they, too, frequently bartered cattle with the colonists. In fact, the first contact between European and Bantu in the eighteenth century was by trade, consisting mainly of an exchange of cattle and some ivory, for pieces of iron, for copper, trinkets, and tobacco. Admittedly, the exchange was not always fair or equitable, but there can be no doubt about its attraction for both parties. This eagerness to barter with the colonists may in part explain the irresistible attraction of European frontier settlements for the Bantus. It may also prove of considerable interest to inquire to what extent cattle stealing at the frontier had been stimulated by opportunities of exchanging the stolen cattle for pieces of metal, beads, etc. Indeed, I am inclined to believe that by the end of the eighteenth century some Bantu tribes, at least those within and on the borders of the colony, had, to a considerable extent, already come within the orbit of the exchange economy of the Cape.

Another point to be cleared up is the use of the term *nomad* with reference to the frontier and interior graziers. It seems to imply that the graziers had reverted to a nomadic stage. But such a notion is misleading.

Every colonist in the Sneeuwbergen, for instance, had "special farms in the low country, which is called Caroo, and which consists of a reddish soil overgrown with shrubs named '*vygebosies*,' the latter being excellent for sheep" (*12*, p. 231). The Sneeuwbergen region, van Reenen points out, is covered with snow in the winter, and is then of no use either to people or for cattle on account of the severe cold. Every stockbreeder had one or more farms in the Karroo for the winter, and for that reason, van Reenen says, the inhabitants often had to take up three or four loan farms (*12*, p. 231).

On the other hand, the colonists of the interior were sometimes accused of being too much anchored to their farms. Thus Percival, who traveled in the Cape at the beginning of the nineteenth century, writes (*13*, p. 210):

A farmer once settled in a farm, with a house ever so wretched, will never leave it though to his advantage, nor would he remove to a spot within three or four miles, although possessing the most eminent advantages in soil and produce; and knowing that he might easily obtain leave to change his abode from the government, who indeed seldom look after their settlements, provided they receive the small tax to the treasury at certain times.

Sparrman, too, writing in the 1770's, says that "in direct contradiction to the custom of the original inhabitants, the Hottentots, the colonists turn their cattle out constantly into the same fields" (*14*, p. 251).

We must therefore reject the widespread notion of lack of attachment to one particular place as having been the cause of "nomadic wandering." The movements of the graziers were not mere wanderings of people who had "little to anchor them to any one place." It is true that they were moving from place to place with their sheep and goats and herds of cattle, but the places they moved from and the places they moved to were their grazing farms, their summer and winter farms, as it were, and they had very good reason for moving.

CITATIONS

1 E. A. Walker, *The Great Trek* (2d ed., London, 1938).

2 E. A. Walker, *A History of South Africa* (2d ed., London, 1940).

3 John Barrow, *Travels into the Interior of South Africa*, 2 vols. (2d ed., London, 1806), II.

4 A. J. H. van der Walt, *Die Ausdehnung der Kolonie am Kap der Guten Hoffnung (1700–1779)* (Berlin, 1928).

5 G. M. Theal, *History of South Africa Since 1795*, 5 vols. (5th ed., 1927), I.

6 G. E. Cory, *The Rise of South Africa: A History of the Origin of South African Colonisation and of Its Development Towards the East from the Earliest Times to 1857* (new impression, London, 1926), II.

7 G. E. Cory, *The Rise of South Africa*, III.

8 S. F. N. Gie, *Die Geskiedenis vir Suid Afrika* (Stellenbosch, 1832), II.

9 J. A. I. Agar-Hamilton, *The Native Policy of the Voortrekkers* (Capetown, 1928).

10 C. W. De Kiewiet, *A History of South Africa: Social and Economic* (Oxford, 1941).

11 D. H. Robertson, "The Cape of Good Hope and 'Systematic Colonisation,'" *South African Journal of Economics*, December 1937.

12 D. G. van Reenen, *Die Journal van Dirk Gysbert van Reenen, 1803* (Van Riebeeck Society Publication, No. 18).

13 Robert Percival, *An Account of the Cape of Good Hope* (London, 1804).

14 Andrew Sparrman, *A Voyage to the Cape of Good Hope from the Year 1772 to 1776* (London, 1785), I.

CHAPTER 4

COMPARATIVE ADVANTAGES OF ARABLE AND PASTORAL FARMING

ARABLE FARMING

Let us examine briefly the economic position of arable farming from the early days of the Cape. Already in van Riebeeck's times the farmers complained that "the price of wheat was so low as not to pay for its cultivation, and desired that it be fixed at 16s. 8d. the muid" (*1*, p. 86). The Dutch East India Company, however, allowed the price of wheat to be raised to only 11s. 8d. per muid, the prices of rye and barley to 9s. 2d., and the price of oats to 6s. 8d. per muid (*1*, pp. 157–58). In 1685 wheat was to be received by the Company at 16s. 8d. per muid in payment of debt or in exchange for goods, but the cash price was fixed at only 15s. per muid (*1*, p. 278). However, these relatively favorable prices could not be maintained long, for soon the supply exceeded the demand and prices had to be lowered to 12s. 6d. for export and 13s. 11d. the muid in the Cape. Yet, even at that price Cape wheat was too expensive to become an article of export to Holland, for wheat was being sold in the Netherlands at 6s. 8d. the muid (*1*, p. 362).

The Cape experienced her first crisis in arable farming in the 1690's when Batavia refused to pay the high prices it had been paying for Cape grain. Temporary relief came when the Council of Seventeen, prompted by the consideration that Batavia's refusal to buy Cape grain would pose a serious threat to the Cape cultivator and the colony as a whole, ordered the Batavian government to buy grain from the Cape regardless of the fact that grain from Bengal and Surat could be obtained at much lower prices (*2*, p. 29). In general, however, the Company's demand for wheat was limited, and in years of bumper crops "all the old troubles arose with Batavia about prices and uncertain quantities" (*3*, p. 77; *1*, p. 501). The market for rye, barley, beans, and peas was hardly more favorable. The market in the Indies for these products was very limited, and in 1703 a notice was issued to the effect that the Company would not purchase either rye or beans any more (*1*, p. 500).

Wine farmers did not fare much better. The Company used to purchase a certain quantity of ordinary wine for the use of the fleets and old wine for the hospital. But the Cape wines, except Constantia, had a bad reputation in Europe (*1*, p. 489). "It was not saleable in India, on account of its being of very inferior quality. Some of it was converted into vinegar for the use of the seamen" (*1*, p. 358). In 1715 the "flood of wine was still pouring forth [at the Cape] in such volume that the Council levied a tax upon it for the first time" (*3*, p. 77; see also p. 60).

In 1717 the position deteriorated to such an extent that, faced with the overproduction of grain and wine at the Cape, the Company was compelled to restrict the issue of freehold land. The only alternative for new settlers or the sons of older colonists who wished to start on their own was to obtain a "loan farm" in the drier regions of the interior on payment of an annual rent, a payment which contributed in no inconsiderable extent to the revenue of the Company (*2*, p. 35).

Despite this check on the expansion of arable farming the position of the established grain and wine farmers showed very little improvement. In 1717 the price of wheat was reduced to 10*s*. 8*d*. per muid and in 1743 to 9*s*. 4*d*. (1, p. 501). In 1743, van Imhoff, who visited Capetown on the way to take up the governor-generalship of India, wrote: "Of wheat, rye and barley the Colony will no doubt be able to export so much to Batavia and India that a glut in the local market will be avoided. This will increase if the price of wheat could be still further diminished, for it becomes a costly matter to supply wheat to the Company's ships while there is an abundance of rice in Java" (*4*, p. 135). Beans and peas "the inhabitants have hitherto been unable to dispose of . . . because the Company required such a small quantity for its homeward bound vessels" (*4*, p. 135).

The demand for wine was little better. With a view to discouraging production the wine tax was raised in the 1740's from 4*s*. to 12*s*. 6*d*. per leaguer (*5*, p. 65). But in spite of the higher wine tax and other considerable deductions, the supply of wine exceeded the demand, with the result that by the 1750's "insolvencies of winefarmers became alarmingly frequent" (5, p. 106).

However, there were also years of prosperity. The first period of prosperity arrived with the outbreak of the Anglo-French war in India, which lasted for four years, from the end of 1758 to the beginning of 1763, and during that time "the officers of French packets from Mauritius and of English packets from St. Helena bid against each other for cattle and meal and wine" (5, pp. 106–07). There was also a much longer period of prosperity which lasted from 1772 to 1795. However, not all farm produce benefited or benefited equally. It is true that the 1770's were marked by "a constant demand for all kinds of farm produce at more than double the prices which the Company was giving" (5, p. 165). But it was the graziers and the wine farmers who benefited most in the period 1772–80. The Company was the sole buyer of wheat for export and the wheat farmers did not receive more than 9s. 9½d. per muid for wheat exported to India, while for wheat sent to Europe the farmers received only 6s. 7d. per muid (5, p. 165), "and the authorities naturally tended to send more to Europe than to the Indies" (3, p. 93; 6, p. 19).

In exceptional years, like the early 1770's, better prices were obtained by the Company for Cape wheat in Holland. This was due to the bad harvests in Europe, particularly in Poland, whence Holland used to import bread cereals. But then the price paid by the Company for export wheat to Holland was only 7s. 2d. Thus Thunberg, writing in 1773, says (7, pp. 231–32):

Small quantities [of wheat] have been exported to the Indies for the use of the better sort of people there; but the voyage has been looked upon as too long, and the freight too expensive to send any to Europe, till the preceding and this present year, when some has been sent to Holland, where it has been found to be much heavier than the European wheat. Poland, the granary of Holland, having for several years past been visited by war, and partly laid waste, and the crops having been in general bad all over Europe, the Dutch East India Company determined to send some small vessels to the Cape to import wheat; and last year they sent one vessel, and this year two frigates. For a freight of wheat the farmer is paid 18 rix-dollars. A freight contains ten muid or about 20 bushels.

It is true that foreigners at the Cape were prepared to pay much higher prices for wheat than the Company, but, as pointed out by Thunberg, "wheat, when it is wanted by foreign nations for exportation, is only to be had of the Company. The French ships frequently exported it in the course of this and the last year to the Isle of France" (*7*, p. 300). In other words, the increased wheat exports from the Cape at higher prices during the nine years 1772–80 did not necessarily bring greater prosperity to the wheat farmers. The controlled price paid by the Company remained unchanged; the Fiscal, having taken control of the grain trade, "permitted nothing to be sold to strangers without his leave," much to the annoyance of the burghers who "protested against this infringement of their rights, but to no purpose" (*5*, p. 167). It was not until the 1790's that the Company raised the price of wheat to 11*s*. 4*d*. per muid, after the tithes were deducted, and allowed the farmers to export the surplus on their own account, provided it was sent in Dutch ships (*5*, p. 270).

There was also some improvement in the market for arable products during the first British occupation. Not only the wine farmers, but also many of the wheat farmers at a distance of not more than two or three days' journey from the Cape were in good circumstances (*8*, p. 114). The price of wine paid to farmers was from 20 to 30 rix-dollars per leaguer (*9*, p. 375),[1] while the price of wheat was never less than 40 to 60 rix-dollars the load of ten muids. During the British occupation there was also a good demand for barley (*9*, pp. 312–14, 319). But this was also a time when, as will be shown later, the already good position of the pastoralist was further improved.

With regard to wine, too, "the average production of wine was 3,244 leaguers, and the Company needed only 945 leaguers for its own use and for sale in Europe and India" (*5*, p. 167). These moderate requirements of wine the Company secured from the farmers, at the same time refusing the burghers the right to export wine to Holland (*5*, p. 167). On the other hand, the directors were only too glad "to know that the surplus could be sold to foreigners at high rates at the Cape" (*5*, p. 167).

It may thus be seen that from the very beginning the economic position of arable farming in the Cape was precarious. This was particularly the case with regard to wheat growing. But even the wine farmer's later prosperity, apart from the short period

---

[1] At the end of the eighteenth century the Company was paying 28 Rds. per leaguer.

of 1758–63, did not properly set in before 1772, only to disappear again in the early part of the nineteenth century. Thus, de Mist, in his *Memorandum on the Cape*, written in 1801, says (*10*, pp. 175–76):

The embargo on freedom of trade, and the difficulty experienced by the farmer in obtaining goods in exchange for the produce which he brought to the Cape Town market in ever increasing quantities, affected the prices of corn [wheat] and wine so adversely that at times the farmer, arriving at the Cape after many a long day's trek at the slow pace of the ox, through the trackless veld, was unable to obtain a purchaser for his grain, and found himself obliged either to sell it, or rather, give it away for next to nothing, or else to store it in hired granaries at a considerable loss to himself. Further, (with shame be it said) the desperate winefarmer had more than once been seen knocking the pegs out of his barrels, and allowing the precious wine to turn to waste, in order that the weary oxen might not have to drag the full casks over the veld back to the farm. And, as if this were not misfortunate enough, the tithes due to the Company's treasury were even more strictly enforced. Every wagon had to pass the military guard at the Castle before it was allowed to enter the town, and the amount to be paid to the Company was estimated on the supposed value of the load. Now, although the load might bring in little or nothing, it was taxed beforehand according to a fixed price, and the tax paid in hard cash, a condition which the farmers found difficult to fulfil before they had disposed of their wares. On that account alone many of them were deterred from bringing their produce to market.

Van Reenen, too, writing of the opportunities in wheat and wine farming in the older districts of the colony at the beginning of the nineteenth century, says (*11*, p. 141):

. . . at present a young man starting to farm cannot expect to make a living on a wine or wheat farm, however hard-working and careful he may be. The high rate of interest and the costliness of all requisites absorb his entire profit. He drudges, toils and moils himself nearly to death but makes no progress whatever.

Yet it must be conceded that the arable farmer was not entirely without some years of prosperity in the first quarter of the nineteenth century. In the first place, there was some improvement in the market for wheat immediately after the second British occupation when Baird, in order to induce farmers to grow more wheat, proclaimed that they would be paid 40 rix-dollars per wagonload of ten muids (*12*, p. 55), which was more than double the price paid in 1773.[2] On the other hand, it is difficult to say to what extent such a price was sufficient to make wheat production more profitable. Apart from "the high rate of interest

2 See above, p. 29.

and the costliness of all requisites," account must also be taken
of the depreciation of the rix-dollar by 1806.[3] Nor, in view of
the low estimation of Cape wines in England (*13*, p. 354), was
there at first any improvement in the market for wine.

More important for the wine farmers were the years following 1813. Theal maintains that "the most flourishing period that
South African wine farmers have ever known" was in the 12
years 1812–25, when the customs duty on Cape wines was reduced from £43 1*s.* to £14 7*s.* for the tun of 252 gallons. This
"gave such an impetus to the planting and enlargement of vineyards that from 7,707 leaguers produced in 1814, the quantity
rose to 19,250 leaguers in 1824, when there were over 30,000,-
000 vines bearing" (*14*, pp. 36–37). The increased quantities
of ordinary wine produced at the Cape were bound to affect the
price. Theal believes that the decline started only in 1825 "when
the difference in the duties on Cape and other wines entering
Great Britain was reduced" (*14*, p. 37). However, there is
reason to believe that this flourishing period actually did not
last until 1825. In fact, the decline in prices set in as early as
1819, as may be seen in the following prices, in rix-dollars per
leaguer, of wine sold in the market in Capetown (*13*, p. 388).

Year	Price	Year	Price
1813	145	1819	82½
1814	145	1820	70
1815	130	1821	45
1816	48	1822	57½
1817	185	1823	55
1818	135	1824	50

In the years 1825 and 1826 the average price of ordinary
wine fell as low as 43 rix-dollars per leaguer (*15*, p. 261).

The following description of the position of the wine growers,
wheat farmers, and stock farmers, by a writer in 1824, is of particular interest (*16*, pp. 226–27):

The Wine Growers have, either belonging to themselves, or upon loan,
large capitals, sunk in slaves, buildings, vineyards, fustage, cattle, and pasture
lands; and are consequently enabled to live at a rate which might be considered by a stranger, who does not perceive their economy, to be extravagant.
But if a very few, who have peculiar advantages, or make a superior descrip-

---

[3] See table of exchange rates, p. xi.

tion of wine, are excepted, they do not receive the average rate of profit on their capital, nor anything like it. Their early habits, and the impossibility of finding purchasers, are the principal causes of their perseverance, at the present low prices of their produce. They can, by means of a very large capital, pay their taxes and live, but that is all.

The profits of the Corn Farmers, within a moderate distance of the Cape markets, are probably somewhat higher; but the difference cannot be great, as there is nothing of moment except the transfer duty, (which to be sure is a serious obstacle in itself,) to prevent the flux and reflux of capital between these two employments.

The Stock Farmers on the Frontier, having acquired few wants, and consequently being less exposed to indirect taxation, and having almost an unlimited range of pasturage, are accumulating capital rapidly, wherever they are able to protect themselves from the depredations of the Bushmen and Caffers.

In the 1820's it was considered that a price of 125 rix-dollars per load, "on years of average produce," would be a remunerative price for wheat grown in the Cape district (*17*, pp. 308, 333, 451, 492). The average prices per load, in rix-dollars, for wheat sold in the Cape market in the years 1813–26 were as follows (*18*, p. 503):

Year	Price	Year	Price
1813	104	1820	93
1814	132	1821	213
1815	93	1822	264
1816	68	1823	104
1817	93	1824	133
1818	174	1825	111
1819	171	1826	224

The average price of wheat in seven out of fourteen years was below what was considered remunerative. In the other seven years it is true that prices were more than remunerative, and in some years even very high, but these high prices are not necessarily an indication of the welfare of wheat farmers. Unfortunately, no production figures are available, but it is known that the high prices of 1821, 1822, and 1826 were the result of crop failures and short supplies (*19*, p. 217). In general, it may therefore be said that the economic position of the wheat farmer at the Cape was adversely affected not only by low prices, but also by the average of poor harvests. The Cape has never been a first-rate wheat-growing country.

Not only had the arable farmer to contend with poor wheat harvests and low prices for grain and wine, but he was also up against high costs of production. In general, the cost of slave labor used in arable farming had always been high compared with the cost of Hottentot labor used in stock farming, while the cost of farm implements increased very considerably in the eighteenth century. The price of a plow, for instance, increased from £2 8s. in 1744 to £4 in 1792, while the blacksmith's charge for a plowshare rose from 12s. to £1 8s. during the same period (*20*, p. 55).

Even more important was the high cost of transport, and one of the factors responsible for making commercial grain growing in the new areas unremunerative at the best of times was the high cost of transport to the market. In the absence of waterways, grain and other bulky farm produce had to be taken by wagon over difficult roads to Capetown, the only market. The ox wagon of the eighteenth century, in itself quite an expensive vehicle, did not last long and often fell to pieces after the first journey; but in most cases it was rendered useless after four or five journeys over rocky and mountainous roads (*2*, p. 41).

Many travelers referred to the unprofitability of commercial grain growing in the Cape at a greater distance than sixty or seventy miles from Capetown. Even at as late a date as the 1820's, J. W. D. Moodie, a traveler who had gained practical farming experience in the Cape, observed that grain carried to Capetown from a distance of more than sixty to seventy miles did not bear the expenses of transport. In short, wheat could not very well serve as a basis for further expansion.

Only livestock was independent of good roads. Livestock, in fact, could walk to market on any road, while, as will be shown later, such animal products as butter, tallow, soap, sheep's tail fat, hides, and skins could make up a load sufficiently valuable to justify high haulage costs.

Aside from the demand for meat and for slaughter stock there was an important market for draft animals for work on the farms as well as for transportation. Indeed, from the early days of the Cape the ox was the chief working and draft animal, while the ox wagon was the universal form of transportation, particularly over longer distances. This demand for draft oxen must, therefore, be regarded as an additional economic link between the Cape and the frontier districts.[4]

PASTORAL FARMING

There is a question whether before 1718 stock farming was the main occupation of farmers. Van der Walt thinks that the newly opened grazing areas were just an extension of the commonage of the older farms around Capetown and Stellenbosch. In his opinion, no colonist was willing to settle in areas remote from Capetown, the only market and trading center of the colony, or to sacrifice the amenities of civilization offered by the settled parts of the colony in the vicinity of Capetown and Stellenbosch for the life of a grazier in the wilds of the interior (*2*, p. 23). On the other hand, the more recent work of van der Merwe suggests the possibility of a number of colonists having become stock farmers exclusively even before the end of the seventeenth century (*21*, pp. 22–26, 30–31). However, it was probably not before the serious deterioration of the Cape market for wheat and wine beginning after 1717 that colonists from the older areas began to settle in the interior in ever-increasing numbers (*2*, pp. 25, 37).

The economic reasons for this migration from the settled areas of the colony are thus obvious. In fact, the expansion movement in the early part of the eighteenth century, if not earlier, *began as a migration of people from the settled areas of the colony*. It is not denied, of course, that the natural increase of the frontier population played an important part in the expansion and settlement of the frontier regions, but it would be fallacious to explain the expansion movement merely in terms of a natural increase of the frontier population. There is no lack of evidence to show that throughout the history of the colony the older areas of the Cape constituted a reservoir from which a stream of population, faster at one time and slower at another, but never drying up, was finding an outlet to the wide spaces of the interior. Nor is there any reason to assume that even in the later years the deterioration in economic conditions of arable relative to pastoral farming, or the opportunities that were opened at the frontier,

---

[4] Somewhat similar conditions with regard to the demand for oxen as working and draft animals also prevailed in the early history of Brazil.

did not result in any migration from older agricultural areas. Yet this is what has been implicitly assumed by many writers up to the present day. Great play has been made of the proverbial fecundity of the frontier Boers as if one could reasonably assume that the fecundity was much less in the older agricultural districts.

There is evidence to show that this migration from the older areas to the interior was not confined to the beginning of the eighteenth century. In 1751 the Heemraaden of Stellenbosch complained (*4*, p. 151):

Some of the settlers, seeing no chance of earning a living in any other way, have already been driven, at the great risk of losing the little they possessed, to removing a considerable distance further inland to see if they could succeed better there.

There is also evidence that in the 1780's, if not earlier, skilled tradesmen from the older parts of the colony were taking every opportunity to migrate to the frontier areas where the chances for earning a better livelihood were much greater (*21*, pp. 189–90). Sparrman tells of a *corn-boer* (wheat farmer) near Capetown who decided to give up the drudgery of the husbandman and wine dresser for the grazing business in the frontier areas (*22*, p. 249). This desire to give up the drudgery of the small arable farmer did not necessarily mean a desire to indulge in a lazy and wandering life. It rather meant that the business of the grazier was more remunerative in terms of human effort than that of the husbandman and the wine dresser.

Barrow speaks of the discharged soldier or runaway sailor who "gets into a boer's family and marries" and becomes a grazier (*8*, p. 123), while, according to Thompson, a young colonist from the older districts who had learned no other trade but farming and whose capital was insufficient "either to purchase or stock a farm in any of the older districts" usually migrated to the frontier (*23*, pp. 324–25). It is true that in Thompson's time the Sneeuwbergen, Tarka, and Bruintjeshoogte were already considered old and settled areas (*23*, p. 327), yet there is no reason to believe that young colonists without sufficient means did not also come from the old arable areas of the Cape, particularly in times when arable farming was depressed.

There is also evidence that poorer farmers in the older districts sold their farms to their next neighbors who wanted them for their sons and daughters, and with the money thus received bought sheep and cattle to stock their new farms in the frontier districts (*24*, p. 25). We also find that in 1825 there were 182 applicants for land in the district of Somerset. It is of interest to note that most of these applicants possessed slaves, some of them as many as 18, suggesting that these, at least, were arable farmers (*25*, pp. 70–73).

THE MAKING OF A GRAZIER

Indeed, it was comparatively easy to set up as a livestock farmer in the interior of the colony without capital. The following citation from Sparrman, who traveled in the frontier districts of the Cape in the 1770's, is of particular interest. While staying on one of the frontier farms Sparrman was enlarging upon the contented life of the colonists. Whereupon the following advice was tendered to him by a well-meaning lady (*22*, pp. 168–69):

You have already a waggon, oxen, and saddle horses; these are the chief things requisite in order to set up as a farmer; there are yet uncultivated places in the neighbourhood, proper either for pasturage or tillage, so that you may choose out of an extensive tract of land the spot that pleases you best. Here are people enough, who will send you that part of their cattle to keep which they cannot conveniently look after themselves, on conditions that you shall have the young ones produced by them for your trouble. In this way many young beginners have acquired a competency in a few years.

Barrow, writing at the end of the eighteenth century, described the making of a grazier in the following terms (*8*, pp. 123–24):

He begins the world without any property, the usual practice being that of the wife's friends giving him a certain number of cattle and sheep to manage, half the yearly produce of which he is to restore to the owner, as interest for the capital placed in his hands. He has most of the necessities of life, except clothing, within himself; his work is done by Hottentots, which cost him nothing but meat, tobacco, and skins for their clothing. His house and his furniture, such as they are, he makes himself; and he has no occasion for implements of husbandry. . . . The only expensive item he has to purchase is a waggon costing about 400 Rix-dollars. He also has to purchase a musquet and a small quantity of powder and lead which will procure him as much game as his whole family can consume. . . . The springboks are so plentiful on the borders of the colony, and so easily got at, that a farmer sends out his Hottentot to kill a couple of these deer with as much certainty as if he sent him among his flock of sheep. In a word, an African peasant of the lowest condition never knows want; and if he does not rise into affluence, the fault must be entirely his own.

In Barrow's time the comparative incomes and outlays of the arable farmer and the grazier were estimated as follows (*8*, pp. 113, 117, 123).

Item	Annual net income (*rix-dollars*)	Annual outlay (*rix-dollars*)	Net income as percentage of outlay
Wine farmer	787	3,212	24.5
Wheat farmer	718	1,423	50.4
Grazier	469	451	104.0

Of further importance is the fact that the grazier required only a small capital to enable him to produce his income. Thus, according to Barrow, while the wheat farmer required a capital of about 12,000 rix-dollars for buildings, slaves, implements, cattle, etc., and the wine farmer a capital of over 24,000 rix-dollars, the grazier's capital investment consisted mainly of two wagons costing only 800 rix-dollars (*8*, pp. 113, 117, 123). The economic position of the grazier was not only a very favorable one, but as Barrow said: "In what part of the world can even a respectable peasant do this?" (*8*, p. 123).

In Thompson's time, too, "a very limited capital" was sufficient to "enable a man to begin the world as a *veeboer* [livestock farmer]" (*23*, p. 325). With 2,200 rix-dollars, or £165, he could buy at the beginning of the 1820's an old wagon, a span of oxen, horses, fifty cows and young cattle, and five hundred sheep and goats. "The above, with a large gun, an axe, adze, and hammer, a couple of waggon-chests, a churn, a large pot for boiling soap, and one or two smaller ones for cooking, are all that is absolutely requisite to establish a stock farmer in South Africa" (*23*, p. 325).

The next step was to pick out a tract of land which, after having complied with the formalities of occupation, would be granted to him upon perpetual quitrent. "Thus he is established; and if no disaster occurs, and he is not very idle or drunken, the progressive increase in his stock, beyond the consumption of his family and servants, will render him, eventually, a *veeboer* of respectable property" (*23*, p. 326).

In other words, the frontier was not only an outlet for landless people and people who did not possess any livestock, it also offered good opportunities for people with some capital.

In 1825 a government commission made the following interesting observations (*25*, p. 195):

> The rearing and feeding of stock in the Colony has we believe at all times been attended with greater, and more certain profit, than the cultivation of grain; and the great extent of pasturage that until lately has been available to proprietors of stock in the Frontier Districts has enabled them to support and increase their numbers, and to defy the influence of continued droughts and unhealthy pasturage during certain seasons of the year, as well as the frequent depredations of wild animals.

Admittedly, the ease with which people from the older areas of the colony could become graziers in the interior played an important part in the expansion movement. But this in itself does not explain why people from the more civilized parts of the colony should have wished to go into the wilds. It can be satisfactorily explained only if account is taken of the deterioration in the economic conditions of arable farming in the older area, on the one hand, and the relative prosperity of stock farming in the interior, on the other.

CITATIONS

1 G. M. Theal, *History of South Africa Before 1795*, 3 vols. (3d ed., London, 1922), II.

2 A. J. H. van der Walt, *Die Ausdehnung der Kolonie am Kap der Guten Hoffnung (1700–1779)* (Berlin, 1928).

3 E. A. Walker, *A History of South Africa* (2d ed., London, 1940).

4 The Reports of Chavonnes and His Council, and of Van Imhoff, on the Cape (Van Riebeeck Society Publication, No. 1).

5 G. M. Theal, *History of South Africa Before 1795*, III.

6 Coenraad Beyers, *Die Kaapse Patriotte, 1779–1791* (Capetown, 1929).

7 C. P. Thunberg, *Travels in Europe, Africa and Asia, Performed Between the Years 1770 and 1779*, 3 vols. (London, 1795), I.

8 John Barrow, *Travels into the Interior of South Africa*, 2 vols. (2d ed., London, 1806), II.

9 G. M. Theal, *Records of the Cape Colony,* 36 vols. (Govt. of the Cape Colony, 1897–1905), XXXII.

10 J. A. de Mist, *Memorandum on the Cape* (Van Riebeeck Society Publication, No. 3).

11 D. G. van Reenen, *Die Journal van Dirk Gysbert van Reenen, 1803* (Van Riebeeck Society Publication, No. 18).

12 G. M. Theal, *Records,* VI.

13 G. M. Theal, *Records,* XIX.

14 G. M. Theal, *History of South Africa Since 1795*, 5 vols. (5th ed., London, 1927), I.

15 G. M. Theal, *Records,* XXXV.

16 G. M. Theal, *Records*, XVII.

17 G. M. Theal, *Records*, XXXIV.

18 G. M. Theal, *Records*, XXVII.

19 G. M. Theal, *Records*, XXVI.

20 C. G. Botha, "Prices in the Eighteenth Century," *South African Journal of Science*, XX, 1923, pp. 552–54.

21 P. J. van der Merwe, *Die Trekboer in die Geskiedenis van die Kaapkolonie (1657–1842)* (Capetown, 1938).

22 Andrew Sparrman, *A Voyage to the Cape of Good Hope from the Year 1772 to 1776* (London, 1785), II.

23 George Thompson, *Travels and Adventures in Southern Africa*, 2 vols. (London, 1827), I.

24 W. M. Macmillan, *Bantu, Boer and Briton* (London, 1929).

25 G. M. Theal, *Records*, XXIII.

CHAPTER 5

THE MARKET FOR MEAT AND
SLAUGHTER STOCK

As we have seen in the preceding chapter, one of the reasons which impelled people in the settled areas of the Cape to take up stock farming in the remote interior was the unfavorable position of arable farming relative to pastoral farming. Whereas the Cape was for a long time in an unrivaled position as a provisioning station for fresh meat, her position as a supplier of grain, wine, and other arable produce was more often than not rather precarious.

The underlying reasons for this have to be sought in the nature of the demand for pastoral products. The Cape, by the very nature of its establishment as a provisioning station for passing ships, was a surplus producer and as such depended on foreign demand. As will be shown later, the expansion movement was to a large extent determined by the demand of passing ships, including the demand of the hospital at Capetown where the sick crews of the passing vessels were treated; the demand of passengers and crews staying at the Cape while their ships remained in the bay; the demand of the garrison and foreign troops staying at the Cape; and, last but not least, the demand of the inhabitants of Capetown. Now this demand was chiefly for fresh provisions, such as fresh meat, live animals, fresh butter, fresh fruit and vegetables. As far as the latter two products are concerned, however, it must be pointed out that owing to their perishability they could come only from the immediate vicinity of Capetown and therefore could not serve as a basis for expansion into the interior. It is true that there was also a demand for products of arable farming, such as cereals, wine, peas, and beans, but it must be borne in mind that neither the passing ships nor the soldiers and sailors on shore were dependent on Cape grain or peas and beans grown in the Cape.

These, as well as rice, could usually be obtained much cheaper elsewhere. Nor were the passing ships necessarily dependent on the not very popular Cape wines. On the other hand, it is important to bear in mind that the Cape definitely held a monopoly in fresh provisions, considering the very long sea voyages of those days. It is not for its grain and wine that the Cape became the *tavern of the oceans*. The seafarers of those days may not have known about vitamins, but they certainly suffered from scurvy and knew that fresh provisions, fresh vegetables and fruit, fresh meat and other animal products, were absolutely essential. It was in these fresh provisions that the Cape held a monopoly. Thunberg, referring to the hospital at the Cape, said: "What most contributes in this place to the recovery of the sick is the excellent refreshments of fresh meat and vegetables that are to be had here" (*1*, p. 248).

Occasionally there was a foreign demand at the Cape for grain and wine, as in the case of French and British troops stationed at the Cape, French troops in Mauritius, and British troops on St. Helena. But even they could have brought along with them all or most of the necessary bread cereals, rice, wine, and brandy from Europe or elsewhere. The only foodstuffs they could not have brought along with them were fresh provisions.

Of all the fresh provisions, meat was the most important single pastoral product that was demanded at the Cape market. At the same time, however, the meat supply, at the prices the Company was prepared to pay, was neither abundant nor always assured. The Company's merchant fleet, the garrison stationed at the Cape, and the Company's hospital in Capetown had first call on the meat supply; the population of Capetown came next; while foreign ships putting in to Table Bay came last. Obviously, such a system of priorities could be effective only under strict control. This, however, could not long be maintained, and it was the failure to control the cattle trade that was in part the measure of success of the expansion movement.

MEAT MONOPOLY

From the early days of the Cape the Company had tried to maintain a monopoly of the meat trade, an attempt in which it had not been wholly successful. For although the Company was theoretically the sole buyer and seller of both slaughter stock and fresh meat, the lucrativeness of the trade and the difficulty with which the law could be enforced encouraged the development of a smuggling trade in slaughter stock and meat (*2*, p. 82). In 1681 the government of the Company decided to lease to two contractors the monopoly for supplying meat to the Company, a system which proved to be much cheaper to the Company (*3*, p. 55). Subsequently, the contract was usually held by three or four men (*4*, p. 110; *3*, p. 56), who were granted grazing rights on extensive government lands where livestock brought from distant parts of the country could be rested and improved in condition.

The prices at which the contractors undertook to supply meat to the Company and to the population of Capetown were prearranged under the terms of their contract, but those chargeable to foreigners were free and exorbitant. It is for this reason that the sale of meat to foreigners was the most profitable part of the meat trade and was for a long time a bone of contention between the meat contractors and other butchers. It was this privilege to charge very high prices to foreign ships, particularly from the 1740's, that enabled the meat contractors to sell meat to the Company at low prices. In addition, the meat contractors had the right to charge higher prices to the burghers than to the Company (*4*, p. 89; *2*, p. 86), whereas the other butchers had to sell to the public at much lower prices (*2*, chap. 7; *5*, pp. 47–48).

MEAT PRICES AND THE EXPANSION MOVEMENT
DURING 1700–50

The early part of the eighteenth century, especially from about the middle of the second decade to about the middle of the twenties, was characterized by fairly high prices for meat. Between 1699 and 1705 the price paid by the Company to its meat contractors for sound and fresh meat was 2½ stuivers per pound. Between 1707 and 1714 the price dropped to only 1 stuiver and 5 duyte per pound, but in 1716 the Cape government had to pay 2 stuivers per pound, while the selling price to the public was fixed at 2½ stuivers per pound for mutton, 2 stuivers per pound for beef, and 5 stuivers per pound for fat. In 1720 the government had to pay 3 stuivers per pound of meat and in

1721 as much as 3½ stuivers per pound (*4*, pp. 89–90, 119; *2*, pp. 83–84). The price to the public was correspondingly higher.

The chief reason for these high prices was the diminution of the sheep numbers at the Cape, caused by a high mortality rate during the years 1713 to 1718, when the sheep population was reduced to about half its former size.[1] Although the Cape government, acting on instructions from the Council of Seventeen, tried its best to keep the price of meat down, it was unable to find a single burgher willing to supply meat at the fixed price. It was only in 1723 that the government was at last successful in concluding a contract for the delivery of meat at 2½ stuivers per pound. The price to the public was fixed at 3½ stuivers per pound (*2*, p. 86).

The most important single measure employed by the Cape government in the 1720's for keeping the price of meat down was the regulation against selling meat to foreign ships. The sale of live animals to foreigners was prohibited in July 1720, while the sale of fresh meat was prohibited in February 1724 (*6*, pp. 490–91). This as well as a series of other measures evolved by the government for the regulation of the meat trade proved quite effective (*2*, p. 86).

However, the lower prices of meat and slaughter stock were bound to affect adversely the livestock breeders and thus to discourage to some extent the expansion of livestock farming in the interior regions of the colony. In particular, it was the regulation against supplying meat and live animals to foreign ships, thus depriving the Capetown butchers of the most remunerative part of the meat trade, that was the most potent factor in depressing the prices of slaughter stock to the farmers.

The prohibition had also other unfortunate consequences. The Cape had already been unpopular with foreign ships as a place of provisioning on account of the excessive prices charged there, and the prohibition on the sale of meat is said to have had the effect of keeping away foreign customers from Table Bay for a number of years.[2] Instead of stopping at the Cape,

---

[1] See Table 3, chap. 8, p. 75.
[2] See Table 1, chap. 6, p. 51.

many French ships went to Mauritius, while many English ships turned to St. Helena. Since trade with foreign ships and boardinghouse keeping were the most important and lucrative occupations of the Cape inhabitants, the avoidance of the Cape by a large number of foreign ships constituted a serious blow to the economic life of the colony as a whole as well as to the frontier graziers.

From 1725 onward there was a continuous fall in the price of meat, both as a result of the measures referred to above and because of the natural increase in the livestock population (2, p. 87). In 1729 the government was able to obtain meat from the contractors at 12 duyte or 1½ stuivers per pound, while in 1743 the price paid by the government was as low as 6 duyte per pound (2, p. 87). In view of this plentiful supply, the regulation prohibiting the sale of meat to foreign ships was no longer enforced and foreign ships could obtain meat at the Cape at as low a price as 1½ to 2 stuivers per pound (7, p. 74). The low prices paid by the government during 1725–43 were perhaps not conducive to a great expansion of stock farming, though, as may be seen from Table 1 (chap. 6), the Cape was not entirely deserted by foreign shipping and the arrivals of Dutch ships during that period were fairly large. It is thus reasonable to assume that the outlet for meat was large though the prices were relatively low.

But that is not the whole story. What was perhaps of decisive importance is the fact that the condition of arable farming during that period was even more depressed than that of pastoral farming. It is therefore reasonable to conclude that on the whole the migration from the arable areas of the colony during the period 1717–43 was due to the relatively more depressed state of arable farming.

FIRST MEAT BOOM

The 1740's marked the turning point from depression to prosperity in the economic life of the colony. This was the time when the long struggle between England and France for trade and possessions in India culminated in the war of 1744–48. French and English ships, particularly English warships and transports, entering Table Bay for the purpose of provisioning brought with them great prosperity not only to Capetown but also to the frontier areas. For the demand of these ships was primarily for fresh meat, live animals, and other animal products, with the consequence that the stock breeder reaped the greatest benefit. Mention must also be made of another event which had a profound influence on the meat position at the Cape. In 1746–47 enormous swarms of locusts made their appearance in the colony, a plague from which it had been free since 1695. On December 28, 1746 the locusts "found their way in such vast numbers into Table Bay that the air seemed filled with them, and in a few days there was nothing edible left, not even leaves on the trees." So serious was the locust plague—it lasted for about four months—that the Council designated February 22, 1747 to be observed as "a day of fasting and prayer that God would be pleased to remove the plague." In the country districts the gardens were completely destroyed, and "as there was nothing left for the cattle to eat, so many oxen and sheep died that meat, which, owing to there having been no diseases among cattle for many years, had been previously sold at less than a penny halfpenny a Kilogramme, at once doubled in price" (7, pp. 80–81).

Although the peace between England and France was concluded at the end of 1748, there is reason to believe that the higher prices for meat and slaughter stock continued right into 1749, when Table Bay was visited by warships and troops on their homeward passage. It may therefore be assumed that it was during these years of prosperity that the expansion movement received its first great impetus.[3]

In 1748 the British Admiral Boscawen with a whole English fleet consisting of 26 men-of-war and transports put into Table Bay on his way to India (7, pp. 77–78). It was the most powerful fleet that had ever appeared on the Indian Ocean (8, p. 538). British troops landed at Capetown "and formed a camp just above the Company's garden, where they drilled for some weeks, as many of them were recruits." In 1749 "some ships of that fleet put into Table Bay when returning home," and a large number of Englishmen were on shore for some time (7, pp. 77–78).

[3] See infra, p. 52.

In other words, the fleet, the transports, and the troops were not just touching Table Bay, but were actually on shore for several weeks, so that the numbers of live animals, the quantities of fresh meat and other animal products both consumed on shore and taken away when leaving Table Bay must have been of such dimensions as to create the first great boom in animal products, especially when it is realized that the increased demand was superimposed on a greatly diminished supply of sheep and cattle.

CITATIONS

1 C. P. Thunberg, *Travels in Europe, Africa and Asia, Performed Between the Years 1770 and 1779*, 2 vols. (London, 1795), I.

2 A. J. H. van der Walt, *Die Ausdehnung der Kolonie am Kap der Guten Hoffnung (1700–1779)* (Berlin, 1928).

3 O. F. Mentzel, *A Geographical and Topographical Description of the Cape of Good Hope*, 3 vols. (Van Riebeeck Society Publication, No. 6), II.

4 *The Reports of Chavonnes and His Council, and of Van Imhoff, on the Cape* (Van Riebeeck Society Publication, No. 1).

5 A. L. Geyer, *Das wirtschaftliche System der Niederländischen Ostindischen Kompanie am Kap der Guten Hoffnung, 1785–1795* (Berlin, 1923).

6 G. M. Theal, *History of South Africa Before 1795*, 3 vols. (3d ed., London, 1922), II.

7 G. M. Theal, *History of South Africa Before 1795*, III.

8 A. W. Ward, G. W. Prothero, and Stanley Leathes, eds., *The Cambridge Modern History*, VI, *The Eighteenth Century* (Cambridge, 1909).

CHAPTER 6

"THE TAVERN OF THE OCEANS"
AND FRONTIER EXPANSION

Thus, one of the most important factors contributing to the increase in demand, at higher prices, for meat and other animal products beginning with the late 1740's was the large number of foreign warships and troops that put in to Table Bay. In order to appreciate the full significance of visiting ships at the Cape as a factor in the demand for fresh meat and slaughter stock, it must be realized that the demand was not limited to the amounts of fresh meat and live animals taken away by departing ships. Account must also be taken of the amounts consumed by crews, passengers, and troops during their long stay at the Cape.[1] An examination of the lists of arrivals and departures of ships shows that the average stay of a vessel at the Cape was about four weeks, thus suggesting that the demand of the ships' crews, passengers, and troops for fresh provisions while at the Cape was very considerable indeed. To this must also be added the demand for fresh provisions of the hospital at Capetown whose requirements generally fluctuated with the amount of shipping, that is to say, with the numbers of sick seamen that were tended there. Thus the *shipping demand* for fresh meat, live animals, and other animal products was comprised of the quantities consumed by the crews, passengers, and troops while staying at the Cape as well as of the quantities that were taken away by the passing ships when leaving the Cape.

How large was this demand for meat and live animals? In what follows, an attempt is made to form some idea of the magnitude of the demand for live animals, and of fresh meat in terms

[1] Major Alexander Gillespie, who visited Capetown in the early part of the nineteenth century, speaking of Capetown's boardinghouses, remarks: "As all passengers to or from India are supposed to disembark while these ships remain in port, those boarding places are much thronged during the whole period of their stay, and they were indeed established with that speculative view" (*1*, p. 21).

of live animals, supplied to the passing ships. Unfortunately, with the scanty information at our disposal, it is impossible to express quantitatively *the whole shipping demand* for meat and other animal products. Therefore, we shall have to confine ourselves solely to the amounts taken away by passing ships when leaving the Cape. Unfortunately even this demand can be estimated only for mutton and live sheep. The available information is insufficient to make a similar estimate of the quantitative demand for fresh beef and live cattle.

In so far as the Company's ships were concerned, in Mentzel's time (mid-eighteenth century) the quantity of mutton required annually was about 300,000 pounds. This quantity included four or more sheep per month for the Governor's table (2, pp. 139, 171). As to the weight of a Cape sheep, Mentzel says that "the average *dead* weight of the Afrikander sheep is about 65 lbs.," a figure which is probably too high. Barrow reports that Cape sheep weighed from 60 to 70 pounds "when taken from their pastures" (3, p. 67), and Bird states that a Cape sheep "if fat, weighs on an average about 45 lbs. without the offal" (4, p. 97). These figures seem to be more correct. The average carcass of a Cape sheep may, therefore, be estimated at about 40 pounds. Converting the 300,000 Dutch pounds given by Mentzel into 342,000 English pounds and deducting 2,000 pounds of meat required for the Governor's table, we get 340,000 pounds of meat annually, amounting to 8,500 sheep for 48 outgoing and 40 homeward-bound East Indiamen (2, p. 171), an average of about 97 sheep for each ship touching the Cape. In addition, each outgoing and homeward-bound ship took about 15 live sheep "in order to have fresh meat for the officers and the sick" (2, p. 171). In other words, the total amounted to about 112 sheep each. To this must be added a large, though unspecified, number of cattle which were required for the passing ships. Mentzel, for instance, says that "the Dutch East India Company takes the greatest pains in the preparation of this corned beef. During the autumn and winter, hundreds of fat oxen are slaughtered for the purpose" (5, p. 103).

The meat requirements of some English ships were estimated in the early part of the eighteenth century at 1,700 pounds per small ship carrying a small crew (6, p. 128). In terms of live sheep it amounted to about 26 sheep per small vessel. This estimate does not include a considerable number of live animals purchased by English captains. Most of these animals were slaughtered and the meat salted on board ship. Generally, a number of live sheep were also taken on board (7, p. 490). Larger foreign vessels, and especially men-of-war, naturally required much larger quantities of meat and much larger numbers of live animals.

The requirements of passing ships, based on an average of 112 sheep per ship, as percentages of the total sheep population of the colonists, are given below. These calculations are based on figures given in the sheep censuses of the eighteenth century and on the annual arrivals of ships in the Cape.

Year	Percentage	Year	Percentage	Year	Percentage
1701	13	1733	7	1768	3
1706	10	1738	6	1773	4
1711	7	1743	5	1778	3
1713	6	1748	5	1783	4
1718	13	1753	4	1788	4
1723	11	1758	5	1793	4
1728	9	1763	4		

The percentages are larger for the first three or four decades of the century because the colonists possessed smaller numbers of flocks during this period. On the other hand, it does not follow that the whole demand for mutton was necessarily met by the colonists from their own flocks. In fact, there is good reason to believe that in the early part of the eighteenth century the largest proportion of that supply came from the flocks of the Hottentots.

Table 1 shows the average number of ships that put into Cape ports throughout the eighteenth century. The increase in shipping, Dutch shipping in particular, during the years 1715–24 coincides with the first period of expansion to the west and south of the mountains, referred to earlier. It is interesting to note that the period during which foreign shipping was at its lowest level, 1725–39, coincides with the period during which the sale of meat to foreign ships was prohibited. At the same time, however, the whole period from 1715 to 1744 is charac-

terized by a high level of Dutch shipping, with the result that
the demand for meat and other animal products between 1725
and 1739 was still considerably higher than during the first fifteen years of the eighteenth century. This also accounts to some
extent for the continuation of the expansion movement from the
1720's to the 1740's, though perhaps at a slower rate than during
the 1715–24 period.

TABLE 1.—AVERAGE NUMBER OF SHIPS ARRIVING AT CAPE PORTS, 1700–99*

Period	Dutch	Foreign	Total
1700–04	48	22	70
1705–09	44	22	66
1710–14	48	21	69
1715–19	61	22	83
1720–24	72	23	95
1725–29	72	10	82
1730–34	65	12	77
1735–39	70	11	81
1740–44	52	18	70
1745–49	53	21	74
1750–54	55	18	73
1755–59	52	12	64
1760–64	50	19	69
1765–69	51	22	73
1770–74	53	53	106
1775–79	52	65	117
1780–84	31	98	129
1785–89	68	100	168
1790–93	58	97	155
1794	37	49	86
1796–99	—	185[a]	185

* Data for 1700–93, compiled from Coenraad Beyers, *Die Kaapse Patriotte, 1779–1791*
(Capetown, 1929), Appendix G, pp. 237–39; 1794 and 1796–99 from G. M. Theal, *History
of South Africa Before 1795*, 3 vols. (3d ed., London, 1922), III, p. 298, and *History of
South Africa Since 1795*, 5 vols. (5th ed., London, 1927), I, p. 41.
[a] Of these ships 73 were non-British.

As pointed out earlier, from 1742 to 1750 the Cape served
as a provisioning station not only for a larger number of foreign
merchantmen but also for foreign warships and transports, so
that the mere number of ships fails to give a true picture of the
demand for fresh provisions needed to supply the larger crews
of the warships. Needless to say, with the sale to foreigners
being the most remunerative part of the meat trade, the pros-

perity not only of Capetown but also that of the graziers was to a considerable extent determined by the number of foreign ships, and the size of their crews, putting in to Cape harbors. As may be seen from Table 1, in the five-year period 1740–44 the average annual number of foreign ships visiting the Cape amounted to 18 as contrasted with an annual average of 12 ships during the 1730–34 period, while the average number of ships during the period 1745–49 amounted to 21.

It is perhaps no mere coincidence that the expansion movement began in earnest in the 1740's. Indeed, at the beginning of the forties by far the greatest number of colonists still lived in the areas west and south of the mountains. Only a few colonists lived in the Bokkeveld, while not more than a few dozen lived in the Little Karroo on the northern slopes of the Langeberge. While it is true that the mountain ranges which form a barrier to the plains of the interior were reached and even crossed by some colonists before the forties, the trek over the mountains assumed large dimensions only in the forties (8, pp. 65–66). In 1746, a year after the first attempt to define the eastern boundary of the colony, the eastern group of colonists was already settled on the northeastern slopes of the Roggeveld across the Karroo, while their pastures extended as far north as the Renoster and the Little Riet rivers (8, pp. 68–69). It was between the years 1745 and 1755 that most of the Swellendam farmers who trekked out of the occupied area settled in the Little Karroo.

By the middle of the eighteenth century "farms were dotted along 160 miles of coast northwards from the Castle to the mouth of the Olifants, and some 200 miles eastward to Mossel Bay and beyond. Cattle farmers were already driving their herds on to the great Karroo and across the confines of the present Calvinia and Namaqualand (1750)" (9, p. 11). "The movement after 1730 and before 1750 to the north-west was over the mountain range running parallel to the west coast. The farmers chose places in the Bokkeveld and occupied the present districts of Ceres and Calvinia. One group pushed due north through the present Van Rhynsberg district and went into Namaqualand. . . . The Roggeveld was occupied during the forties" (10, p. 577). (See Map 2.)

As indicated in Table 1, the shipping position continued to be favorable up to about the middle of the 1750's. There was a drop in foreign shipping during 1755–59 when an average of only 12 foreign ships called at the Cape; but during that short period at least three of the foreign ships took on more than usual amounts of provisions as they were specially sent from Mauritius to procure provisions for the French troops there (*11*, p. 106). At any rate, foreign ships began to arrive in larger numbers again in 1758. This time it was the French who brought prosperity to the Cape, and from the end of 1758 until the termination of the Anglo-French war in India in 1763 the Cape experienced boom conditions. Indeed, at the end of 1758 and the beginning of 1759 a fleet of seventeen French men-of-war and transports with troops arrived from Mauritius "to refresh and lay in a supply of provisions. . . . At once the price of farm produce doubled or trebled, all the surplus stock was disposed of, and everything was paid in money. . . . French men-of-war until 1761, and after that date ships of both nations, came to the Cape to refresh and take supplies. The officers of French packets from Mauritius, and of English packets from St. Helena, bid against each other for cattle and meal and wine" (*11*, p. 106). In fact, so eager were the burghers to sell at high prices to the French that "on more than one occasion the government was unable to procure as much provision as was needed for the Company's ships" (*11*, pp. 106–07). In 1763, for instance, the government was compelled to prohibit the sale of butter to foreigners (*11*, p. 107).

As was shown in chapter 4, during this short period 1758–63, arable farmers who had their farms within a certain distance of Capetown were also in prosperous circumstances. Beyond certain limits, however, transport conditions rendered arable farming unprofitable, and the only way farmers in the more distant areas could participate in this prosperity of the Cape was to send livestock and livestock products to Capetown.

LONG PERIOD OF PROSPERITY

The 1758–63 boom was only a forerunner of a long period of great prosperity to come. The late 1760's marked the beginning of a most spectacular increase in foreign shipping, a development which assumed ever-larger dimensions in the following three decades, particularly in the 1770's and 1780's.[2] But,

[2] See Table 1.

as was pointed out in chapter 4, this increased demand did not benefit the wheat farmers. It was also during this long period of prosperity that the Company was able to obtain meat from the contractors at low prices. In 1775, for instance, the directors expressed satisfaction at the fact that the Company had succeeded in obtaining the meat contract at reduced prices. This was possible because the Company allowed contractors to fleece foreigners. Thus Moodie reports that because of the increased number of foreign vessels calling at the Cape, meat could be supplied to the Company at as low a price as 1*d.* a kilogram, while foreigners were charged as much as 4⅖*d.* per kilogram (*12*, p. 50 n.; *11*, p. 167). Thunberg, too, reports that in 1773 the price paid by foreigners for meat was five times as high as that paid by the Company (*13*, p. 262). Thunberg described the manner of conducting the victualing contract in 1773 as follows (*13*, p. 299):

He that bids the lowest at the auction is appointed the farmer general of this monopoly; viz. he that offers to furnish the Company with fresh meat for its ships and its other exigencies at the lowest price. From this contract, it is true, the Company receives no pecuniary advantage; but then it gets all its meat at a much lower price than it otherwise could possibly be obtained. It is in consequence of this contract also, that the burghers as well as strangers, are obliged to pay an extravagant price for butchers meat. Thus, whilst the company gets butchers meat for two doits per pound, the burghers must pay at the rate of four or more, and strangers two stuivers: and while a bullock, fit for slaughter, is commonly sold for five Dutch rixdollars, strangers must pay at the rate of ten or more.

Although the burghers were charged a relatively higher price for meat than the Company, they nevertheless benefited greatly from the lower price differential. Moodie, too, records that in 1775 the increase in foreign shipping to the Cape contributed to the lowering of meat prices to the public (*12*, p. 50). As late as 1796 the prices of meat provisions to foreigners, burghers, Dutch shipping, and soldiers were as follows (*14*):[3]

Item	Mutton and beef (lb.)	Sheep (head)
Strangers	4*d.*	4 Spanish dollars
Inhabitants	2*d.*	2 Spanish dollars
Dutch shipping and soldiers..	1½*d.*	———

[3] The weight of a sheep is given at 65–70 pounds.

What was the effect of this new prosperity on the expansion movement into the interior regions? We have no exact data for correlating the rate of expansion with the increase in foreign shipping or with the expansion of the market for pastoral products. Unfortunately, no information is available as to the number of farms that were actually occupied by colonists, irrespective of government permission, during the second half of the eighteenth century. Nor is any information readily available as to the number of loan farms granted in each of the years of that period. The following table shows the number of loan farms granted for each of the years 1768–78 (*12*, p. 73).

Year	New farms	Changes in residence	Year	New farms	Changes in residence
1768	53	41	1774	31	49
1769	138	40	1775	41	76
1770	91	56	1776	59	99
1771	88	60	1777	44	116
1772	88	58	7778	23	101
1773	73	60			

These were all farms occupied with government permission; but many more farms were probably occupied without it. For instance, many of the farms that were granted in the Zuurveld and beyond the Bruintjeshoogte after 1775 had been occupied earlier without official permission (*12*, p. 73).

In spite of the lack of complete quantitative data relating to the occupation of new farms, the large extent of the expansion during that period as well as the speed with which it took place can hardly be in doubt. Thunberg, writing of Kaffraria in 1774, said (*13*, pp. 106, 124–25):

It is not long since that this whole tract of land from Hartequas-Kloof down to Gamtous-rivier, which is now filled with settlements, was first peopled; and twenty-three years ago there was not a single farm, when, in the year seventeen hundred and fifty, Governor Tulbagh sent a caravan out to this coast, with a view to gain certain intelligence with respect to the country and its inhabitants. . . . Within these last 30 years, the colony has increased to such a degree, and with such rapidity, that not only the country from Roode Zand and Hottentot's Holland mountains, has been occupied and inhabited as far as Zwellendam, but also as far as Mosselbay, Houtniquas, Lange-Kloof, Krommeriver, and all the way to Gamtous-river, the Bokke- and Rogge-velds, Cambedo and the Snowmountains.

Walker considers the period between 1750 and 1795 "the

most rapid stage of the dispersion" (*9*, p. 11; see Map 2). It is
common knowledge that the eastern boundary of the colony had
to be moved four times within a period of 16 years, i.e., between
1770 and 1786. Walker explains the great rapidity of the expansion by the existence of the semiarid Great Karroo. "The old
name of Droogeveld [dry veld] tells why the farmers skirted
the Karroo" (*9*, p. 11). However, there is no complete una-
nimity even today as to the confines of the Great Karroo. In the
second half of the eighteenth century it was probably the driest
parts, in the center, that the farmers skirted. At any rate, even
without the arid part of the Karroo plains, the area occupied in
the second half of the eighteenth century must be considered very
large. Moreover, the Karroo, though not permanently settled in
the eighteenth century, was used by the colonists for winter
grazing.

However, the most interesting piece of evidence is the rapidity with which the boundary of the colony was moved between
1770 and 1786. Indeed, so rapid was the expansion during that
period that five years after the Stellenbosch and Swellendam
boundaries had been moved to the Gamtoos River in 1770, they
had to be moved again, in 1775, to the Bushmans River on the
south, and to the Fish River on the north. Five years later the
boundary was moved to the lower Fish River, and in 1786 it was
shifted to the Tarka and Baviaans rivers.

This successive shifting of the frontier within such a short
period by a government opposed to dispersion is rather surprising. There is reason to think that during this period of great
prosperity the government itself had a vital interest in the expansion of the frontiers of the colony. The Cape was now entirely
dependent on the colonists of the interior regions for its supply
of meat and other pastoral products for the Company's own needs
as well as for the very lucrative trade with foreigners, a trade
by which both the public and the government greatly benefited.
There was also a pressing need for an increased revenue. Government expenditures were rising and the treasury was becoming
empty (*11*, pp. 187, 207).

CITATIONS

1 Major Alexander Gillespie, *Gleanings and Remarks Collected During Many Months of Residence at Buenos Ayres and Within the Upper Country with a Prefatory Account of the Expedition from England until the Surrender of the Colony of the Cape of Good Hope* (Leeds, 1818).

2 O. F. Mentzel, *A Geographical and Topographical Description of the Cape of Good Hope*, 3 vols. (Van Riebeeck Society Publication, No. 4), I.

3 John Barrow, *Travels into the Interior of South Africa*, 2 vols. (2d ed., London, 1806), I.

4 W. W. Bird, *State of the Cape of Good Hope in 1822* (London, 1823).

5 O. F. Mentzel, *A Geographical and Topographical Description of the Cape of Good Hope* (Van Riebeeck Society Publication, No. 6), II.

6 *The Reports of Chavonnes and His Council, and of Van Imhoff, on the Cape* (Van Riebeeck Society Publication, No. 1).

7 G. M. Theal, *History of South Africa Before 1795*, 3 vols. (3d ed., London, 1922), II.

8 A. J. H. van der Walt, *Die Ausdehnung der Kolonie am Kap der Guten Hoffnung 1700–1779* (Berlin, 1928).

9 E. A. Walker, *Historical Atlas of South Africa* (Oxford, 1922).

10 C. G. Botha, "The Dispersion of the Stock Farmer in Cape Colony in the Eighteenth Century," *South African Journal of Science*, XX, 1923, pp. 574–80.

11 G. M. Theal, *History of South Africa Before 1795*, III.

12 D. Moodie, *The Record: or a Series of Official Papers Relative to the Conditions and Treatment of the Native Tribes of South Africa* (Capetown, 1838–41), Pt. III.

13 C. P. Thunberg, *Travels in Europe, Africa and Asia, Performed Between The Years 1770 and 1779*, 3 vols. (London, 1795), I.

14 Macartney Papers, Shipping and Trade, 1795–96 (The Gubbins Collection of Africana, University of the Witwatersrand Library).

CHAPTER 7

THE NATURE OF THE DEMAND FOR
OTHER ANIMAL PRODUCTS

Slaughter stock and draft oxen were not the only products that were sent by farmers of the interior to the Cape market. There was a variety of other products, mostly of animal origin, which played a very important part in the frontier economy. Apart from such animal products as butter, fat, tallow, hides and skins, and hoofs and horns, consideration must also be given to a variety of products derived from wild animals, such as venison, the famous South African biltong (jerked beef), skins, ivory, teeth and fat of the hippopotamus, ostrich feathers, and ostrich eggs. Particular attention is also drawn to the production of soap and candles, soda ash, and berry wax, which came to the Cape markets from the interior and frontier districts. The significance of all these products in the frontier economy has generally been entirely overlooked.

BUTTER

There was always a good demand for butter at the Cape both for local consumption and for the passing ships. Significant quantities of butter were first exported from the Cape to India in 1754. Thereafter, for a period of eighteen years, the quantity of butter exported averaged 10,125 kilograms per annum. It was usually purchased at the Company's stores at 13 to 17½ pence per kilogram, but in times of scarcity as much as 2s. 1½d. per kilogram was paid for it (1, p. 163).

In the early 1770's fresh butter was sold in Capetown at from 7 to 16 stuivers, and salted butter at from 2 to 6 stuivers per pound, the prices varying with market conditions in Capetown (2, p. 251). Sparrman reports that Swellendam butter (probably salted) sold in Capetown at from 3 to 6 stuivers per pound, the resale price to ships being 20 to 100 per cent higher (3, p.

245). At the end of the eighteenth and the beginning of the nineteenth century, butter from the Swellendam district fetched 6*d*. per pound in Capetown (*4*, p. 201; *5*, p. 207).

Sparrman also reports that an average Swellendam farmer produced from 1,800 to 3,500 pounds of butter a year, which he took to Capetown in one or two journeys (*3*, p. 245). This would mean that at the end of the eighteenth century the cash receipts of an average Swellendam farmer producing, say, 2,600 pounds of butter a year were, from the sale of butter alone, as high as £66 per annum. Such a state of affairs is a far cry from a self-sufficient economy; and even if the price of salted butter had been as low as 3*d*. per pound, cash receipts would have amounted to £33 per annum.

Some farmers derived the main part of their cash income from butter production; some sold both butter and cattle; while others again, notably young graziers and managers of large grazing farms, sold butter and wethers (*6*, p. 63; *7*, pp. 111, 114). At the end of the eighteenth century and the beginning of the nineteenth, the best butter came from the Sneeuwbergen (*8*, p. 330). Considerable quantities of this butter, "salted and put up in casks," sold at a premium in Capetown (*8*, p. 204). The bulk of the butter, however, came from the Swellendam district, where some farmers derived "their whole income and support from this line of farming" (*5*, p. 206).

With the expansion of the colony to the east and the northeast, and the emergence of Port Elizabeth as a new shipping center, and Graaff Reinet, Grahamstown, and Uitenhage as new trading centers, butter production shifted to the eastern and northeastern areas of the colony (see chap. 12).

The importance of butter production in the Eastern Province may be seen from the following list of the quantities of butter exported direct from Port Elizabeth (*9*, p. 201):

Year	Pounds	Year	Pounds
1835	37,882	1839	62,420
1836	60,339	1840	123,063
1837	128,931	1841	179,815
1838	67,299		

From the early 1820's the best butter in the whole colony was shipped from Port Elizabeth. Mauritius provided a ready and constant market long after St. Helena had lost its importance as a market for Cape butter. In the early 1840's butter was generally shipped in small casks of about 50 pounds, and was valued at Port Elizabeth at about 9*d.* per pound, exclusive of casks and charges. Butter exported for the Capetown market contained less salt than butter destined for long voyages (*9*, p. 164). The value of butter exported from the Albany district rose from £1,486 in 1828 to £3,300 in 1829 and £5,389 in 1830 (*10*). In the late 1830's butter was one of the important products of the district of Somerset and one of the staple products of the district of Cradock (*9*, pp. 55, 65, 72).

TALLOW

During the eighteenth century the export of tallow from the Cape was probably of little importance. In 1772, 2,404 kilograms of tallow, purchased by the Company at 44*s.* per 100 kilograms, were sent to Holland as part of a cargo of other Cape produce, and during the nine-year period 1772–80 over 5,245 kilograms of tallow were exported to India. The price paid by the Company—4½*d.* per kilogram—was considered very low (*1*, p. 162). But the production and export of tallow did not assume importance until the nineteenth century. Before that, there is reason to believe that very little tallow was available for export from the Cape. In spite of the fact that the meat contractors had at their disposal the Groene Kloof, a large government farm for fattening stock near Capetown, most of the slaughter stock killed in Capetown was in poor condition, largely owing to the fact that most of the animals were killed "the moment they arrived from a journey of forty or fifty days" (*4*, p. 39). While it is true that Cape mutton was of excellent quality, Cape beef was said to be tough and tasteless (*11*, pp. 83–84). Barrow spoke of the quality of Cape beef as "very bad" (*4*, p. 39), while Percival complained that the Cape beef was "seldom fat and in good order, but generally tough and lean" (*5*, p. 262). Although this long journey through the arid Karroo was made by both sheep and cattle, sheep, especially the fat-tailed sheep, could stand such a journey without impairing the quality of the meat, though even sheep would lose some 20 to 30 pounds in weight (*4*, p. 67). In other words, despite the fact that the price of tallow was higher than the price of meat, the whole animal had to walk to the Cape market—marching on its fat, as it were.

All this meant that comparatively little tallow was produced in Capetown itself; it also seems that the quantities of tallow brought to the market by ox wagon from the country districts were probably not very large. Indeed, the fact that tallow was scarce in Capetown at the end of the eighteenth century and the beginning of the nineteenth is confirmed by Barrow, who states that "the tallow to be purchased at the Cape is barely sufficient for the consumption of the town and the garrison, and the candles made from it are seldom lower than fifteen pence a pound" (4, p. 332). It is true that quantities of tallow were produced on the frontier farms, but, as will be shown later, they were used mostly for making soap, as it was easier to transport soap from the farms than tallow. The latter could be carried only in casks, which were always in short supply and utilized in carrying products of higher value. It was soap rather than tallow that the farmers carried to Capetown.

The establishment of coastal trading between Capetown and the cattle districts in the east could have solved the problem of transporting tallow and salted meat as well as other salted provisions. But coastal trading was a comparatively late development in the history of the Cape.

Indeed, van Reenen, writing in 1803, refers to the "most delightful and excellent regions" of the eastern part of the colony, such as Zeekoe, Gamtoos, and van Stadens River, Winterhoek, Sunday and Bushmans rivers, Bruintjeshoogte, the Zuurvelden, and the Great Fish River, most of which were "most suitable for sheep and cattle" (12, p. 139). These districts, van Reenen thought, "could become very flourishing if shipping were introduced for the transportation of products" (12, p. 139). Van Reenen also observed that the pure and plentiful supply of salt from the saltpan "at an hour's distance" from the Bay of Algoa could be used for establishing a factory for preserving meat there. "At present," van Reenen says, "owing to the distance of transport, the cattle become thin and get into poor condition before they arrive at the Capital." Given shipping facilities and the establishment of a factory for preserving meat, van Reenen rightly believed that "it would be possible to supply the garrison at the Cape with good meat quite successfully" (*12*, p. 137). However, it was not before the 1810's that meat was first shipped from Algoa Bay to the Cape, and not before the 1820's that coastal trading between Table Bay and Algoa Bay was more fully developed. It was only from the 1810's or 1820's that it became possible to send salted meat, butter, and other salted provisions from Port Elizabeth to Capetown. In fact, with the improvement of the harbor facilities at Port Elizabeth, not only were all kinds of provisions taken by passing ships, but also salted provisions were shipped from there direct to St. Helena and Mauritius.

A regular export of tallow from the Cape to England and other countries began only in the late 1820's. In 1828 tallow was already one of the principal export products from the Albany district, its export value from that district alone having risen from £1,400 in 1828 to £1,600 in 1829, and to £4,500 in 1830. The total quantity of tallow exported from the colony in 1832 amounted to 662,630 pounds, valued at £10,742 (*13*, 1834, p. 106).[1]

SHEEP'S TAIL FAT

Sheep's tail fat, derived, as its name implies, from the tails of the aboriginal Cape sheep, was for a long time the staple fat of the colony. Tail fat was not only a very important article of food, but also was used extensively for lighting, for making candles and soap, and as wagon grease. "Many people, and particularly sailors, instead of butter, used to purchase the fat that had been melted down from the large tails of the African sheep." The fat was put into little tubs "with some salt and pepper, and used at sea with bread in lieu of butter" (*2*, p. 300; see also *5*, p. 164). In the early part of the nineteenth century, too, "the fat-tail was a very useful article in the household affairs at the Cape. . . . Salted it is used to lard the venison of the Colony, which is somewhat dry; for frying and pastry, it is excellent, and it is often employed as a substitute for butter. The tips of the tail, when melted down, give a very pure and transparent oil" (*9*, p. 171). The fat was considered too oleaginous, however, to be employed alone as tallow for making candles, and had to

---

[1] See also Appendix Table III.

be mixed for that purpose with the hard tallow of the goat, or with berry wax (*14*, p. 332).

Apart from being sold to the crews of passing ships, sheep's tail fat and sheep's tail oil were also articles of export from the Cape. In 1832, for instance, 2,710 gallons of sheep's tail oil were exported at a value of £375, or about 2*s*. 8*d*. per gallon (see Appendix Table III). There is reason to believe that sheep's tail fat (unlike cattle tallow) was produced in large quantities on the farms of the interior, since two sheep, and sometimes more, were slaughtered daily on the farms for family consumption (*15*, p. 113; *16*, p. 19). Some of this fat was brought to the Cape, where it found a ready market, but most of it was used for making soap and candles on the farms.

OSTRICH FEATHERS AND OSTRICH EGGS

Ostrich feathers and ostrich eggs represented another source of income. Ostrich feathers, in fact, were exported from the Cape as far back as the first half of the eighteenth century.

Thunberg reports that ostrich eggs were purchased mostly by the naval officers (*2*, pp. 300–01).

These eggs sold in general for a skelling a piece, or about sixpence English. They are fittest, and most used for cakes and oeufs perdus; and they are particularly good when eaten with a large quantity of butter. One single egg is sufficient for several people. And whereas hens eggs will seldom keep for any length of time on board of ship, and require great pains to be taken with them in order to turn them every day, ostriches eggs are easily preserved at sea on account of their size, and of their thick and strong shells.

In the years (1803–06) of Lichtenstein's visit to the Cape, ostrich eggs sold in Capetown for one rix-dollar each (*17*, p. 27).

Percival reports that at the beginning of the nineteenth century the price of a fine ostrich feather in Capetown was as high as 1½ to 3 rix-dollars. He also reports that in consequence of the high prices obtained for the feathers, "the farmers and country people killed a great number of ostriches, and sent them to town. . . . Sir George Young, fearing they might all be destroyed, except in the very remote part of the Colony, issued strict orders to prevent their being killed, and enacted a very severe penalty against those who disobeyed" (*5*, p. 167). At the beginning of the 1820's, ostrich feathers constituted an important article of trade in the eastern parts of the colony, and were shipped from Port Elizabeth to Capetown (*18*, p. 121).

Even in later years, ostrich feathers were procured not only by professional traders from the natives at Fort Willshire fair and in Kaffirland, but also by farmers of the interior and frontier districts (*19*, p. 124). In the early 1830's, farmers from the most distant parts of the colony could be met at the Grahamstown public market "with various curiosities for sale, such as skins of wild animals, ostrich feathers, and ivory" (*20*, p. 455). Pringle reports that on the northern border of the Karroo, Boers "made the pursuit of the ostrich, for the sake of its plumage, one of their chief occupations, thus combining profit with pass time." An ostrich's skin, in the 1820's, brought in from 15 to 25 shillings sterling, while the fine feathers, about 45 in number, brought in from 6*d*. to 1*s*. each (*16*, p. 58). The trade in ostrich feathers must have been profitable to the frontier farmers, since feathers were obtained mostly in barter with the natives for beads, buttons, and other articles of comparatively little value.

IVORY AND SKINS

As in the case of ostrich feathers, ivory and skins of wild animals, too, came to market from the frontier areas. While many colonists at the frontier combined the business of a grazier with that of a trader, bartering cattle, ivory, skins, etc., with the native tribes, others combined cattle farming with hunting (*6*, pp. 67–68). The abundance of game on the frontier farms and in the areas beyond the frontier undoubtedly played an important part in the expansion movement. In some places game was so abundant that venison could be procured with the greatest of ease (*8*, pp. 123–24). Without having to encroach on their flocks and herds, farmers could provide themselves not only with meat, but also with skins of wild animals.

The following citation from Thunberg's description of the life of the frontier farmers in the 1770's demonstrates the importance of game in the economy of the frontier colonists (*2*, pp. 194–95).

The whole roof in the kitchen was hung with thick slices of buffalo's flesh, which, being dried and smoked, they ate as hung beef. . . . Buffaloes were shot here by a Hottentot, who had been trained to this business by the farmer, and in this manner found the whole family in meat, without having recourse to the herd. The balls were counted out to him every time he went ashooting, and he was obliged to furnish the same number of dead buffaloes as he received of balls. Thus the many Hottentots that lived here were supported without expense, and without the decrease of the tame cattle, which constituted the whole of the farmer's wealth. The greatest part of the flesh of the buffalo falls to the share of the Hottentots, but the hide to that of the master.

In many other parts the farmer's meat supply was provided by springboks. They were abundant, and out of their skins the farmers made large karosses.[2] In other parts, again, the presence of elephants and hippopotamuses presented at least as big an attraction as good grazing, and ivory and skins of wild animals were exported from the Cape as far back as the first half of the eighteenth century (*1*, p. 81).

Most of the ivory came from Kaffirland, a fact which to some extent accounts for the eastward direction of the expansion movement during the second half of the eighteenth century. As pointed out by van der Merwe (*21*, pp. 28–29), elephant hunting was encouraged by the Company as there was a great demand for ivory in Batavia. But van der Merwe rather tends to minimize the importance of ivory as a source of income during the eighteenth century. He states that right through the eighteenth century ivory had to be delivered to the Company at only 16 stuivers (or about 1*s*. 4*d*.) per pound for first-grade ivory, 8 stuivers per pound for second-grade, and 16 stuivers for three pounds of third-grade ivory (*21*, p. 37). He also quotes figures to show that in the decade 1769/70 to 1778/79 only 8,889 pounds of ivory was sold to the Company at a value of £451 13*s*. 0*d*.

As regards the quantities of ivory sold, van der Merwe himself admits that in view of the smuggling trade in ivory the above figures do not give a true picture of the actual situation. Although he quotes Sparrman to the effect that farmers used to bring ivory hidden in butter vats to Capetown for sale, he nevertheless seems to doubt whether the smuggling trade in ivory was of such dimensions as to make elephant hunting sufficiently profitable.

Admittedly, information on this point is lacking, but Batavia and the Dutch East India Company were not the only buyers of ivory, and, considering the fact that nearly everybody in eighteenth-century Capetown was a trader (*11*, p. 75), and that a very brisk trade was carried on with both Dutch and foreign naval

---

[2] Kaross—mantle made of the skins of animals with the hair on.

officers (*2*, p. 261), it would have been surprising if the colonists had not sold a large proportion of their ivory at prices higher than those fixed by the Company. Second, as mentioned already, a large proportion of ivory was obtained through barter with the native tribes for articles of comparatively little value, so that even 16 stuivers (1*s.* 4*d.*) per pound was not an unprofitable price. In fact, this price could hardly have been unprofitable even to the European elephant hunters themselves, for it seemed to have been profitable in Sparrman's time to produce and deliver butter at 3 to 6 stuivers per pound. Finally, there is evidence that the Company paid higher prices than those mentioned by van der Merwe. Thus Thunberg, writing in 1773, says (*6*, pp. 39–40): "Each elephant's tooth weighs from thirty to one hundred and thirty pounds. They are bought up by the Dutch Company at the rate of one gilder [one guilder equal to 1*s.* 8*d.*] per pound."

Mentzel, too, speaking of the expeditions to barter cattle with the natives, said that they bartered mostly elephant tusks with the natives, cattle bartering being "only a secondary matter which is postponed until the return journey" (*7*, p. 126). The Company paid 20 stuivers per pound for large elephant tusks, and 12 or 16 stuivers per pound for the smaller ones (*7*, p. 127).

The price of ivory at Fort Willshire in 1824–25 was on an average 1 to 1½ rix-dollars per pound (in 1824–25 the rix-dollar was equal to only 1*s.* 6*d.*), varying with the price given for beads, buttons, etc. The price of beads varied from 4½ to 20 rix-dollars and upward per pound. Buttons varied in price from 4 to 10 rix-dollars and upward per gross (*22*, p. 182). The articles given by the colonists for ivory were: beads, buttons, knives, tinder boxes, axes (large and small), blankets, and handkerchiefs. The market price of elephant teeth in Capetown in 1826 was 3*s.* to 3*s.* 9*d.* per pound (*23*).

The value in pounds of ivory exported from the Cape to Great Britain in the years 1813–17 was as follows (*25*, p. 293):

Year	Value
1813	3
1815	59
1816	282
1817	4,091

The following figures show the quantities in pounds, and the values in rix-dollars, of ivory (elephant and hippopotamus teeth) exported from the Cape during the years 1820–26 (*24*, p. 502):

Year	Quantity	Value
1820	9,510	17,560
1821	4,538	8,350
1822	24,420	46,750
1823	19,855	42,576
1824	20,061	44,587
1825	106,778	221,146
1826	48,258	103,996

HIDES, SKINS, AND HORNS

For a long time there seemed to have been very little demand at the Cape for hides and skins of domestic animals. All the skins and hides required for the Company's stables and ships were supplied gratis by the meat contractors (*11*, p. 55). In the eighteenth century the prices of hides and skins were rather low, "ranging from one rijksdaalder [rix-dollar] for an ox-hide to half a stuiver for a sheepskin, and this only in fresh condition, since a dried sheepskin is useless for any leather manufacturer" (*11*, p. 55). In later years, however, dry oxhides and calfskins were sold together with skins of wild animals to foreigners, especially to Americans (*26*, pp. 55–56), while considerable quantities of hides and skins were also exported to Holland (*27*, p. 243). But it was only with the development of coastal trading in the 1820's that an outlet was found for the hides and skins produced in the frontier districts. The following tabulation shows the exports of hides (ox and horse) from the Cape of Good Hope, 1820–26 (*24*, p. 502):

Year	Quantity (*pieces*)	Value (*rix-dollars*)
1820	3,819	30,990
1821	2,732	15,880
1822	16,391	127,304
1823	15,017	110,311
1824	12,126	104,829
1825	29,722	313,920
1826	40,097	280,413

The demand for horns, too, was a comparatively late development in the history of the colony. The trade developed in the 1820's when "a keen-sighted merchant adventured a few to England, and the trial proved successful" (*9*, p. 163).

The development of the export trade in hides, skins, and horns in the fifteen years between 1822 and 1837 is shown in the following table:

TABLE 2.—EXPORT OF HIDES, SKINS, AND HORNS, FROM CAPE PORTS, 1822–37*

(Value in pounds sterling)

Year	Hides (ox, horse, cow)		Skins (sheep, goat, calf)		Horns	
	Number	Value	Number	Value	Number	Value
1822[a]	16,638	13,581	115,860	8,386	...	...
1823	15,011	11,031	97,277	8,257	...	1,797
1824[a]	12,126	9,804	44,896	4,325	48,436	948
1825[a]	29,722	23,544	98,939	10,780	62,554	1,456
1826[a]	40,099	21,054	120,715	9,134	66,615	1,681
1827[a]	75,210	27,092	110,179	6,588	78,289	2,502
1828[a]	55,729	22,675	112,484	6,683	95,069	3,322
1829	79,035	33,723	...	12,506	302,032	6,621
1830[a]	39,483	20,251	133,575	8,900	156,077	4,400
1831[a]	32,766	22,536	113,909	7,673	147,095	4,887
1832[b]	54,989	40,821	173,611	11,394	167,024	6,110
1833[a]	36,836	27,326	185,572	12,193	63,715	2,318
1834[a,c]	20,664	13,906	309,630	18,611	234,253	4,572
1835[d]	57,603	25,685	339,808	20,895	129,378	3,303
1836[e]	17,947	15,476	79,793	5,571	58,571	2,115
1837[d]	32,767	19,402	268,536	22,045	145,672	3,415

* Data from Colonial Secretary's Office, *Cape of Good Hope Blue Book*, 1822 to 1837 (Capetown), unless otherwise stated.

[a] Exports from Table Bay only. The export value of hides and skins from Simon's Bay in 1822 amounted to £516, consisting of 1,290 hides and skins.

[b] George Greig, compiler, *South African Directory and Almanac*, 1834 (Capetown).

[c] The total export value of hides, horns, and skins in 1834 was £83,435 (*9*, p. 198).

[d] The figures represent totals of exports from Capetown and Port Elizabeth; the export figures from Port Elizabeth are those given by Chase (*9*, p. 201).

[e] Exports from Port Elizabeth only. The total export value of hides, horns, and skins from Capetown and Port Elizabeth in 1836 amounted to £74,246 (*9*, p. 198).

As may be seen from the above table, the export trade in hides, skins, and horns advanced rapidly from the early 1820's; it soon became the most important export item after wine and brandy. As we have seen earlier, the export market for tallow, salted meat, and butter developed along similar lines. In what manner and to what extent these developments influenced the pastoral economy of the frontier, and what bearing they had on the expansion movement, we propose to examine later.

CITATIONS

1 G. M. Theal, *History of South Africa Before 1795*, 3 vols. (3d ed., London, 1922), III.

2 C. P. Thunberg, *Travels in Europe, Africa and Asia, Performed Between the Years 1770 and 1779*, 3 vols. (London, 1795), I.

3 Andrew Sparrman, *A Voyage to the Cape of Good Hope from the Year 1772 to 1776* (London, 1785), II.

4 John Barrow, *Travels into the Interior of South Africa*, 2 vols. (2d ed., London, 1806), I.

5 Robert Percival, *An Account of the Cape of Good Hope* (London, 1804).

6 C. P. Thunberg, *Travels in Europe, Africa and Asia*, II.

7 O. F. Mentzel, *A Geographical and Topographical Description of the Cape of Good Hope*, 3 vols. (Van Riebeeck Society Publication, No. 25), III.

8 John Barrow, *Travels into the Interior of South Africa*, II.

9 J. C. Chase, *The Cape of Good Hope and the Eastern Province of Algoa Bay* (London, 1843).

10 Colonial Secretary's Office, *Cape of Good Hope Blue Book* (Capetown), 1829.

11 O. F. Mentzel, *A Geographical and Topographical Description of the Cape of Good Hope* (Van Riebeeck Society Publication, No. 6), II.

12 D. G. van Reenen, *Die Journal van Dirk Gysbert van Reenen, 1803* (Van Riebeeck Society Publication, No. 18).

13 George Greig, compiler, *South African Almanack and Directory* (Capetown), 1832.

14 W. J. Burchell, *Travels in the Interior of Southern Africa*, 2 vols. (London, 1822), I.

15 W. J. Burchell, *Travels in the Interior of Southern Africa*, II.

16 Thomas Pringle, *Narrative of a Residence in South Africa* (new ed., London, 1840).

17 Henry Lichtenstein, *Travels in Southern Africa, in the Years 1803, 1804, 1805 and 1806*, 2 vols. (Van Riebeeck Society Publication, No. 11), II.

18 W. W. Bird, *State of the Cape of Good Hope in 1822* (London, 1823).

19 Andrew Steedman, *Wanderings and Adventures in the Interior of Southern Africa*, 2 vols. (London, 1835), I.

20 Stephen Kay, *Travels and Researches in Caffraria* (London, 1833).

21 P. J. van der Merwe, *Trek: Studies oor die Mobiliteit van de Pionersbevolking aan die Kaap* (Capetown, 1938).

22 G. M. Theal, *Records of the Cape Colony*, 36 vols. (Govt. of the Cape Colony, 1897–1905), XX.

23 *Cape Gazette*, May 5, 1826.

24 G. M. Theal, *Records*, XXVIII.

25 G. M. Theal, *Records*, XI.

26 G. M. Theal, *Belangrijke Historische Dokumenten Over Zuid Afrika*, 3 vols. (Govt. of South Africa, 1911), III.

27 J. A. de Mist, *Memorandum on the Cape* (Van Riebeeck Society Publication, No. 3).

CHAPTER 8

SHEEP, SOAP, BERRY WAX, AND THE FRONTIER ECONOMY

The preceding chapters dealt with the demand for livestock and livestock products as well as with the demand for other frontier products. This chapter examines the structure of the frontier economy of the Cape as it evolved under the influence of market demand and natural environment. It also considers the part played in the expansion movement by such products as soap, candles, berry wax, and soda ash.

UTILIZATION OF ARID LANDS

Already in the early part of the eighteenth century we find colonists in possession of extensive areas of land and large numbers of livestock. The size of the farms was determined not so much by the abundance of available land as by the natural conditions of the regions in which the land was situated. In the last resort it was the aridity of these regions and the consequent low carrying capacity of the natural pasture that determined the nature of farming which the colonists had to pursue as well as the size of the farm unit.

But that was not all. There was also the question as to the kind of animal to be employed for the best utilization of the extensive grazing areas of the interior. This, too, depended to a large extent upon natural conditions. Generally speaking, sheep farming will be favored in arid and semiarid conditions, while cattle farming will require more humid conditions. Thus, for example, the drier regions of South Africa and Australia favored sheep farming, while the mild, temperate climate and the abundant rainfall prevailing in the Argentine Pampas made that region more suitable for cattle farming.

The natural pasturage of the arid and semiarid territories of the Cape was more suitable for sheep and goats than for cattle,

MAP 3

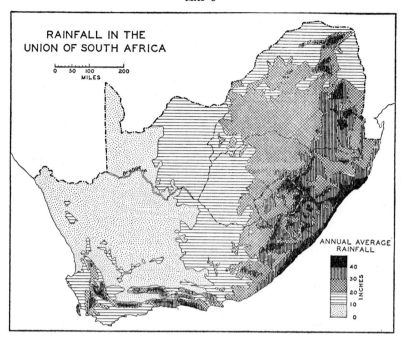

MAP 4*

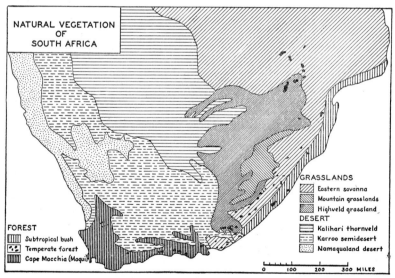

* Based on Map in W. R. Thompson, *Moisture and Farming in South Africa* (South Africa: Central News Agency, Ltd., 1936), facing p. 96.

with the result that animal husbandry in those regions was based
largely on sheep farming. While it is true that in some of the
better-watered areas cattle farming was important, the fact remains that sheep farming was the most important animal industry of the Cape and that it played the most decisive part in the
occupation of the interior regions and in the continual expansion
of the frontier of the colony.

Indeed, the suitability of the interior regions of the Cape for
sheep had been recognized very early by the colonists, and the
Karroo was known as excellent sheep country. Thunberg reports
that the Middle Roggeveld "produces good fodder for sheep and
horses only, of which there are great numbers, but very little
horned cattle, on most of the farms" (*1*, p. 168).

But even the country about Bushmans River, Sunday River,
and Bruintjeshoogte was more suitable for sheep than for cattle
on account of the small salty bushes which were found there,
though the country between the lower Fish and lower Sunday
rivers was good cattle country (*2*, p. 195). The Zoete Valley
along the Zeekoe River, too, was good sheep country, but only the
country along the Gamtoos and Van Stadens rivers was good for
both cattle and sheep. This dual suitability also applied to the
regions from the foot of the Sneeuwbergen to the Orange River
(*2*, pp. 139, 237, 241). On the other hand, the upper Fish River,
Zak River, and the Sneeuwbergen districts actually produced
more sheep than cattle (*2*, p. 277).

Only parts of Albany were good cattle country. In fact, the
northeastern division of Albany was considered better suited for
sheep than for cattle (*3*, p. 175). Even in areas where the pasture
was more suitable for cattle, large numbers of sheep were raised
for the extensive domestic requirements of the farmer (*2*, p. 75).
Indeed, as Pringle reports (*4*, p. 19; see also *5*, p. 113):

. . . two sheep, and sometimes more, were daily slaughtered for family consumption, the Hottentot herdsmen and their families, as well as the farmer's
own household, being chiefly fed upon mutton, at least during summer, when
beef could not be properly cured.

In other words, sheep farming rather than cattle farming
fitted in best both with the natural conditions of the dry regions
of the interior and the domestic economy of the colonists.

What makes sheep more suitable for the utilization of scanty pasturage is, above all, the fact that the sheep is essentially an animal of arid and semiarid regions. Second, the sheep is generally distinguished by its nimble movements and its capacity to cover long distances in search for food, qualities which make the sheep a migratory animal *par excellence*. Third, owing to their manifest herd instinct, sheep can be easily kept together in flocks and thus more easily handled than cattle.

But what makes the sheep particularly valuable for the utilization of scanty pasturage is the fact that its great mobility, coupled with its pointed mouth and nimble lips, enables it not only to pick up thinly scattered blades of grass, but also to select from among the vegetation the best individual plants or the best parts of the same plant with much greater ease than any other domestic animal except perhaps the goat. In fact, sheep thrive well on pastures which could hardly sustain cattle.

Indeed, there is a certain relationship between the scantiness of the pasture and the degree of mobility of the animal, a relationship which has been expressed by Aereboe in the following rule: the scantier the pasture the greater must be the mobility of the animal if the pasture is to be utilized to the best possible advantage.[1]

It may also be noted here that, as far as mobility is concerned, the goat is in no way inferior to the sheep, and where the pasture consists mainly of bushes, as it does in the more arid regions of South Africa, the goat answers the purpose even better, since it browses the foliage of bushes and trees even more greedily than the sheep. Moreover, owing to its being a much better climber than the sheep, the goat is particularly suited for utilization of the vegetation on steep mountain slopes (6, p. 76).

In view of these considerations, it is of particular interest that the breeds of sheep and goats which the early colonists had found in the Cape proved eminently suitable for the mountainous and arid areas of the interior. This is particularly true with regard to the fat-tailed Hottentot sheep and the Cape goat, which are able to subsist on scanty pasturage. A typical animal of arid regions, the fat-tailed sheep stores up the whole of its fat in its

---

[1] "*Je spärlicher die Weide, desto beweglicher müssen die Weidetiere sein, um sie auszunutzen, auf ihnen noch erzeugen zu können, das ist ein Grundsatz von weittragendster Bedeutung für die Wahl der Nutzviehzweige und deren Rassen*" (6, p. 75).

broad tail and rump, thus rendering the animal a very efficient fat producer. Moreover, owing to its strong and robust constitution, the Hottentot sheep is very resistant to disease, while its strong and long legs enable it to cover a more extensive area of scanty range than any other breed of sheep.

As to the African goat, we have it from Barrow that it was the most profitable animal[2] for home consumption (7, pp. 67–68).

The African goat is the finest of the species I ever saw, and so wonderfully prolific that it is considered as the most profitable animal for home consumption that can be kept. They go twenty weeks with young, and seldom have less than two at a birth, very commonly three, and frequently four. The flesh, though much inferior to mutton, is quite good enough for the Hottentots in the service of the farmer; and the choice pieces, well soaked in the fat of sheeps' tails, are served upon his own table.

The first European colonists were also very fortunate in having found in the Cape long-horned cattle which served as draft oxen. But what was of no less importance was the fact that the colonists had found in the Hottentots careful shepherds and herdsmen. The Hottentots also proved to be skilled trainers of draft oxen (8, pp. 177–80; 1, p. 65). Indeed it was with the assistance of the Hottentot herdsmen and shepherds, trainers of draft oxen and wagon drivers, that the vast territories of the interior could be utilized. Without the Hottentots no such rapid expansion of the colony could have taken place.

CATTLE AND SHEEP NUMBERS IN THE EIGHTEENTH CENTURY

The relative numbers of cattle and sheep in the Cape in the eighteenth century are shown in Table 3. The figures in this table were derived from the annual returns (*opgaaf*) of the colonists who, being liable for a tax assessment on their flocks and herds, were said to have been inclined to underestimate the numbers of livestock they actually possessed.[3] On the other hand, the figures demonstrate the predominant importance of sheep farm-

---

[2] The fact that the goat is now universally condemned as a cause of erosion is beside the point here.

[3] On the disparity that existed between the *opgaaf* returns and the actual numbers of livestock, see 9, pp. 77–78. Attention is also drawn to the disparity between the figures given by Barrow for 1798 and the *opgaaf* figures for 1793. (See infra, p. 76.)

TABLE 3.—CATTLE AND SHEEP NUMBERS IN THE CAPE COLONY, ACCORDING TO ANNUAL (OPGAAF) RETURNS, IN SPECIFIED YEARS 1701–93*

Year	Total	Cape	Stellen-bosch	Draken-stein	Swellen-dam	Graaff Reinet
			CATTLE			
1701	9,704	4,204	2,931	2,569	...	...
1706	12,671	5,696	3,227	3,748	...	...
1711	20,743	10,358	4,543	5,842	...	...
1713	16,557	5,650	4,606	6,301	...	...
1718	16,202	5,224	3,901	7,077	...	...
1723	21,888	7,799	4,864	9,225	...	...
1728	21,083	6,689	5,098	9,296	...	...
1733	26,824	6,514	5,832	14,478	...	...
1738	33,876	9,029	6,173	18,674	...	...
1743	34,916	8,807	6,921	19,188	...	...
1748	31,375	8,145	4,299	9,691	9,240	...
1753	36,243	8,748	5,594	10,207	11,694	...
1758	34,586	7,904	5,273	10,298	11,111	...
1763	33,523	6,875	4,539	10,667	11,442	...
1768	36,786	6,059	5,603	12,867	12,257	...
1773	39,019	6,103	5,487	15,367	12,062	...
1778	61,961	7,135	7,366	24,417	23,043	...
1783	62,762	7,398	7,827	26,067	21,470	...
1788	80,921	7,290	23,399	—[a]	17,764	32,468
1793	82,110	6,570	22,155	—[a]	18,462	34,923
			SHEEP			
1701	53,126	30,693	12,470	9,963	...	...
1706	79,314	39,080	20,074	20,160	...	...
1711	116,256	50,468	30,318	35,470	...	...
1713	120,208	42,860	32,279	45,069	...	...
1718	64,381	21,414	15,036	27,931	...	...
1723	88,837	32,776	18,469	37,592	...	...
1728	97,570	34,742	21,907	40,921	...	...
1733	134,714	36,830	25,865	72,019	...	...
1738	151,075	43,174	25,451	82,450	...	...
1743	169,440	44,740	31,150	93,550	...	...
1748	152,092	38,542	19,375	49,775	44,400	...
1753	191,511	41,260	28,420	59,951	61,880	...
1758	151,812	39,986	30,720	21,616	59,490	...
1763	199,339	38,548	26,160	66,719	67,912	...
1768	250,978	34,448	38,698	101,185	76,647	...
1773	285,094	41,060	42,335	127,380	74,319	...
1778	376,433	28,560	49,594	194,670	103,609	...
1783	310,904	21,390	29,405	183,319	76,790	...
1788	445,557	24,537	128,885	—[a]	61,110	231,025
1793	475,205	19,581	111,217	—[a]	63,212	281,195

* Data from Coenraad Beyers, *Die Kaapse Patriotte, 1779–1791* (Capetown, 1929), Appendix H.

[a] Included in the district of Stellenbosch and probably also in that of Graaff Reinet.

ing in the Cape throughout almost the whole of the eighteenth century. It is true that in terms of "animal units"—six sheep to one head of cattle—this predominance would appear less conspicuous, but the device of the "animal unit" would be useful only under grazing conditions which are equally suitable to both cattle and sheep, and not when, as in our case, the largest proportion of the land represents "absolute sheep pasture."

The figures show a definite trend in the distribution of livestock in the Cape. At the beginning of the eighteenth century most cattle and sheep were concentrated largely in the Cape and Stellenbosch districts. From about the end of the 1710's the numbers of both cattle and sheep increased very slowly or remained stationary in the Cape district as well as in the Stellenbosch district, but increased rapidly in the then frontier area of Drakenstein. From the 1740's the increase in cattle and sheep numbers was most pronounced in the new district of Swellendam. The shift of livestock to the interior and frontier areas is thus quite apparent. From about the end of the 1760's, while the Cape and Stellenbosch districts show very little change in their cattle population, the frontier areas show rapid increases. This coincides with the eastward and northeastward expansion into some good cattle country. Finally, Graaff Reinet, which became a district in the 1780's, shows the largest number of cattle and sheep.

The relative numbers of cattle and sheep in the Cape in 1798 were, according to Barrow, as follows (*10*, p. 83):

District	Cattle	Sheep
Cape	20,957	61,575
Stellenbosch	59,567	451,695
Swellendam	52,376	154,992
Graaff Reinet	118,306	780,274
Total..........	251,206	1,448,536

The distribution of the cattle and sheep population at the beginning of the nineteenth century may be seen from Table 4. It also demonstrates the relative importance of sheep farming, especially in the vast frontier area of Graaff Reinet where the sheep population was from six to twelve times as large as the cattle population.

So far, we have stressed the supply factor, i.e., the natural

TABLE 4.—CATTLE AND SHEEP NUMBERS IN THE CAPE COLONY,
SPECIFIED YEARS, 1806–21*

District	1806	1811	1816	1821
	CATTLE			
Cape	18,461	15,946	12,106	14,808
Stellenbosch	28,173	25,146	23,169	24,325
Swellendam	52,429	54,265	36,350	30,018
Graaff Reinet	54,556	68,477	76,472	147,260
Uitenhage	37,948	34,867	39,561	61,976
Tulbagh	16,878	32,646	40,097	45,292
George	...	33,096	32,983	31,933
Albany	...	...	...	13,825
Total..............	208,445	264,443	260,738	369,437
	SHEEP			
Cape	32,239	20,474	8,529	11,259
Stellenbosch	21,108	62,357	20,115	23,563
Swellendam	137,036	142,978	92,131	59,183
Graaff Reinet	665,889	1,273,664	842,629	1,452,279
Uitenhage	229,305	291,171	148,310	122,446
Tulbagh	168,807	303,564	414,980	45,383
George	...	56,886	40,714	29,821
Albany	...	...	...	111,634
Total..............	1,254,384	2,151,094	1,567,408	1,855,568

* Data from G. M. Theal, *Records of the Cape Colony*, 36 vols. (Govt. of the Cape Colony, 1897–1905), VI, p. 75; VIII, p. 233; XI, p. 239; XIV, p. 247.

conditions of the semiarid and arid areas which favor sheep ranching rather than cattle ranching. The demand factor pointed in the same direction. Indeed, as mentioned earlier, Cape mutton was of excellent quality, while most of the Cape beef was tough and tasteless, with the result that beef was much less in demand than mutton. It was only from about the 1820's that the quality of beef began to improve. However, before slaughter cattle or salted beef could be delivered to Capetown or otherwise sold in good condition, sheep farming was the principal source of the colony's meat supply. This, of course, in no way detracts from the importance of the cattle industry as a source of both draft oxen and butter.

IMPORTANCE OF SHEEP RANCHING IN THE GRAZIER'S ECONOMY

That sheep breeding played a most important part in the economy of the graziers of the interior and frontier districts is confirmed by many eighteenth- and nineteenth-century travelers in the Cape. Sparrman, who traveled in the Cape in the 1770's, reports that only the wealthier farmers in the Swellendam district—an area better suited for cattle than for sheep—could sell some eight or ten oxen every other, or every third year, "some to the butchers, others to the people that carry wood between the town and shore, and others again to other farmers that live nearer to the Cape" (*11*, p. 247), i.e., to the wine and wheat farmers who used them as draft oxen. Each grazier in the Cambedo, Roggeveld, and Bokkeveld possessed from one to three thousand sheep. Mentzel, too, speaks of the young grazier selling wethers and butter (*12*, pp. 111–14). He also speaks of the meat contractors employing butchers "who travel round the country to buy the wethers," without any mention anywhere of butchers buying oxen (*12*, p. 212). Sparrman reports that the graziers of the Swellendam district derived a considerable income from the sale of wethers, of which they disposed of "from 20 to 100 yearly at the rate of from six shillings [schillings or skillings] to a dollar [rix-dollar] per head" (*11*, p. 247–48). The farmer had very little trouble in disposing of the wethers,

. . . as the butchers' men go about, buying them up, and afterwards drive them in flocks consisting of several hundreds, and sometimes even thousands, to the slaughter-houses at the Cape, about the times when the fleets are chiefly expected. A great number of the peasants in this country are termed grazing farmers or graziers, the chief, and sometimes the whole of their income depending on their breeding of sheep.

In the 1770's each farmer in the Roggeveld, the Bokkeveld, the Karroo, and the Cambedo possessed from 1,000 to 3,000 sheep (*11*, p. 248). At the close of the eighteenth century the farmers in the Graaff Reinet district possessed on an average at least 1,100 sheep each (*10*, p. 122). Barrow reports that there were in Graaff Reinet at the end of the eighteenth century 700 families who possessed a total of 118,306 head of cattle and 780,274 sheep, while a farmer in the Sneeuwbergen had "seldom fewer than from three to four thousand sheep" (*10*, p. 204). Lichtenstein reports that at the beginning of the nineteenth century the breeding of sheep was the most important occupation of the colonists of the Sneeuwbergen, and that "some farmers have flocks to the amount of six or seven thousand, and few have less than three thousand" (*13*, p. 6). Burchell, who traveled in the Cape Colony about a decade later, reported that many farmers in Achter Sneeuwbergen possessed from 4,000 to 6,000 sheep (*5*, pp. 112–13), while Thompson, who traveled in the 1820's, reported that in the northern parts of the colony, on the lower parts of the Zeekoe River, some farmers possessed as many as 10,000 sheep and goats (*14*, p. 58).

It may thus be seen that the pastoral economy of the frontier graziers was based mainly on sheep ranching, a circumstance which has a direct bearing on the expansion movement. For in the light of what has been said about the arid nature of most of the frontier areas, it is doubtful whether the expansion of the frontier would have been possible at all without sheep. Yet, while it is true that the fat-tailed sheep made such an expansion *technically* possible, the importance of the factors which made such an expansion *economically* advantageous can hardly be over-emphasized.

SOAP AND CANDLES

In an earlier chapter we considered the demand that existed at the Cape for such pastoral products as tallow and sheep's tail fat. We have to examine now another outlet, namely, the manufacture of soap, an important industry which for a long time had its location not in Capetown but in the interior districts of the colony. The manufacture of candles, too, played an important part in the domestic economy of the colonists, but, as will be shown later, candles for the Cape market were produced only on farms situated at no great distance from Capetown.

The development of an early soap and candle industry in the Cape has, as far as I know, never received the attention of investigators of South African history, nor is there more than the most casual reference to its existence. Theal, for instance, in describing conditions in the colony at the end of the eighteenth century, merely says (*15*, pp. 363–64):

Nearly every family made soap and candles for its own use. In the manufacture of the first the ashes of a common shrub were used with animal fat, and for the last either pure tallow, or tallow hardened with a vegetable wax obtainable in many parts of the country. Thrifty housewives often kept themselves supplied with little articles of domestic use by sending blocks of coarse soap of their own making or dipped tallow candles to Cape Town for sale.

The prevailing view has thus been to regard both soap and candles as articles which were produced on the farms primarily for home use and as having very little significance from the point of view of an exchange economy. While this may be more true with regard to candles, it is not true for soap. Indeed, the available evidence shows not only that large quantities of farm-made soap were sold in Capetown and in all the other trading centers of the colony, but also that quantities of soap made on the farms were actually exported to St. Helena and Mauritius. Moreover, the income derived from the sale of soap constituted a not unimportant part of the income of the farmers of the interior.

With regard to candles, the accepted view is much nearer the truth. Some candles were brought in from the farms to Capetown for sale, but probably only from farms at no great distance from Capetown, as the transporting of candles required a certain amount of care, and farmers residing on the other side of the mountains found it impracticable to carry candles to Capetown over the difficult roads. Indeed, being an unsafe article to transport by land carriage, candles were seldom brought out of the country (*10*, p. 332). It is therefore safe to conclude that, unlike soap production, the making of candles, except for the family's use, played a very small part in the economy of the frontier farmers.

Soap, however, was in a different category. In the early days of the Cape, soap was imported from Holland. Information on this point is very scanty, but there are very good reasons to believe that up to about the 1750's or 1760's the Cape, at least Capetown itself, was largely dependent on imports for its soap supply. To what extent the Cape was dependent on soap imports during the second half of the eighteenth century is difficult to say. Mentzel considered imported tobacco and soap as the "staple merchantable articles at the Cape." He gives two reasons why soap and tobacco were brought to the Cape by all ships' officers, of whatever rank. First, "because there is always a ready market for the goods at the Cape." Second, because soap and tobacco could be obtained in Holland on long credit and sold in the Cape for cash (*16*, pp. 77–78).

Soap and tobacco do not yield as much profit as other articles but as they are purchasable on long credit and as they are sold for cash the business is attractive. Ready money is of good value to a ship's officer on the Eastern Station, since on his numerous voyages to and from the various East India islands—Japan, China and the Indian mainland—he has opportunities of purchasing local products advantageously. In this respect the ship's officer is better off than the landsman. Another factor that adds to the importance of the Cape trade is the readiness with which the Company gives her officials permission to import goods for sale at the Cape.

The price of soap at that time was subject to wide fluctuations owing to fluctuations of supply. Mentzel cites the case of a Cape burgher "who laid in a stock of 20,000 lbs. at 6 stuivers per lb. at a time when the market was glutted, owing to an unusually large number of shipments that came in within a short space of time. Some weeks later it became known that no fresh soap was likely to arrive within the next three months, and then this astute speculator sold out at 20 stuivers per lb., netting within a short while a profit of *f*14,000" (*16*, p. 76). As the above narrative relates to Mentzel's own experience at the Cape, it may be taken to refer to the 1730's.

The development of soap production within the colony was closely connected with the expansion of the frontier, which, as we have seen earlier, was very rapid from about the middle of the eighteenth century. From that time onward soap could be produced on the farm not merely for the family use but also for the Cape market. The chief reason for this comparatively late development of a soap industry at the Cape was neither a lack of demand for soap at the Cape nor the competition of imported soap,[4] but the relative scarcity of raw materials. Such a statement may at first sound somewhat surprising when it is considered that the chief raw material for making soap was fat, and that the colonists had in the fat-tailed sheep such a convenient source of raw material. Yet when it is remembered that the most rapid pastoral development of the colony did not start before the middle of the century and that sheep's tail fat was essentially an article of food not only of the Hottentots but also of the slave population and of the Europeans, it may be doubted whether at that state of development any considerable surplus of fat for soap making was

[4] Compare *9*, p. 81. See also Egbertus Bergh, "Memorie over de Kaap de Goede Hoop," in *17*, p. 55. Bergh's opinion about the market for soap at the Cape as well as about the quality of Cape soap seems to be contrary to all the evidence that is available from numerous contemporary sources.

available (*18*, p. 65). In fact, the tail fat was used by the poorer
Europeans and all the slaves instead of butter, "from which indeed, when melted, it is not easily distinguished." It must also
be remembered that all attempts at cultivation of the olive in the
Cape had been unsuccessful and that no other oil-bearing plants
were grown there. Animal fat was thus the only fat produced in
the colony.

Another important reason for the slow development of the
soap industry in the Cape before the 1740's or 1750's is probably the fact that very little soda ash, an essential raw material
in making soap, was available. Indeed, Le Blanc's process of
manufacturing soda was unknown before the end of the eighteenth century, and alkali for soap making was still obtained by
the incineration of wood. The Cape, however, had very little
wood to spare for that purpose.

It is true that in the Cape soda could be obtained from the
ashes of some species of salt plants which grew abundantly in
certain regions of the colony. These plants did in fact play a
most decisive part in the subsequent development of the early
soap industry of the Cape. But, as will be shown here, until
about the second half of the eighteenth century this source for
obtaining soda was either not yet available or available only in
very small quantities. The reason is that these plants were found
in abundant quantities only in the interior regions of the Cape,
in the Karroo, the Roggeveld, the Bokkeveld, and further on in
the eastern and northeastern regions of the Cape. As has been
pointed out earlier, even the Bokkeveld, the Roggeveld, and the
Karroo were not occupied before the 1740's.

SODA ASH

There were two species of salt plants which served the colonists as sources of soda ash: the *Salsola* and the *Salicornia*. The
first has as its habitat the saline soils of semiarid inland areas,
while the second is found mostly on salt marshes near the seashore. The Swedish botanist Thunberg, traveling in the Cape in
the years 1772–74, mentions that on certain farms around the
Lange Kloof area soap was made "from a ley, prepared from
the *Canna bush* (*Salsola aphylla*)." The plant "was boiled a long

time and inspissated; when mutton suet was added till the mass acquired a proper consistence. . . . It was then poured out, and formed into long squares" (*19*, p. 199). In Thunberg's time the *Salicornia* species was probably not used for soap making. His reference to that species is as follows (*19*, p. 292): "The *Salicornia fruiticosa* (Zee koral, or sea coral) grew on the sea shore, and notwithstanding its brackish taste, was eaten by the soldiers and some few others as a salad, dressed with oil and vinegar."

Detailed descriptions of the methods of preparing soda from the ashes of these two plants and of making soap are given by Barrow, Lichtenstein, Burchell, and others. According to Barrow, who traveled in the Cape in the late 1790's, the *Salsola* species was known to the colonists by the Hottentot name of *Canna*. Almost all the soap that was used in the colony was made from the ashes of this plant (*7*, pp. 42–43). "These ashes, when carefully collected from the burnt plants, are a pure white caustic alkali, a solution of which, mixed up with the oily fat of the large broad tails of the sheep of the Colony, and boiled slowly for five or six days, takes the consistency and the quality of an excellent white soap." Barrow also mentions another "shrubby plant, the ashes of which also give a strong alkaline lie," stating however that the soap made from that plant, thought to be an *antriplex* species, "is said to have a bluish colour, and to be of a very inferior quality to that made of the former" (*7*, p. 43).

Of the *Salsola* species Barrow says that it grows "in almost every part of Southern Africa, but particularly on those plains known by the name of Karroo, and in such abundance that, supposing the plant, after being cut down and burnt, to be reproduced in five years, the quantity of soda, or barilla, that might annually be made from the ashes would be sufficient, beside serving the Colony, for the whole consumption of Great Britain" (*7*, p. 43).

Lichtenstein, who traveled in the Cape at the beginning of the nineteenth century, speaks of the abundance of the *Salsola* and *Salicornia* species in the Roggeveld (*13*, p. 447). According to him, the *channa* or *ganna* bush is indigenous to the Roggeveld and the Bokkeveld (*20*, p. 154).

Burchell, traveling through the Roggeveld in 1811, observed there an abundance of *kanna-bosch*, *Salsola aphylla* or *Caroxylon*

Salsola, the ashes of which "are much used by the Colonists as an alkali in making soap" (*21*, p. 419).

In Barrow's time the plains of the Achter Sneeuwbergen were covered with tall bushes of the *Salsola* (*7*, p. 267). He also suggested the collection of barilla "in the plain through which the Olifant River flows at no great distance from the bay" (*10*, p. 159), the reference being apparently to Mossel Bay. Barrow states that most of the soap was brought to Capetown from the district of Graaff Reinet (*10*, p. 331).

Although great interest was shown at various times in the production of soda ash or barilla from the *kanna-bosch*, there is very little evidence that any considerable quantities of it were ever brought to Capetown for soap making. Indeed, it was not until the 1830's that soap was manufactured in Capetown. The *South African Almanack* for 1831 mentions a soap boiler in Capetown by the name of D. Rynbach, but it is possible that he was already using imported soda from England for soap making. There is thus good reason to assume that the colony's soap industry was located in the interior and the frontier districts, not only because of the fat produced there, but also because these regions possessed the *kanna-bosch*, the source of soda ash, which was indispensable for the production of soap. When the first soap factory was established in Capetown in 1834, not only had coastal trading ensured Capetown's supply of tallow, but caustic soda, imported from England, could already compete very successfully with the barilla obtained from the *kanna-bosch*.

With the opening up of coastal shipping some barilla was exported from the Cape to Europe in the early 1820's (*22*, p. 119), but the export did not develop in subsequent years. Cape barilla had also to contend with high import duties in England. For instance, the English import duty on Cape barilla in 1830 was from £5 to £13 per ton, according to the quantity of mineral alkali it contained, while the price of barilla in England was £14 per ton (*23*, p. 126; *24*, p. 397).

SOAP PRODUCTION AND THE FRONTIER ECONOMY

The importance of soap production in the economy of the farmers of the interior districts may be gathered from the descriptions given by travelers already mentioned as well as from many other sources. Swellengrebel, too, in describing the conditions under which a certain colonist, F. Botha, lived on the eastern frontier of the colony in the 1770's, refers to the fact that he could not make soap because he could not obtain barilla (*25*).[5] Barrow states that soap manufacture by the farmers in some of the districts of the colony formed "a considerable part of their surplus revenue, which is appropriated to the purchase of clothing and other necessaries at their annual visits to Cape Town" (*10*, p. 330). He also says (*7*, p. 267): "The soap that the inhabitants make from the ashes of this plant, and the fat of sheep's tails, is no inconsiderable article of their revenue. Cattle and sheep are purchased by butchers upon the spot, but soap and butter are carried in waggons to the Cape."

As to the quality of soap produced on the farms, we have it from Barrow that it was of "excellent quality," and that, in fact, it generally commanded the same price as salted butter. "Being mostly brought from the district of Graaff Reinet at the same time with the butter, they rose and fell together according to the quantity on the market, and the demand there might happen to be for them" (*10*, p. 331).

Barrow states that the proceeds from a wagonload of soap and butter taken to Capetown were used for purchasing "clothing, brandy, coffee, a little tea and sugar, and a few other luxuries." A great wagonload of soap consisted of about 1,500 pounds of soap which, when sold in Capetown at 6*d.* per pound (which is a low price) to the retail dealers, would yield the farmer £37 10*s.* 0*d.* It is true that a journey from the Sneeuwbergen to Capetown and back, for instance, took about 60 days, but the farmer had no choice, for Capetown was the only market and there was no other way of proceeding to the Cape (*10*, pp. 331–32).

The collection of *kanna* bushes and the manufacture of soap also provided a good distribution of labor throughout the year. Thus Lichtenstein reports that in the winter "the children and slaves are sent to collect the young shoots of the *channa* bushes (*Salsola aphylla*, and *Salicornia fruiticosa*)" (*20*, p. 154). This

---

[5] "*Zeep kon hy nog niet maken, omdat er hier omstreeks geen Kanna boschjes wassen, maar hij hoopte dat werkstellig te kunnen maken, schoon hij dan hout en schoft ver moest halen.*"

utilization of labor during the slack period for the production of soap was an additional advantage.

Lichtenstein testifies both to the quality of the soap produced on the farms and to its economic importance to the farmers (*20*, p. 154): "The ashes of these saline plants produce a strong ley, and of this, mixed with the fat of the sheep, collected during the year, the women make an excellent soap, from the sale of which a considerable profit is derived; large quantities are sent to Cape Town where it is sold at a high price."

Burchell reports that the fat of the sheep "was considered almost equal in value to the rest of the carcass, by being manufactured into soap." This was particularly the case on the remoter frontier farms where the *slagters knegt*, or butcher's agent, would not make his appearance, despite the fact that many farmers possessed from 4,000 to 6,000 sheep. Under such circumstances it was more profitable to kill the sheep for the purpose of producing soap "than to sell them to the butchers at so low a price as a rix-dollar or less" (*5*, p. 113). Burchell saw on the farm to which he is referring "a great number of cakes of this soap, piled up to harden, ready for their next annual journey to Cape Town; whither they go, not merely for the purpose of selling it, but for purchasing clothing and such other articles as are not to be had in the country districts, but at an exorbitant price" (*5*, p. 113). Admittedly, selling the whole sheep on the hoof was much better than selling sheep's fat in the form of soap. Yet the Cape colonists who were able to sell soap were better off than colonists in Australia where, at one time, the only marketable part of the sheep was tallow.

Theal states that in the eighteenth century the farmers of the interior "occasionally sent a wagon load of butter and tallow and soap, consigned to an agent, who forwarded in return ammunition, coffee, sugar, pieces of calico or prints, and perhaps a dozen metres of cloth or something else that was needed" (*15*, p. 370). While it is to be doubted whether the quantities of tallow sent from the interior to Capetown were in any way commensurate with those of butter and soap—hardly any mention of tallow sent from the interior to Capetown in the eighteenth century and the beginning of the nineteenth is to be found in the literature of that period—Theal's statement in the above quotation that butter and soap were consigned to an agent who forwarded in return ammunition, coffee, sugar, etc., is of particular interest. For it means that the supply of soap and butter to Capetown was not always dependent upon the annual journeys of the individual farmers to the capital. Nor did the frontier farmers always have to be absent from their homes for months when they wished to exchange their farm products for Cape merchandise.

We may thus see the close interdependence that existed between sheep farming and soap production in the frontier economy from about the third quarter of the eighteenth century. Indeed, sheep farming to a large extent also meant fat production and soap manufacture, for the fat-tailed sheep was a most efficient fat producer. Thunberg wrote that in the winter the sheep in the Karroo sometimes grew so fat that their flesh could not be eaten. "When a butcher has purchased a flock of sheep and driven them 130 to 150 miles to the Cape, they are generally reckoned fat enough to be killed" (*1*, p. 153).

The significance of the Hottentot fat-tailed sheep thus lay not only in the fact that it was an animal eminently suited to utilize the fleeting vegetation of the arid and semiarid regions, but also in the circumstance that it was able to convert that vegetation into fat. Yet fat production alone would not have been sufficient had it not also been for the circumstance that the *kannabosch* was readily available in those regions as a source of alkali for soap making. This also demonstrates the close connection between soap production and the expansion of the frontier. For it was the combination of these two circumstances that contributed greatly to the opening up of the arid regions and to the expansion of the frontiers of the Cape.

SOAP AND TALLOW PRICES

Although no information is available as to the quantities of soap produced in the second half of the eighteenth century and the beginning of the nineteenth, there is reason to believe that considerable quantities were manufactured in the soap-producing areas. Unfortunately the earliest available figures relating to the Cape soap trade are those of the 1820's, when the soap industry in the frontier and interior areas began to show signs of decline. Increasing competition from imported soap as well as the greater facilities provided by coastal trading for selling tallow caused a shift in production on the farms from soap to tallow. In spite of these developments, however, soap production for the market continued to play for some considerable time an important part in the economy of the districts of Uitenhage, Cradock, Swellendam, and Somerset.

The quantities and prices of soap and tallow sold on the public markets of Capetown and Grahamstown in the years 1826–34 are shown in Table 5; quantities and values of soap exported

TABLE 5.—SOAP AND TALLOW SOLD ON PUBLIC MARKETS AT
CAPETOWN AND GRAHAMSTOWN, 1826–34*

Year	Capetown market		Grahamstown market	
	Quantity (lbs.)	Price (d/lb)	Quantity (lbs.)	Price (d/lb)
	SOAP			
1826........	54,630	3¾–4½	...	...
1827........	42,755	...	...	...
1828........	19,912	...	...	...
1829........	13,911	...	42,427	...
1830........	33,280	...	43,817	4
1831........	34,951	...	35,000	3½
1833........	47,127	...	...	...
1834........	24,653	...	...	...
	TALLOW			
1826........	32,245	3–3¾	...	...
1827........	33,966	...	...	...
1828........	8,726	...	...	...
1829........	13,969	...	31,327	...
1830........	38,590	...	68,952	5
1831........	93,791	...	53,204	3
1833........	77,459	...	...	...
1834........	32,222	...	...	...

* Data from *Cape of Good Hope Government Gazette*, Jan. 19, 1827; George Greig, compiler, *South African Almanack and Directory*, 1830–33; George Greig, compiler, *South African Directory and Almanac*, 1834–35; Stephen Kay, *Travels and Researches in Caffraria* (London, 1833), II, p. 465.

from the Cape, mostly to St. Helena and Mauritius, and the values of soap imported into the Cape for the period 1822–34 are given in Table 6.

TABLE 6.—SOAP EXPORTS AND IMPORTS OF THE CAPE, 1822–34*

	Exports			Imports		
Year	Quantity (*lbs.*)	Value (£)	Price*a* (*d/lb*)	Quantity (*lbs.*)	Value (£)	Price*a* (*d/lb*)
1822	31,050	493	3.8	...	2,412	...
1823	1,500	72	11.5	...	901	...
1824	...	...	...	...	3,000	...
1825	880	18	4.9	...	2,200	...
1826	...	...	...	...	2,000	...
1827	2,500	12	1.1	...	1,483	...
1828	6,280	217	8.3	...	1,771	...
1829	1,218	24	4.7	...	3,739	...
1830	1,000	20	4.8	...	5,265	2.5*b*
1831	1,500	30	4.8	592,928	5,914	2.4
1832	12,907	218	4.1	...	...	...
1833	14,114	227	3.8	1,954,736	4,218	.5
1834	2,760	58	5.0	...	2,718	...

* Data from Colonial Secretary's Office, *Cape of Good Hope Blue Book*, 1822–34 (Cape-town). The export figures for the year 1832 are those given in George Greig, compiler, *South African Directory and Almanac*, 1834, p. 126.

a Average value of exports, or imports.

b The 1830 price of imported soap has been calculated on the basis of 4,356 cwts. valued at £5,105, the difference between this sum and that given in the table being made up by imports of 73 boxes of soap to the value of £113, and 5 cases of soap to the value of £47, landed in Simonstown and Port Elizabeth, respectively.

Although there are no statistical records of soap exports prior to 1822, it is not unreasonable to assume that in the years before 1822 soap exports from the Cape had been much larger, in view of the fact that the bulk of exports of Cape soap went to St. Helena to supply the garrison guarding Napoleon. Napoleon died in 1821, but exports of soap to St. Helena still continued in 1822 as the evacuation of the large garrison and squadron took some time. After 1822, however, soap exports declined.

From about 1822 the Cape soap industry not only lost its most important foreign market, but it was also experiencing the ever-increasing competition from the English soap industry, despite an import duty of 15 rix-dollars per hundredweight on British soap. This competition became particularly severe from the 1820's when soda and soap began to be manufactured in Britain on a much larger scale and at lower costs than before, and when the exports of these two commodities from Britain began to dominate world markets. The abolition of the excise duty on salt, the raw material for soda production by the LeBlanc process, contributed to the lowering of the cost of production of soda in Britain, while the cost of fat in soap manufacture in Britain was reduced by the increasing use of West African palm oil as a substitute for the higher-priced tallow (*26*, p. 31).

Soap production in Britain increased from 57 million pounds in 1801 to 98 million in 1821, to 123 million in 1831, and 199 million in 1841. These increases in production were accompanied by price reductions and increased exports. The price of soap in England dropped from £74 per ton in 1801 to £68 in 1821, to £53 in 1831, and to £48 in 1841, while exports increased in weight from 4 million pounds in 1821 to 16 million in 1831, and 29 million in 1841 (*27*, p. 542).

Whether and to what extent the greater cheapness of British soap was achieved by lowering its fatty-acids content is impossible to say. However, as may be seen from Table 6, the average prices of imported soaps were about half those of soap produced in the Cape. That Cape soap was able to sell at twice the price must have been due to a large extent to its greater fat content and superior quality. Yet, the cheapness of the imported article could not have failed to depress the demand for the Cape soap, with the result that the farmers found it more advantageous to sell tallow than soap.

BERRY WAX

According to all accounts, berry wax was an important article in the Cape, and small quantities were exported from time to time.[6] Professor L. Pappe (*28*, p. 45) stated that the first information on the usefulness of the waxberry myrtle in the Cape Colony was contained in a letter addressed to the Reverend A. Buurt at Amsterdam by the Reverend J. F. Bode, then minister of the Dutch Reformed Church in Capetown. From his letter it appears that for a long time the shrub, or waxbush, which grew on the sandy hills between Capetown and Stellenbosch, received little notice and that it was not until October and November 1776 that the berries were collected for wax making. Bode predicted that in the course of time the wax would become an article of com-

---

[6] Even as late as 1911 and 1914 berry wax was exported from the Union of South Africa, the quantities exported having increased from about 3,000 pounds at 8*d.* per pound in 1911 to 21,000 pounds at 11.4*d.* per pound in 1914.

merce, as "the plant grows in the dry sands, where nothing else will thrive, and of that description of soil we have over-abundance. Who can tell what more may be discovered?" (*28*, pp. 45–46).

It would seem, however, that Bode was not quite correct in reporting 1776 as the year in which the usefulness of the waxbush had been discovered, for in 1772 Thunberg had already mentioned its use in the interior of the colony. Thunberg's description of the wax and its uses on the farms around the Leeuwe River is as follows (*19*, pp. 166–67; my italics):

The branches of the wax-shrub (*myrica cordifolia*) the berries of which are covered with a fat substance resembling bees-wax, were put whole into a pot of boiling water, in order to melt and skim off the wax. It resembles grey impure wax, is harder than tallow, and somewhat softer than wax. *The farmers use it for candles*, but the Hottentots eat it like a piece of bread, either with or without meat.

Thunberg informs us also about its uses near Capetown (*19*, p. 249):

Near Muysenberg (or Mouse Mountain) the wax-shrub (*myrica quercifolia* and *cordifolia*) grew in abundance along the shore. The berries of them are quite round, full of knobs, soft and of the size of a pea. The berries themselves are quite black, but covered with a farina of a whitish-grey colour. They are gathered in their ripe state in the month of March, and boiled in water till all the white powder is melted off, and floats on the surface of the water like fat; this, then skimmed off and cooled, grows hard, almost like wax, and is of a greenish-grey colour. The farmers use it for candles, when they get any quantity of it, and the Hottentots eat it like so much cheese.

Pappe reports that the waxbush was common in the sandy tracts along the shores of the colony and in the downs of Algoa Bay (*28*, p. 47). In Lichtenstein's time the plant was "exceedingly abundant in the Black Mountain" (*13*, p. 179). "The wax is of no other use but for making candles; it is then commonly mixed with an equal quantity of tallow, since, at the same time that it burns out slower, it does not give so good a light as animal wax or greese. Used by itself it gives a sort of bluish flame" (*13*, p. 180). This is also confirmed by Burchell who states that without this vegetable wax it was difficult to make candles from the soft tallow of the Cape sheep, particularly in warm weather (*21*, p. 332). Barrow adds that the plant was plentiful near the seashore, and that the wax was sometimes sent up from there to the Cape in large green cakes, to be sold at between a shilling and 15*d.* per pound (*10*, p. 332). J. W. D. Moodie, who was farming in the Swellendam district in the late 1820's, also reports that he occasionally employed his people "at spare time in gathering wax-berries, that grow in great abundance upon small bushes in the sandhills near the sea, and yield a substance partaking of the nature of wax and tallow, which is mixed with common tallow, and used by the colonists for making candles" (*29*, p. 197). In Moodie's time berry wax was selling at the same price as tallow (*29*, p. 197). The plant itself was used as sheep feed (*13*, p. 180).

A more exact account of the properties of berry wax is found in a paper read by John Read at the South African Institution and published under the title "Experiments of Candles Wicks; and on the Effects of Chlorine upon the Combustible Properties of the Wax of the Candle Berry Myrtle." The following extracts from the above paper may be of some interest (*30*):

The wax procured from the Candle-berry Myrtle of which there are several species indigenous in the Colony, and from which a large quantity is collected by the farmers, is frequently used for making candles. The wax possesses a pleasant smell and burns without emitting that unpleasant empreumatic odour which renders the combustion of animal fat disagreeable. It is naturally white, but acquires in the process of manufacturing it, a deep green colour derived from the soluble matter of the seeds. It is much harder than Bees' Wax; is brittle and sonorous. It burns with a bluish flame giving a comparatively faint light, and candles made of it, in burning are even more apt than tallow candles to run. Mixed with an equal quantity of tallow, it forms a candle which differs but little in its combustive properties from a tallow candle.

Thus it may be seen that the waxbush was found not only in localities near Capetown, but that it was also abundant in the interior, in the Swellendam district, and in the sandy downs of Algoa Bay. The berries were collected in large quantities by the farmers of the eastern frontier, and the wax was sent to Capetown and elsewhere for sale, commanding a comparatively high price as an essential material in making candles. We may therefore conclude that the proceeds from selling berry wax constituted a not unimportant addition to the income of the frontier farmers.

CITATIONS

1 C. P. Thunberg, *Travels in Europe, Africa and Asia, Performed Between the Years 1770 and 1779*, 3 vols. (London, 1795), II.

2 D. G. van Reenen, *Die Journal van Dirk Gysbert van Reenen, 1803* (Van Riebeeck Society Publication, No. 18).

3 George Greig, compiler, *South African Almanack and Directory* (Capetown) 1831.

4 Thomas Pringle, *Narrative of a Residence in South Africa* (new ed., London, 1840).

5 W. J. Burchell, *Travels into the Interior of South Africa*, 2 vols. (London, 1824), II.

6 Frederich Aereboe, *Allgemeine Landwirtschaftliche Betriebslehre* (Berlin, 1923).

7 John Barrow, *Travels into the Interior of South Africa*, 2 vols. (2d ed., London, 1806), I.

8 Peter Kolbe, *The Present State of the Cape of Good Hope*, 2 vols. (London, 1731), I.

9 A. J. H. van der Walt, *Die Ausdehnung der Kolonie am Kap der Guten Hoffnung (1700–1779)* (Berlin, 1928).

10 John Barrow, *Travels into the Interior of South Africa*, II.

11 Andrew Sparrman, *A Voyage to the Cape of Good Hope from the Year 1772 to 1776* (London, 1785), I.

12 O. F. Mentzel, *A Geographical and Topographical Description of the Cape of Good Hope*, 3 vols. (Van Riebeeck Society Publication, No. 25), III.

13 Henry Lichtenstein, *Travels in Southern Africa, in the Years 1803, 1804, 1805 and 1806*, 2 vols. (Van Riebeeck Society Publication, No. 11), II.

14 George Thompson, *Travels and Adventures in Southern Africa*, 2 vols. (London, 1827), II.

15 G. M. Theal, *History of South Africa Before 1795*, 3 vols. (3d ed., London, 1922), III.

16 O. F. Mentzel, *A Geographical and Topographical Description of the Cape of Good Hope* (Van Riebeeck Society Publication, No. 6), II.

17 G. M. Theal, *Belangrijke Historische Dokumenten Over Zuid Afrika*, 3 vols. (Govt. of South Africa, 1911), III.

18 Peter Kolbe, *The Present State of the Cape of Good Hope*, II.

19 C. P. Thunberg, *Travels in Europe, Africa and Asia, Performed Between the Years 1770 and 1779*, I.

20 Henry Lichtenstein, *Travels in Southern Africa, in the Years 1803, 1804, 1805 and 1806* (Van Riebeeck Society Publication, No. 10), I.

21 W. J. Burchell, *Travels in the Interior of Southern Africa*, I.

22 W. W. Bird, *State of the Cape of Good Hope in 1822* (London, 1823).

23 George Greig, compiler, *South African Almanack and Directory*, 1830.

24 William Tooke and William Newmarch, *A History of Prices and of the State of Circulation*, 6 vols. (London, 1928), II.

25 P. J. van der Merwe, *Die Trekboer in die Geskiedenis van die Kaapkolonie (1657–1842)* (Capetown, 1938).

26 Allan McPhee, *The Economic Revolution in British West Africa* (London, 1926).

27 M. G. Mulhall, *Dictionary of Statistics* (4th ed., London, 1903).

28 L. Pappe, *Silva Capensis* (London, 1862).

29 J. W. D. Moodie, *Ten Years in South Africa* (London, 1835).

30 John Read, "Experiments of Candles Wicks; and on the Effects of Chlorine upon the Combustible Properties of the Wax of the Candle Berry Myrtle," *The South African Quarterly Journal*, Jan.–Apr. 1830.

CHAPTER 9

THE CATTLE TRADE WITH THE
NATIVE TRIBES

The history of the cattle trade with the native tribes is interesting in more than one respect. Besides being the first important point of contact and friction between black and white in South Africa, the cattle trade was an integral part of the frontier economy and was responsible for drawing the native tribes into the exchange economy of the Cape.

A distinction is made here between trade with the Hottentots and trade with the Bantus. The Hottentots possessed not only cattle but also flocks of sheep and goats, and the cattle trade with them included these categories of livestock. The Bantus possessed cattle only.

Cattle barter with the Hottentots at the Cape is known to have taken place as early as 1595, when the Dutch, sailing to and from India, bartered iron, knives, etc., for cattle and sheep (*1*, p. 75). In the early 1620's the crew of the wrecked Portuguese ship *S. Jao Baptista* obtained cattle from both the Hottentots and the Bantus in exchange for pieces of iron (*2*, p. 133), while in 1647 the stranded crew of the Dutch ship *Haarlem* obtained cattle and sheep from the Hottentots.

TRADE WITH THE HOTTENTOTS

After the first settlement of the Cape in 1652, cattle trade with the Hottentots remained for a long time the chief source of the Company's meat supply. From the outset the Company was determined to reserve the cattle trade for itself lest competition should lead to a rise in the price of cattle, and beginning with the year 1658 the colonists were prohibited from bartering for cattle with the Hottentots. There was also fear that the Hottentots might be mistreated by the colonists and thus become unwilling to barter cattle. Only government trading parties were entitled to engage in the cattle trade. In this, however, the

Company was only partly successful, for the cattle trade proved too lucrative to both the colonists and the Hottentots, and the prohibition was too difficult to enforce. In the late 1690's trouble arose with the Hottentots over the actions of "parties of men of loose character," who "were often guilty of conduct that cannot be distinguished from robbery," and Governor Simon van der Stel renewed the prohibition under a *placaat* issued in 1697 prohibiting bartering for cattle with the Hottentots "under penalty of whipping, branding, banishment, and confiscation of property" (*3*, p. 400).

In 1700, however, the Company decided to relinquish its trade with the Hottentots and throw it open to the burghers, on the condition that the Hottentots should suffer no ill treatment as a result of the change. The Company was to obtain its meat requirements by tender (*3*, p. 400). In order to encourage cattle breeding among the burghers, the Company "accepted a meat tender for five years at a price which in those days was considered exorbitant." No rent was charged for grazing land until 1714, "and no other tax than the one for district purposes was laid upon their stock" (*3*, p. 402).

But the unrestricted cattle trade with the natives did not last long. In 1702 a cattle-plundering expedition from Stellenbosch, consisting of forty-five Europeans and as many Hottentots, left for the eastern parts of the interior and fell afoul of Bantu tribesmen in the neighborhood of the Fish River. The cattle raiders then attacked the Hottentots of that region, drove away their cattle, and committed other acts of violence against them. When the criminal conduct of this party became known, free barter was suspended again. But as usual the new prohibition was ineffective.

A new scandal arose in 1726, when the Hottentots at the river Zonderend complained to the government that they were exposed to the depredations of vagrant Europeans, "who professed to visit them for purposes of trade, but in reality robbed them of cattle" (*2*, p. 24). The result was another very strict *placaat* forbidding, under most severe penalties, all dealing by private persons "with the uncivilised inhabitants" (*2*, p. 24).

In 1739 a new outrage was revealed. A party of European farmers, living north of Piketberg, bartered for a large number of cattle from the Namaquas on the southern bank of the Orange River on the most friendly terms. The party had no sooner left than "their coloured servants went back stealthily, fell upon the Namaquas and robbed the Kraal of all its cattle" (*2*, p. 43). This resulted in the 1739 proclamation prohibiting barter for cattle with the natives "on pain of bodily and capital punishment" (*4*, p. 5). The proclamation was later followed by other *placaaten,* but the cattle barter with the Hottentots, and later with the Bantus, continued all the time, especially in the frontier and interior regions of the colony where government control was weak or entirely absent.

The colonists, however, were not the only culprits. Government officials, too, were involved, and the government would not or could not always exercise its control over them, even if they were guilty of injustice and violence in their dealings with the Hottentots. The following quotation from Thunberg, written in 1774, is of considerable interest (*5*, pp. 156–57):

With these as well as other Hottentots who live farther up the country near Roggeveld, and were once more numerous and rich than they are at present, the Dutch company formerly carried on a bartering trade; but, on account of the injustice and violence which the factors that were sent to them were guilty of, and which the governors frequently connived at, not deeming it their duty to contend for the rights of nature and humanity, when neither the Company's nor their own private interest was concerned, it has now entirely ceased. When a corporal was sent out by the governor with a few men to barter with the Hottentots for their oxen, against arrack, glass-beads, iron and tobacco, he not only got their oxen for slaughter, but their calves, cows and sheep. And this exchange was not always with the Hottentots' goodwill and consent, but by compulsion and frequently by force. Besides this, they were base enough to dilute the arrack with water, and thus to adulterate it. This mode of bartering occasioned by degrees such a disgust that some of the Hottentots neglected to augment their stock, and others entirely left the places of their residence, and ran away; after which they sometimes stole cattle from the farmers who by degrees seized upon their land. Not long ago, Corporal Feldman procured by barter 500 oxen, with the greater part of which he enriched himself, returning only fifty into the Company's slaughterhouse. This bartering traffic, which was not very advantageous to the Company but unjust and cruel towards the Hottentots, has now quite ceased as well in this North Western, as in the South Eastern part of Africa, especially since the land is well peopled, and the farmers who abound in cattle, are now capable of delivering as many soever as may be wanted. Should such traffic ever take place again, it ought to be with the Caffers and Namaquas, who are possessed of a great quantity of cattle, and whose lands have not hitherto suffered in the least by the encroachments from the colonists.

The above quotation shows also that the disintegration of the Hottentot tribal organization was already advanced in the early 1770's. In the early days of European settlement in the Cape the Hottentots were said to have been extremely rich in livestock—sheep, cattle, and goats—which supplied them with their daily food in the form of milk, meat, and fat, and with skins for clothing. In losing their livestock, the Hottentots lost both their livelihood and their independent tribal existence.

The Hottentots also lost their land, but that was a minor calamity compared with the loss of their livestock, for land is of value to nomads only so long as they have livestock to graze on it. Indeed, land was not the limiting factor in a country where land for grazing was still in abundance in the interior. Some Hottentot tribes saved themselves by withdrawing into the interior with their flocks and herds, but this was no solution for the Hottentot tribes bordering on the settlement of the colony who had already lost their livestock.

THE BANTUS

It is uncertain when and where exactly the first contact between the colonists of the Cape and the Bantus was made. The presence of Bantu tribesmen as far west as the Buffalo River was probably known in the Cape as early as the 1680's, when the first report was received in the Cape about the men of the wrecked ship *Stavenisse* who traded arm rings, beads, and neck rings to the Bantus for cattle (*3*, p. 298). As mentioned earlier, the first encounter with the Bantus is known to have taken place in 1702, and there is reason to believe that cattle bartering between Cape colonists and the Bantus was going on intermittently from the beginning of the eighteenth century. By then "the country must already have been explored far inland, for parties of elephant hunters were sometimes absent from the colony for eight or nine months at a time before returning with their wagon laden with ivory." It seems safe to assume that hunting and trading went together, although no records of these early exploits are available, probably because "these people were usually very reticent upon the subject of routes and hunting grounds" (*2*, p. 36). The records of a party of elephant hunters headed by one Hermanus Hubner, which left the colony for Kaffirland in 1736 (*2*, pp. 36–39), are the only notable exceptions.

The first official record concerning the Bantus came sixteen years later, in 1752, when Ensign R. v. d. Beutler, in command of an expedition sent by the Cape government to explore the country east of the Cape Colony, followed the way of the hunters and traders into Kaffirland (*"het padt der togtgangers tot naar de Caffers"*) (*6*, p. 16). Beutler says that the Bantus were very eager to barter cattle for trinkets (*snuijtserrijen*) (*6*, pp. 38–39).

But the most conclusive official evidence of an extensive cattle trade carried on between the colonists and the Bantus was gathered in 1768 by the commission appointed by the Cape government to define the boundaries of the colony. Not only had they found the road from the district of Swellendam leading "eastwards to the abode of the Kaffirs" (*4*, p. 3), but they were also told of a narrower road running the same way. This road was "merely a track frequented only by hawkers" using horses and horse carts instead of ox wagons (*4*, pp. 1–2).

Between the Fish and Gamtoos rivers the commission found colonists with considerable herds of cattle several days' journey from their loan farms. These colonists were not only grazing their cattle on land not possessed on loan from the government, but also carrying on an illicit cattle traffic with both the Hottentots and the Bantus (*4*, p. 5). The commission met Hottentots who were carrying on cattle bartering with the Bantus, and with other Hottentots, presumably on behalf of the colonists by whom they were employed. The commission also had evidence of three Europeans with wagons from the colony who in 1768 had bartered cattle with the Kaffirs, though it turned out later that these Europeans had permission from the authorities to do so (*4*, pp. 2-3).

As in the earlier days, the ostensible reason for prohibiting free barter with the natives was the fear that unfair trading might lead to trouble. The government renewed the old prohibitions, and the colonists were instructed "[not] to prosecute any the least cattle barter with the Hottentots or Kaffirs, however trifling in amount the same may be, not to proceed in person for that purpose with waggons and merchandise into the interior, neither to employ any other person on pain, if detected after this date, even although they may have bartered the cattle in friendship and without violence, but so much the more when trouble have been caused to the said Hottentots or Kaffirs, besides the confiscation of their property taken with them, as also of the cattle bartered, waggons and merchandise, [they] shall, as disturbers of public peace, and violators of Law and Liberty, without any connivance, be arbitrarily punished upon the body, aye, even with death" (4, p. 6).

This stern prohibition is of interest in that it refers to the employment of persons other than the trader himself, and to connivance, presumably on the part of government officials. As in the past, however, this stern warning was of little avail. There seemed to have developed the practice of taking the cattle thus obtained from the Hottentots and the Bantus to Capetown for sale, and to take back a variety of merchandise from Capetown to the Cambedo, and thence to Kaffirland, where it was again traded for cattle, which was in turn taken to Capetown, and so forth (4, pp. 21–22). Among the articles bartered for cattle were not only beads, copper, and arrack, but also iron, clothes, linens, baftas, knives, tobacco, and pipes (4, pp. 21–22, 40). Thunberg speaks of the eagerness of the Bantus to obtain iron, "which they forge and grind to make heads for their javelins" (5, p. 94).

The mode of bartering with the Bantus is reported by Moodie in a narrative relating to a period before 1778. A number of colonists first proceeded "northwards to the Great River, in order to shoot elephants on the other side of it, but as the river was impassable, they turned southwards into Kaffirland, where each of those burghers bartered cattle for himself from the people, giving for each head of cattle four bunches of beads and two copper plates, and a string of beads for each calf" (4, p. 73).

Coinciding with the increased demand for fresh meat in the 1770's is the more frequent occurrence of cattle-bartering with the Kaffirs—more accurately, of abuses in connection with that trade (4, pp. 21–22, 24, 33). In 1774 a number of colonists who were in possession of Kaffir cattle were ordered by the government to dispose of them in order to facilitate the government's control over cattle smuggling from Kaffirland. Cattle bartering was also carried on by persons who "have made it their business to wander about everywhere in the interior, from one District to another, with goods and merchandise, conveyed on wagons, cars, horses, or pack oxen, thus also causing many irregularities in the said districts" (*4*, p. 24). The position became so acute in 1774 that, owing to the competition of the smugglers, the Company found it difficult to procure enough cattle for itself, with the result that the Cape government had to send one of the Company's officials "to the Gamtoos River, and thereabouts, to barter cattle for the Company" (*4*, pp. 33–35).[1]

In fact, Thunberg reports that the Bantus inhabited at that time "the most delightful meadows, that can be imagined, along the coast," and that they possessed "large herds of tame horned cattle" (*7*, p. 205). Even before 1774 the Company obtained from the Bantu tribesmen "a great number of cattle, fit for slaughter, in exchange for tobacco, brandy, glass-beads and bits of iron" (*7*, p. 206).

Although the Bantus had large numbers of cattle, some of which they were prepared to exchange for trinkets, tobacco, and various other merchandise with the colonists, it is doubtful whether they had large numbers to spare, for, unlike the Hottentots, they had only cattle and no sheep or goats, whose natural rate of increase is much greater than that of cattle. Sparrman, who visited the eastern territories at the beginning of the 1770's, says (*8*, p. 152): "The country of the Caffers lies to the east of the Great Visch River, next the coast. Its inhabitants, the Caffers, have no notion of the breeding of sheep, employing themselves only in rearing horned cattle." Thunberg mentions that, unlike the Hottentots, who wore sheepskins, the Bantus were dressed in calfskins.

It is also important to bear in mind that to the Bantus cattle were not only a source of food, clothing, shields, and other useful objects, but also the only means of securing wives and the principal medium of paying fines to the tribal authorities. Finally, the possession of cattle is also closely linked up with the whole Bantu social and religious organization. For all these reasons the relative number of cattle that the Bantus were prepared to part with annually by free and voluntary exchange was probably

---

[1] Although the reference here is to procuring cattle from the Hottentots, it is known that Hottentots were procuring cattle from the Kaffirs (*4*, p. 2).

not very large. If the number of cattle bartered in any particular year was in excess of the natural increase, fewer cattle could be spared in the following years. This was the position confronting the European cattle farmers *cum* cattle traders when they first came into contact with the Bantus residing within the boundaries of the colony and across the frontier. An attempt to obtain cattle from these people by robbery or other unfair means was bound to lead to war, an emergency for which the Bantus, unlike the Hottentots, were well organized.

Thunberg states that "in order that the colonists might not be induced to wage war with the courageous and intrepid Caffers, or the Company suffer any damage by that means," the crossing of the boundary was strictly prohibited by the government (*5*, p. 79). However, as we have seen earlier, this prohibition was often ignored, for the simple reason that it interfered with cattle bartering, in which both Boers and Bantus were vitally interested. The following passage, contained in the Instructions for the Commandant of the Eastern Country issued by the Council in 1780, is of particular interest (*4*, p. 101):

. . . there is good reason to suppose that notwithstanding the prohibition and severe penalties of the existing laws against bartering cattle from the Kafirs or Hottentots, the practice is still carried on by some refractory and avaricious inhabitants, and that on these occasions much injury and violence is done to the Kafirs in which, however, it seldom happened that any one could be so far detected, as to receive his well earned punishment according to law; and that the inhabitants are as little deterred by fear of the prescribed penalties, as are the Kafirs by the injuries and violence aforesaid; but that, nevertheless, hence arises enmity between this people and our inhabitants, of which the injurious consequences have been experienced even by those who are entirely innocent.

Indeed, so keen were the Bantus to barter cattle with the colonists for European merchandise that it is probable their movements in the eastern frontier districts were to a large extent influenced by this one desire. In 1786 Woeke, first landdrost of Graaff Reinet, reported that the Bantus were everywhere lying among the Boer settlements, and were still coming over from the other side of the mouth of the Fish River in order to barter their cattle (*9*, p. 292). Collins, who visited the eastern parts of the colony at the beginning of the nineteenth century, expressed the view that "the continuance of the Caffers within

or near the boundary has been occasioned in a great degree by
the facility thereby afforded them to trade, beg and plunder"
(*10*, p. 18).

But cattle stealing or cattle plundering by the Bantus of the
eastern frontier was a rather late development and does not
appear to have been of any consequence before the 1790's. In
other words, the westward movement of the Bantus toward the
European settlements cannot be attributed to predatory motives,
at least not before that time.

It is true that it was the vagrant element of the Bantus that
was responsible for stock theft (*9*, p. 317); yet the appearance
of vagrant Bantus on the frontier requires some explanation.
The question arises whether the Bantus did not turn vagrant
after they had lost their cattle. As a cattleless proletariat, the
Bantus, like the Hottentots earlier in the century, had two alterna-
tives—to go into European service or to turn vagrant. The latter
alternative was probably the more feasible one, especially in
view of the fact that the employment of Kaffir servants was prohibited by the government, quite apart from the fact that the
Kaffirs were, on the whole, mistrusted by the colonists themselves.
It is thus possible that the emergence of the vagrant Bantu class
at the frontier was closely connected with a mode of "barter"
which deprived some Bantus of their cattle (*11*, p. 17). Indeed,
we know how some of the Xosa were so deprived. Marais mentions a burgher who was alleged to have locked up the Xosa
chief Langa and forced him to barter cattle. It was further
alleged that when Langa's sons complained that a certain burgher
gave them too few beads for cattle, the cattle were nevertheless
taken away from them by force (*11*, p. 24). The Kaffirs also
accused the colonists of employing Hottentots "expressly to
steal" Kaffir cattle (*4*, p. 92).

We cannot here go into the details of cattle raiding, cattle
stealing, and other irregularities connected with the cattle trade of
those days, which ultimately led to the outbreak of the first Kaffir
war in 1779. Nor are we concerned here with the details of the
wars that followed.[2] What is important to note here is the fact
that the first Kaffir war was not about land or frontiers, for neither

[2] The interested reader should consult *9*, chap. VII, and *11*, chaps. I and II.

Bantus nor Boers, least of all those at the frontier, were interested in maintaining a frontier which only hampered the cattle trade. It was a war about cattle, or more precisely, a war caused by cattle plundering, cattle stealing, unfair exchange, and coercion. These irregularities were both the immediate and the basic causes of the first Kaffir war (*11*, p. 7).

Indeed, the complaints by the colonists about land and grazing, e.g., that the Xosa cattle were devouring their pastures, must not be taken too literally. It seems more likely (*9*, pp. 291–317) that at the back of most of the farmers' requests for commandos to drive out the Xosa from the Zuurveld was the expectation of the spoils of war in the form of captured cattle. There is no lack of evidence to support this view. In the 1780's Woeke was at first led to believe in the necessity of driving out the Xosa from the Zuurveld (*9*, p. 292), but he changed his mind in 1792 (*11*, pp. 25–28). Again, when Woeke was absent from the drostdy, the Secretary, Waegener, received an urgent request from nine Boers to help them stave off alleged aggression from the Kaffirs. But, as it appeared later, this was only an excuse for a planned attack on the Kaffirs, with cattle plunder as the real objective.[3]

Woeke, in fact, was of the opinion that the Zuurveld was in itself not worth a quarrel with the Kaffirs, and it was more strongly a government than a Boer point of view that the Xosa should be driven out of the Zuurveld. Prestige was undoubtedly one of the reasons which prompted the government to drive them out; the Xosa had to be removed from the Zuurveld in order not to create a precedent for further encroachment upon the colony. But the most important consideration was perhaps the intention to prevent the colonists from carrying on an open cattle barter with the Kaffirs (*9*, p. 311). Needless to say, this was not exactly the opinion of the frontier colonists, many of whom were concerned less with the territory of Zuurveld than with the convenience of the cattle trade with the Bantus. Indeed, from the farmers' point of view, the Zuurveld was a more convenient place for bartering cattle than the territories on the other side of the Fish River to which the government wished to confine the Kaffirs.

The second Kaffir war, which broke out in 1793, was due to

---

[3] "*Een goede buijt te maken, daar hen tog altoos 't Hoornvee dat de Caffers besitten in de oogen steekt*" (*9*, pp. 293–94).

the same causes, though the severe drought of 1792–93 and the acute grazing shortage that resulted were probably important contributory factors. Maynier, landdrost of Graaff Reinet at that time, gave the cattle barter as one of the causes of the second Kaffir war. But "cattle barter" is a very vague term for what had actually taken place. Free and voluntary barter could hardly have been the cause of hostilities. Maynier's contemporary, Campagne, referring to the same event, was certainly more precise when he said that the honest Boers made tolerably decent use of that trade "while others fell into abuses which richly deserved punishment" (*11*, p. 14).

The third Kaffir war (1799) probably had little to do with the cattle trade, for, as pointed out by Marais (*11*, pp. 104–07), it was "a Hottentot at least as much as a Kaffir war," in which many Hottentot farm servants joined Xosa tribesmen living within the colony. There was no Kaffir invasion from outside the colony. To what extent the 1799 war was a revolt of disintegrated Hottentot and Bantu elements against their European masters cannot be gone into here.

In this as well as in the previous chapters, our aim has been to show that the frontier economy of the eighteenth century, including that of the native tribes, was largely linked up with the trade of the Cape, and that the cattle trade was the pivot around which the economic life of the frontier revolved. Indeed, from the beginning of the eighteenth century the meat supply of Capetown, including that of the garrison, the hospital, the Company's ships, and foreign ships, was drawn more and more from the graziers of the frontier districts beyond the mountains and from the native tribes beyond the frontiers. By the end of the 1760's or the early 1770's, the western Hottentots had lost most of their livestock, and the cattle trade shifted to the east, to the eastern Hottentots and to the Bantus. Many colonists who had farms in the interior were combining stock farming with cattle trading, while others had farms in the interior for the sole purpose of being able to carry on the cattle-smuggling trade with greater ease. The burghers A. Heyring and H. L. Crouse, so often mentioned by Moodie in connection with the cattle-smuggling trade, are good cases in point (*4*, p. 34).

From the late 1760's the Cape's meat supply was dependent

upon livestock produced by the colonists in the interior and frontier districts as well as upon the livestock obtained from the eastern Hottentots and the Bantus, particularly the latter, through barter. The combination of stock farming with cattle trading was thus destined to play a most important part in the expansion of the colony to the east and the northeast, especially during the last quarter of the eighteenth century when the Cape experienced the largest increase in foreign shipping. Needless to say, the cattle trade carried on by frontier farmers did not exclude cattle trading as a separate function, carried on largely by butchers and their agents who were also the ultimate buyers of livestock. In fact, the butchers or meat contractors who had a large amount of capital at their disposal and were also in a position to obtain as many loan farms as they wanted, were also graziers on a very large scale (*12*, p. 88), thus contributing greatly to the expansion movement. The expansion of the frontier was thus aimed not only at opening up new areas for grazing, but also at tapping the cattle resources of the native tribes for the ever-widening Cape market. It was probably this factor more than anything else that accounts for the rapidity of the expansion movement. When in the middle of the seventies this expansionist movement reached the Fish River, it met with formidable obstacles. The colonists were now up against the Bantu tribesmen, who were militarily better organized than the Hottentots to defend their cattle. Nor were the Bantus so prone as were the Hottentots to succumb to arrack and brandy.

The expansion of the colony now took a northeasterly direction, and in 1786 the boundary was moved to the Tarka and Baviaans rivers, while in the south the boundary remained the Fish River. The northeasterly boundary, which included Bushman and Bantu territory, was moved not only because the government wanted to take in the more remote Boers who had established themselves beyond the old frontier, but principally because it was necessary to forestall the possibility of a foreign power's depriving the Company of an indispensable source of cattle.[4]

---

[4] ". . . *den van daar niet meet te ontbeerende toevoer van slagtvee herwarts afsnijde.*" See C.78 Resoluties, 28.8.1785 (*9*, p. 161). Although the quotation refers also to recognition fees, it does bear out the fact that the northeastern territory was an indispensable source of livestock to the Company. Recognition fees were important, but were certainly not indispensable.

In spite of a succession of Kaffir wars—in 1793, 1799, 1812, and 1818—and incessant frontier troubles in the intervening periods, the 1786 boundary was not materially altered. The shifting of the frontier in 1824 was to the drifts of the Orange River "in the wake of the advancing cattle-farmers" (*13*, p. 186), while in the east the frontier was not altered until 1829, when it was shifted up to the "hills west of the Tyumie and a line drawn thence to the Kat below Fort Beaufort" (*13*, p. 189). All the time, however, there was peaceful penetration of the Boers into Griqualand, and many graziers were living at the beginning of the 1830's in Adam Kok's country "on land sold or leased to them by Griquas in defiance of missionary-Griqua law" (*13*, p. 186). The cattle trade and the expansion movement were shifting to the north and northeast, to the cattle resources of the Griquas and Bechuanas.

SOME CONCLUDING OBSERVATIONS

While the need for meat and cattle (and hence for new grazing land and native cattle) was the primary cause of expansion, there were also other causes which, in the aggregate, were of great importance. There had always been a good demand for tallow, tail fat, and soap at the Cape. The grazier also derived an income from selling berry wax, ostrich feathers and ostrich eggs, ivory, karosses, leather, skins, and the teeth and fat of the hippopotamus. In some areas the sale of draft oxen was very important, while in others butter production was the chief source of income. As might be expected, this great variety of articles, originating from such heterogeneous economic pursuits as manufacturing, grazing, hunting, and collecting, had no uniform bearing on the expansion movement. For instance, those products derived from collecting (barilla, berry wax, ostrich eggs) and hunting (ivory, skins of wild animals, ostrich feathers) required areas of even greater dimensions than those required for a purely grazing economy.

However, all these commodities did have one important thing in common, their mode of being taken to market. Unlike sheep and cattle, which walked to market, they were transported by ox wagon over long distances and difficult roads. While the value of an article per unit of weight and volume was one important consideration, another was the ease with which an article could be transported. As shown earlier, soap, for instance, could be transported with much greater ease than tallow. In general, however, the cost of transport played a decisive part in determining not only what articles and how much of them should be taken to market, but also what and how much should be produced for the market. While soap, salted butter, some leather, dry hides, and berry wax made up the bulk of the products taken to market, the value of the load was increased when accompanied by ivory, ostrich feathers, skins of wild animals, and other high-priced products. Since, moreover, the grazier at the frontier relied to a large extent upon game for his meat, the products of hunting became complementary to the products of the pastoral economy, and hunting and stock breeding interrelated pursuits.

CITATIONS

1 The Early Cape Hottentots (Van Riebeeck Society Publication, No. 14).

2 G. M. Theal, *The History of South Africa Before 1795*, 3 vols. (3d. ed., London, 1922), III.

3 G. M. Theal, *The History of South Africa Before 1795*, II.

4 D. Moodie, *The Record: or a Series of Official Papers Relative to the Conditions and Treatment of the Native Tribes of South Africa* (Capetown, 1838–41), Pt. III.

5 C. P. Thunberg, *Travels in Europe, Africa and Asia, Performed Between the Years 1770 and 1779*, 3 vols. (London, 1795), II.

6 G. M. Theal, *Belangrijke Historische Dokumenten Over Zuid Afrika*, 3 vols. (Govt. of South Africa, 1911), II.

7 C. P. Thunberg, *Travels in Europe, Africa and Asia, Performed Between the Years 1770 and 1779*, I.

8 Andrew Sparrman, *A Voyage to the Cape of Good Hope from the Year 1772 to 1776* (London, 1785), II.

9 P. J. van der Merwe, *Die Trekboer in die Geskiedenis van die Kaapkolonie (1657-1842)* (Capetown, 1938).

10 "Journal of a Tour of Lt. Colonel Richard Collins to the North-Eastern Boundary, the Orange River and the Storm Mountains," in 4, Pt. V.

11 J. S. Marais, *Maynier and the First Boer Republic* (Capetown, 1944).

12 A. J. H. van der Walt, *Die Ausdehnung der Kolonie am Kap der Guten Hoffnung* (Berlin, 1928).

13 E. A. Walker, *The Great Trek* (2d ed., London, 1938).

CHAPTER 10

THE CAPE OF GOOD HOPE MARKET AND THE FRONTIER ECONOMY, 1793–1826

The great prosperity of the colony which had begun in the early 1770's (see chap. 6) came to an end in the early 1790's; the years 1793–1826 were characterized by short depressions and longer periods of prosperity. In what follows we shall examine the market demand at the Cape for the products of the frontier districts during this interval and its effect on the development of the frontier economy.

Economic conditions deteriorated as a result of the withdrawal of the garrison in 1790 and the stoppage of all work on fortifications. In 1793–94 "ocean commerce past the Cape was greatly diminished" (*1*, p. 298), and a depression set in. The fall in foreign shipping and the reduction of the garrison were undoubtedly the most serious factors affecting the demand for live animals and animal products from the interior.

The economic depression at the frontier also had certain political repercussions, among them the Kaffir war of 1793. The fact that this war coincided not only with a severe drought at the frontier, but also with a very severe depression at the Cape, may perhaps demonstrate once more the close link between the Cape and the frontier economy.

It is also necessary to point out that most of the cattle and sheep consumed in Capetown came from the distant frontier district of Graaff Reinet, the "storehouse of meat and cattle" of the Cape. While Capetown was thus dependent upon Graaff Reinet for most of its meat supply, Graaff Reinet was no less dependent upon Capetown for articles needed by the farmers, particularly ammunition. In 1796, for example, the rebellious farmers of Graaff Reinet were easily forced into submission as soon as General J. H. Craig cut off their supply of ammunition. It is true that the farmers could in their turn cut off Capetown's meat supply. In fact, this was perhaps implied in the original offer made by the farmers of Graaff Reinet when they promised to send to Capetown livestock and such articles as their land produced, "according to the ancient custom," and to observe all reasonable laws and orders, "provided the English governor would supply them with powder, lead, clothing and such other articles as they needed" (*2*, pp. 9–10). But apparently the need for ammunition was too great and the market for cattle and sheep, which had in the meantime improved very considerably, too lucrative to make an embargo on livestock to Capetown very effective.[1] General Craig evidently had the upper hand.

GENERAL PROSPERITY, 1795–99

The depression of the early nineties did not last long, however, for after the coming of the British in 1795 the colonists were promised the opening up of overseas trade on the best possible terms and free internal trade for the first time (*4*, p. 128), and farmers were invited to send their livestock and other farm produce to Capetown for sale (*2*, p. 4). It is true that no provisions were allowed to be exported without special permission, but the large garrison and squadron provided an excellent market for all farm produce (*2*, p. 40). British ships putting into Table Bay also brought a revival to Capetown's trade in imported wares (*4*, p. 133). Although in 1798 the price of meat was fixed at only $2\frac{2}{3}d.$ per pound, it did not compare unfavorably with the prices fixed at the height of the boom at the beginning of the eighties when meat prices were very high.[2] The prices of other farm produce, with the exception of wine and wheat, were also very high (*4*, p. 133). The following figures show some prices of animal products in the Cape in 1783 and in the early years of the nineteenth century (*6*, p. 280, and for 1801, *7*, pp. 397–98):

---

[1] For a detailed account of the Boer insurrection at Graaff Reinet, the reader should consult Marais (*3*, particularly chap. VII). Marais concludes that the acute shortage of ammunition was a very important factor in bringing about the collapse of the resistance movement, and points out that the surrender of a Dutch fleet in Saldanha Bay could not have had anything to do with the submission (*3*, p. 91).

[2] At the beginning of the 1780's the price of beef was fixed at $4\frac{2}{3}d.$ and mutton at $2\frac{1}{5}d.$ per kilogram (*5*, p. 203).

Item	1783			1801			1803 or 1806		
	Rd.	Sch.	St.	Rd.	Sch.	St.	Rd.	Sch.	St.
Sheep	—	6	—	...	...	...	2	2	—
Ox, 500 lbs....	6	—	—	...	...	...	26	—	—
Cow, 300 lbs....	4	—	—	...	...	...	15	—	—
Butter, lb.	—	—	5.0	—	2	2–4	—	4	—
Soap, lb.	—	—	5.0	—	3	—	—	4	—
Meat, lb.	—	—	.5	—	—	2	—	—	3
Tallow, lb......	...	...	...	—	3	0–2	...	...	...

The extent of the demand for livestock created by the army and navy may be seen from the following figures of cattle and sheep consumed in Capetown in 1797 (*8*, p. 50):

Consumer	Cattle	Sheep
Civil population............	5,000	130,000
Army and navy.............	6,372	31,856

The above figures do not include the number of cattle and sheep required by passing merchant ships. Barrow reports that the farmers in the Graaff Reinet district received in those years about 6–8*s*. (1½ to 2 rix-dollars) for a sheep and 48*s*. (12 rix-dollars) for an ox (*9*, p. 67), prices which compared very favorably with those given by van Reenen for the year 1783 (*6*, p. 280). In Barrow's time there were 5,000 troops and a large fleet stationed at the Cape (*8*, p. 29).

The market for other animal products was not less favorable. Salted butter from the interior, for instance, was "a very marketable article both for the consumption of the town, the garrison and the navy, as also for exportation" (*8*, p. 330). There was also a good market for salted mutton and mutton hams, which were prepared in Capetown (*8*, p. 329). Barrow reports that the exportation of hides and skins "both dried and salted raw has been increased to a very considerable degree under the British government, and the price has consequently augmented in proportion to the demand for them" (*8*, pp. 323–24). In fact, the price of oxhides rose from half a rix-dollar to 2 rix-dollars per piece, and the quantity exported was estimated at 2,000–3,000 annually. Most of these skins and hides, however, originated from animals killed in and around Capetown, and very few were exported from the interior. There was also a good market for ostrich feathers (*10*, p. 167), skins of wild animals, and ivory—the teeth of the hippopotamus being considered the best ivory (*8*, p. 335).

SERIOUS SETBACK TO EXPANSION MOVEMENT

The Batavian government between 1803 and 1806 held out great promise for the development of the colony, but was too short-lived to put its beneficial reforms into practice. Its immediate effect on the market for Cape produce was circumscribed by its limited spending power. The garrison under the Batavian government consisted only of some 1,500–1,600 regular European troops (2, p. 191), and Barrow asserts that a total stagnation of trade had set in following the surrender of the colony in 1803. "The merchant of the town was clogged with a heavy capital of foreign goods, for which there was no vent; and the farmer had little demands for his produce" (8, p. 341).

Lack of markets, however, was not the only trouble the farmers of the frontier districts had to contend with. Indeed, the Kaffir war in 1799 was so disastrous to the farmers of Graaff Reinet, and the Hottentot and Kaffir depredations that followed so widespread and ruinous, that most of the colonists had hardly anything to take to market.

In his special remarks concerning the areas[3] which suffered very severely van Reenen says (6, p. 275):

These districts have been destroyed and burnt by the Kafirs and Hottentots whereby quite 500 families have suffered. The statement of the lost livestock could be found in the returns of Graaff Reinet. The quantity is enormous, and even if no further disturbances occur in the next fifteen years, these districts will not yet have attained their previous prosperity. The wealth of the Colony in cattle and sheep depends, for the greater part, on this area.

In other words, the high prices of livestock and livestock products that prevailed during the period under review were due chiefly not to an increase in demand but to a shortage of supply. Van Reenen recommended that the farmers in these devastated areas be assisted "in the restoration of their devastated property in order that agriculture and stock-farming in those parts, which are so beneficial and indispensable to this Colony, may again flourish" (6, p. 290). Van Reenen's emphasis on the importance of these livestock areas to the colony are of particular interest, for he was not only well acquainted with the general conditions

---

[3] Krom River, Zeekoe River, van Stadens River, Zwartkops River, Sunday River, Bushmans River, Little Fish River, Zuurvelden, Winterhoek, Bruintjeshoogte, Baviaans River, Great Fish River (6, p. 275).

of the colony, but able to speak with authority on its agricultural and pastoral problems. "The reparation of these devastated farms," he says, "is all the more necessary because in those districts most of the cattle and the heaviest animals are produced, the pasture being exceptionally rich and luxuriant. This would save the slaughter of sheep and so overcome the existing shortage of them" (*6*, p. 291–93).

However, in spite of these shortages and high prices, very little development in stock farming took place in that period. The reasons are not far to seek. In the interior, "many families, whose houses and lands were burnt and destroyed in the last Caffer War, have been compelled through necessity to adopt a wandering life" (*11*, pp. 83–84), while well-to-do residents in Capetown, "owing to the shortage of specie in circulation . . . [were] unable to raise any money on mortgage wherewith to encourage their children to devote themselves to profitable agriculture and stock-raising" (*6*, p. 287). In addition, owing to the desertion of the Hottentot farm servants, the frontier districts were also suffering from an acute labor shortage. In fact, it was this rising of the Hottentot farm servants that made the war of 1799 and the subsequent widespread risings in 1801 and 1802 so disastrous to the colonists of the frontier districts. Their desertion must have had a paralyzing effect on the whole farm economy of the frontier colonists, quite apart from the fact that, as an internal enemy trained in the use of firearms, the Hottentot servants were able to inflict much greater losses upon their former masters than the Xosa. We have it from van Reenen that the Hottentot farm laborers were indispensable to the frontier farmers both as cattle herdsmen and in ordinary agriculture (*6*, p. 289):

On these [frontier] farms slaves cannot be used on the account of the proximity to the Kafirs; for often they desert, taking with them the arms with which they have been supplied for the protection of the live-stock entrusted to their care, and then join the Kafirs, from whom they cannot be recovered again. The Hottentots are faithful, are good shots, and the farmer has nothing to fear from them. The slaves on these distant farms, on the contrary, often assassinate and rob their masters; of this more than one sad example is at hand. In Kafirland they enjoy the same privileges as the Kafirs and moreover the loss of a slave means a loss of from 500 to 600 Rds. to the poor farmer. Slaves are often even murdered by the Kafirs when the latter wish to seize the cattle of the masters.

In other words, the frontier farmers had no substitute for Hottentot farm labor and, so long as the Hottentots were in revolt against the colonists, restoration of the devastated areas was hardly possible.

Until the end of the eighteenth century the Hottentots were rendering the frontier farmers an invaluable service, and it is doubtful whether such an expansion of the colony as had taken place would have been possible without the Hottentot shepherds, Hottentot cattle herdsmen, and Hottentot wagon drivers. It is doubtful also whether the colonists could have defended themselves effectively against the attacks of Bushmen and other hostile native tribes without the help of their numerous and faithful Hottentot servants. But at the close of the eighteenth century and in the early years of the nineteenth century the Hottentots, for reasons which cannot be entered into here, were in revolt, and events took a different turn. Indeed, the rising of the Hottentot farm servants against their masters must be regarded not only as the most serious calamity that had befallen the frontier farmers, but also as the first great reverse in the whole history of the expansion movement.

GOVERNMENT INTEREST IN THE FRONTIER

The devastation of the frontier areas soon made itself felt in the form of a meat shortage in Capetown, for, as we have seen earlier, these areas were Capetown's chief source of meat supply. The dependence of the capital, the army, and the navy on the frontier areas for their meat supply was also one of the chief reasons why the government was bound to keep the peace there by all available means. An insurrection of colonists could be suppressed easily by withholding the supply of ammunition, but Xosa depredations and the revolt of farm servants proved a more complicated affair.

The first attempt to solve the Hottentot-Kaffir problem was made by the British government at the Cape in 1800 when Major General R. Dundas tried "to break off the confederacy or league which had been unhappily formed for the first time between the two sets of savages," a combination which threatened the whole colony with destruction (quoted in 7, p. 52). Maynier, the landdrost, was directed by Dundas "to convince the Hottentots and Caffres that it was the intention of His Britannic Majesty's Government to alleviate the sufferings of the former, and to prevent in future the injustice which upon many occasions has been done the latter on the part of the farmers in their dealings with them." Second, a register of the Hottentots in the farmers' service was to be established "and kept at the Drosdy by the Landdrost in which is to be specified the names of the parties, farmer and Hottentot, with the age, condition and term of service of the latter." Third, the landdrost was instructed "not to suffer with impunity any acts of violence or cruelty as have been usual on the parts of the farmers towards the Hottentots" (quoted in 7, p. 53). Finally, Maynier was also given the task of persuading "as many as possible of the runaway Hottentots to return to the service of the farmers under the protection or guarantee of the Register with the exception of a few of the Hottentot Captains whose individual safety would be endangered by returning to the Boers, as they have become particularly obnoxious to them." These Hottentot captains with their adherents were to be given unoccupied lands for their use (quoted in 7, p. 55).

At the same time a post was established at Fort Frederick, furnished with a cannon and a garrison consisting of 300 men, not so much as a measure of security against future Xosa attacks—for this the small garrison was inadequate—as "in order to awe the turbulent inhabitants and for supporting the civil magistrate in the execution of his office" (quoted in 7, p. 56).

FARM LABOR

But the Hottentot farm labor policy of 1800 proved a failure. For one thing, the measures taken were too feeble to break off what Dundas had called "the league between the Hottentots and the Caffres." The latter still remained in the Zuurveld. The opportunities for stealing cattle were certainly not diminished, while the protection the Hottentots were offered in the form of a register, held at the drosdy of Graaff Reinet, was hardly adequate to induce disaffected farm laborers to return to their masters, although some Hottentots did come back. Maynier's was a heroic effort to solve a difficult problem with inadequate means.

The farm labor situation remained unchanged during the short rule of the Batavian Republic. The Governor of the Cape, J. W. Janssens, journeyed to the interior. He was motivated chiefly by the desire "to remove the inconvenience occasioned by the unsettled state of the Kaffres and Hottentots," but his reforms did not go beyond prohibiting the missionaries at Bethelsdorp from sheltering runaway Hottentots (*12*, pp. 52, 110).

Janssens thought that the missionaries did a considerable amount of mischief (*13*, p. 24; see also *14*, p. 163). "The attraction which the savages really find in the missionaries is that the latter distribute presents and allow their pupils to continue living in that complete idleness which these people so dearly love. They leave the farmers or are prevented remaining with them: they prefer, for their daily and sole work to pray and listen in idleness to a few hours preaching." The concern of the missionaries about the welfare of the Hottentots in the midst of a labor shortage proved somewhat awkward even to British government officials. Collins, for instance, recommended that the Bethelsdorp mission be closed because it had a detrimental effect on the farm labor supply of the eastern frontier districts (*12*, p. 109).

However, after the second British occupation in 1806 a more active policy with regard to Hottentot farm labor was pursued. Thus in a letter to Caledon, dated July 17, 1807, the landdrost of Graaff Reinet requested the governor not to recruit Hottentots from the district for military service, since their enlistment would deprive the farmers of their best herdsmen, "which cannot but have fatal consequences in those parts of the country exposed to the Wandering Hords" (*15*, p. 183). At the end of that year Caledon recommended to Castlereagh, the secretary of state for war and colonies, the disbanding of the Hottentot Corps in order to restore 700 men to the service of the farmers, stating that "on account of an encreased demand for agricultural products, owing to a numerous garrison as well as the more frequent resort of Shipping to the bays, an additional supply of fresh provision is requisite, and consequently an encrease of labour to procure it" (*15*, p. 233).

In an earlier letter to Castlereagh, dated July 25, 1807, Caledon had explained that the reduction of the Hottentot Corps would benefit the farmers who "would gain the advantage of some useful Labourers, a consideration of some importance, especially since the abolition of the Slave Trade" (*15*, p. 182).

The next step was to put the Hottentots under colonial law. As a modicum of protection, the laws of 1800, providing for written contracts, were strengthened, and in 1811 the circuit judges were instructed to receive complaints from the Hottentots. At the same time, however, their freedom of movement was restricted. In 1809 Caledon proclaimed that Hottentots should have a fixed abode and that they should not be allowed to change their place of abode from one district to another without a certificate from the Fiscal or landdrost. Hottentots going about the country without a pass would be "considered and treated as vagabonds" (*12*, pp. 211–16). In 1812 Cradock further directed that Hottentot children, born while their parents were in service and maintained by the master to the age of eight, were to be apprenticed to that master for ten years to come (*16*, p. 386).

As regards the Xosa, it was decided to drive them across the boundary and to settle the Zuurveld with a dense European population (*4*, pp. 159–60):

The clearing of the Zuurveld was carried out by Cradock. A large force of troops and burghers swept 20,000 Ndhlambis and Gunukwebes beyond the Fish, and, to hold the frontier, Cradock built a double line of block-houses, garrisoned them with troops and burghers, placed a deputy landdrost behind each wing of the line at the new villages of Cradock and Grahamstown, and offered quit-rent farms of 2000 morgen, two-thirds the usual size of a farm, near each military post.

In fact, in 1812 Cradock proclaimed the government's intention to "found extensive settlements from Algoa Bay, the future naval mart of those quarters, to Uitenhage and Graaff Reinet" (*16*, p. 374). Farms which previous to the expulsion of the Xosa had been abandoned were not to be reoccupied on loan but "upon the tenure of Perpetual Quit Rent" (*16*, p. 375), the idea being to encourage a permanent occupation of the frontier farms.

However, the settling of the freed territories with a dense European population proved a much more difficult problem than Cradock and his advisers had thought. Quite apart from the fact that good land was also available in the northeastern districts of the colony, it was impossible to get the necessary numbers of people within the colony to fill up the frontier.[4] But the more immediate, and perhaps more serious, problem was that of Hottentot farm labor. The difficulty of procuring Hottentots in the grazing districts was already great, and the reoccupation of the farms in the freed areas of the eastern frontier required more and not less farm labor. It is true that, in spite of numerous proclamations and warnings, increasing numbers of Kaffirs were employed on the eastern frontier as herdsmen and agricultural laborers (*17*, pp. 407–09).[5] However, the expulsion of the Kaffirs from the colony deprived the farmers of even that source of labor.

The scarcity of labor was an important factor in diverting the expansion movement from the eastern to the northeastern frontier. Moreover, it compelled the colonists to treat their Hottentot servants better. Thus, the Commission of Circuit was able to report in 1812 that the farmers had an "essential interest" in the satisfaction and willingness of the Hottentots, "as they [the farmers] have not any other persons for herdsmen, neither can they easily obtain people even for other work, in consequence of the present daily encreasing dearness of slaves" (*18*, p. 72). The Commission of Circuit report for 1813 also states that the Hottentots were well treated by the inhabitants (*19*, p. 86).

THE NORTHEASTERN BORDER

Until the beginning of the nineteenth century very little was known in Capetown about the northern border territories of the colony and even less about the areas beyond the Orange River, though a considerable amount of information had been gathered by graziers living in the Sneeuwbergen, and along the Zak and the Zeekoe rivers. The occasion for exploring the northeastern territories arose in 1801 when, owing to a long drought, large numbers of livestock were lost in the wheat-growing districts of the Cape. A survey of 223 wheat farms revealed that owners of these farms alone had lost 3,000 draft oxen, 1,400 head of cattle,

---

[4] Collins thought that 6,000 settlers were necessary for the eastern frontier, but he considered it useless to look for these people within the colony (*12*, p. 103).

[5] Collins, for instance, reports that the farmers were gradually forgetting the misfortunes they had suffered from the Kaffirs and were receiving many of them into their service (*12*, p. 53).

2,600 horses, and 14,400 sheep (*20*, p. 195). Since it was feared that the loss of livestock, particularly draft oxen, might affect Capetown's supply not only of wheat, but also of other farm produce, the lieutenant governor requested that the special commission appointed for regulating the consumption of grain in the colony "would seriously deliberate on the state of the Colony with regard to cattle, and propose some plan for replacing the vast numbers that have perished in the course of the late unfavourable season" (*20*, p. 198).

The commission decided that it was necessary to "open up a trade by the way of barter with some of the natives bordering the Colony" (*20*, p. 199). But which of the native tribes still had cattle to spare and, having any, were willing to barter them? The answer to this question did not appear at all easy. As the commissioners put it (*20*, p. 199):

The people from whom the former government were most in the habit of supplying the Colony in times of scarcity were the Kaffers on the east side, and the Namaquas on the north; with the former it appeared by no means advisable to the Commissioners that at the present moment any communication ought to be attempted by way of traffick; and the latter being reduced by the neighboring Bosjesmans and by a former trade with the Colony to very few hords, and these not possessed of abundance of cattle, policy required that this nation ought not to be tempted to part with their remaining stock, as the consequences would lead to their becoming Bosjesmans or Marauders either upon the colonists or upon the neighbouring tribes of natives.

The possibility of obtaining cattle from the European farmers of the Graaff Reinet district was apparently ruled out on account of the heavy losses in livestock sustained by them in the 1799 Kaffir war (see above, p. 111).

The only part of the country that was considered worth exploring was "the belt of the country extending behind the Colony from the Kaffers to the Namaquas" (*20*, p. 199). Information was also obtained from a Roggeveld farmer that although the Koranas and other tribes on the banks of the Orange River had no cattle, "among or very near to the Koranas were dwelling certain Bastards or men sprung from Europeans and Hottentots, who were in the constant practice of frequenting and trading with a populous nation called the Beriquas [Griquas], situated about ten days journey beyond the said Orange River" (*20*, p. 199).

The Griquas were said to be "exceedingly rich in horned cattle," and were very willing to barter them for trinkets, knives, buttons, pieces of iron, etc.

This information being confirmed also from other sources, the commission sent an expedition "into the country of the Beriquas" (*20*, p. 201), which left Capetown in October 1801 and returned in August 1802. Although the number of cattle brought back from the country beyond the Orange River was not very large, the expedition did bring back a detailed account of "everything remarkable that occurred in the course of their journey in the unfrequented North-Eastern part of this continent" (*20*, p. 359). The members of the expedition also discovered that the tribes they called "Beriquas" were the same as Bechuanas.

We have stressed this event because it shows not only the great scarcity of livestock that then prevailed in the colony, but also how it came about that the colony was compelled to tap the cattle resources north of the Orange River. This foreshadowed the future direction of the expansion movement, though the latter did not actually follow the route of the 1801 expedition. In subsequent years colonists were to find in the areas south of the Orange River not only better grazing land but also new sources of labor and game, and, in the cattle resources of the Griquas and Bechuanas beyond the Orange, new opportunities for cattle trading.

As regards grazing and game, Collins, who visited the country around Rhinocerosberg during the summer rainfall season of 1809, reported that the area abounded not only with "fine pasturage and good water" but also with game. Near the Orange River antelopes and springboks were particularly plentiful, while in the river he saw large numbers of hippopotamuses. "The country we had just visited," Collins says, "is one of the finest I had ever seen. It is bounded on the west by the colony and the Zuurberg stream, on the north by Orange River, on the east by Grey River, and on the south by the Storm Mountains. . . . The country beyond Orange and Grey Rivers, as far as we could see, is not inferior to that on this side of them." The small plains of the Storm Mountains offered fine water and pasturage and the summits were covered with a superior quality of grass (*12*, pp. 21, 22, 23, 29).

Collins met there in 1809 new settlers who came from other

parts of the country, one from Hantam, who were well satisfied with the change (*12*, p. 21). Collins himself found the Bushmen friendly and helpful, and found the farmers in that part of the country as well as in the Tarka living in peace with the Bushmen (*12*, p. 23). He also reports that (*12*, p. 36): "Since the year 1797, several inhabitants of the northeastern districts appear to have exerted themselves with as much zeal to acquire the friendship of the Bosjesmen, as they had before done to blot them from the creation. They have experienced the most happy results from this line of conduct."

A year earlier, in 1808, Collins reported that farmers were getting on well with some Bushmen (*15*, pp. 340–41), that many farmers had Bushmen in their service, that they treated the Bushmen humanely, and that the latter served the farmers faithfully (*15*, p. 344; *12*, pp. 21–23, 29). Collins also reported that on the borders of the Koup and of Sneeuwbergen Bushmen "frequently engage in the service of the farmers"[6] (*15*, p. 349). The Tarka, which was deserted in Barrow's time on account of Bushmen (*8*, p. 80), was being reoccupied in Collins' time (*16*, p. 31). Thus, while in the east Kaffir depredations and cattle lifting continued, and many Hottentot herdsmen were deserting either to Bethelsdorp or across the border, in the northeast the little Bushmen were receiving ever greater praise.

Kaffir depredations in the eastern areas of the colony continued even after the Xosa were driven across the Fish River in 1812. At the end of 1813, Cradock himself spoke of "the fatal consequences that result from the almost unceasing incursions of the Kaffer Tribes into His Majesty's Territories." He adds unhappily that "the extent and nature of the country to be guarded, and the facility with which the Great Fish River can be forded at almost all points, render it next to impossible to prevent the entrance of the Kaffers" (*18*, p. 285), and that "a third of the scanty population of those Districts are employed on Commando service, and thus withdrawn from domestic avocations, to the almost total interruption of agricultural improvement" (*18*, p. 286). His remedy was to discontinue permanent

---

[6] See also *11*, chap. XXXI, on the amicable relations that were found by Governor Janssens to exist between some Bushmen and colonists in the neighborhood of the Orange and Zeekoe rivers.

commandos and to entrust the protection of the frontier to the Cape Regiment, consisting of Hottentot levies. But this could hardly solve the farm labor problem, for it now became necessary to augment the strength of the Cape Regiment by another 200 Hottentots, recruiting them from the different districts of the colony, including those of Graaff Reinet and Uitenhage (*18*, p. 286). Thus, while the returned farmers could now attend better to their farms, they could hardly dispense with their all-too-scarce Hottentot herdsmen. While these conditions continued in the east, the Commission of Circuit found that the Bushmen in the northeastern districts "conduct themselves very peaceably," that "they seem to accustom themselves more and more to the Christians," and "that they are even of very essential service to the inhabitants in whose neighbourhood they live, by taking care of their cattle, for which on account of their great fidelity they are considered as superior to the Hottentots" (*19*, p. 94).

TRADING WITH THE NORTHERN TRIBES

As in the eighteenth century, the northward expansion movement was initiated by a combination of trading and livestock farming. Lichtenstein reports that about the middle of the first decade of the nineteenth century some Bastard-Hottentots beyond the Orange River carried on a sort of contraband trade with some Capetown burghers who had "cattle places on the borders of the Colony," exchanging "horned-cattle, elephants' teeth, ostrich feathers, and hides of animals" for powder and firearms (*11*, p. 325).

George Thompson, in his evidence on the state of the Bushmen, Griquas, and other frontier tribes in the 1820's, said that the native tribes of the northern frontier "labour under the belief that they are not allowed to proceed to Cape Town, or indeed to come within the Colony, an impression which the Boers upon the frontier have given them, in order that they might enjoy the whole traffic themselves; and the independent tribes are thus obliged to dispose of their goods at the lowest rates to the Boers" (*14*, p. 136).

The cattle-plundering element was provided by Coenraad Buys and his Griqua band who were raiding "Beriqua tribes." They too bartered the plundered cattle for firearms and gunpowder with farmers of the Tulbagh district (*21*, pp. 34–35), from whom the cattle were eagerly snatched up by the Capetown butchers to supply the army and navy with meat. History repeated itself.

It was with a view to stopping this illicit traffic that the government decided in 1818 that the deputy landdrost of Beaufort should take measures for establishing a market within the Beaufort district, and that he should take every measure "to invite and entice the neighbouring tribes of Briquas, Bochuanas, or Bastards, to come to the same periodically with such cattle or effects as they might wish to dispose of" (*22*, p. 328). But the Beaufort fair proved a failure and the bulk of the trade continued to be carried on by the border colonists and by hawkers at or beyond the borders of the colony. In 1825 the government had to legalize "intercourse or Traffic, of every kind, with the Griqua nation, or neighbouring Tribes, beyond the Northern Frontier of the Colony . . . by means of Passports, for every Person or Party so Trafficking." These passports had to be signed either by the government agent (or in his absence by any of the resident missionaries) or by the landdrost of Graaff Reinet, or the deputy landdrost of Beaufort (*22*, p. 227).

The traffic in firearms and powder with the northern tribes, though strictly prohibited, went on all the time. In fact, the Commission of Inquiry on Finance in its 1826 report thought that such a restriction was futile, and even suggested that the traffic should be legalized, particularly in view of the immense extent of the northern frontier, "and the absence of all control over it. . . . That this restriction has not had the effect of preventing the smuggling trade in arms and gunpowder upon the frontier is apparent from the supplies of both that are obtained by the Griquas or Bastards who are settled beyond the Orange River" (*23*, p. 437).

The part played by the illicit trade in firearms and gunpowder in the northward expansion movement may also be seen from the following quotation from the report of the Commission of Inquiry upon the Administration of the Government. In its report of September 1826 the commission stated (*23*, p. 384):

The application of the graziers for occupancies have followed the course of the Sea Cow River, to the place where it falls into the Orange or Groote

River. The pursuits of the people to whom the occupation of tracts under the name of "request places" has been granted by the magistrate of the district, and which are yet unconfirmed and unsurveyed, consist altogether of grazing sheep and cattle during certain parts of the year, and keeping up an illicit trade in firearms and gunpowder with the Griquas and Bechuana tribes.

It is of interest to note that the supply of firearms and gunpowder to the Griquas by the farmers of the northern frontier was decisive in defeating the hordes of native tribes who were coming down from the north toward the Orange River. Were it not for these firearms in the hands of the Griquas the invasion from the north would probably have proved much more disastrous to the colony than the Kaffir wars. Curiously enough, the illegal traffic in ammunition thus served not only to secure slaughter cattle for the colony but also to ward off invasion.

In this connection it is interesting to observe how little smuggling of ammunition was going on between the colonists and the Kaffirs on the eastern frontier. This cannot be explained by the greater vigilance of the patrols on the eastern border, since this vigilance did not halt the constant cattle smuggling "between the Kaffers and some of the worst description of Settlers located near the Frontier" (*24*, p. 447). In fact, it was this illegal and uncontrollable cattle traffic with the Kaffirs that prompted the government in 1825 to make the cattle trade legal at Fort Willshire (*25*, p. 332). Thus, Lieutenant-Colonel Henry Somerset, in a letter to the Governor, said (*24*, p. 449):

The dreadful manner in which some of the Settlers are leagued with the Kaffers in order that they may carry on the illicit Trade in Cattle has induced me to beg I may be authorised to allow a free Trade in Cattle entirely. Cattle are brought in at night by Kaffers to these Traders, and as the Kaffers return they sweep up the Country of all they find, take them into the Kloofs, skin them and take the hides to the Fair, and these Traffickers watch for them so that the Patroles can scarcely ever detect them.

That the colonists at the eastern frontier abstained, as they probably did, from trading firearms and gunpowder to the Kaffirs must be attributed to a keen sense of responsibility and self-preservation even among the "worst description of settlers." (The traffic in firearms with the Griquas had no such implications.) As in the case of cattle trading on the eastern frontier, government prohibition did not correspond to the realities of the situation and was therefore ignored.

CITATIONS

1 G. M. Theal, *Belangrijke Historische Dokumenten Over Zuid Afrika,* 3 vols. (Govt. of South Africa, 1911), III.

2 G. M. Theal, *History of South Africa Since 1795,* 5 vols. (5th ed., London, 1927), I.

3 J. S. Marais, *Maynier and the First Boer Republic* (Capetown, 1944).

4 E. A. Walker, *A History of South Africa* (2d ed., London, 1940).

5 G. M. Theal, *History of South Africa Since 1795,* III.

6 D. G. van Reenen, *Die Journal van Dirk Gysbert van Reenen, 1803* (Van Riebeeck Society Publication, No. 18).

7 G. M. Theal, *Records of the Cape Colony,* 36 vols. (Govt. of the Cape Colony, 1897–1905), III.

8 John Barrow, *Travels into the Interior of South Africa,* 2 vols. (2d ed., London, 1806), II.

9 John Barrow, *Travels into the Interior of South Africa,* I.

10 Robert Percival, *An Account of the Cape of Good Hope* (London, 1804).

11 Henry Lichtenstein, *Travels in Southern Africa, in the Years 1803, 1804, 1805, and 1806,* 2 vols. (Van Riebeeck Society Publication, No. 11), II.

12 G. M. Theal, *Records,* VII.

13 W. J. Leyds, *The First Annexation of the Transvaal* (London, 1906).

14 *Papers Relative to the Condition and Treatment of the Native Inhabitants of Southern Africa,* Imperial Blue Book, 1835.

15 G. M. Theal, *Records,* VI.

16 G. M. Theal, *Records,* VIII.

17 H. M. Robertson, "150 Years of Economic Contact Between Black and White," *South African Journal of Economics,* II (4), 407–09.

18 G. M. Theal, *Records,* IX.

19 G. M. Theal, *Records,* X.

20 G .M. Theal, *Records,* IV.

21 G. M. Theal, *Records,* XII.

22 G. M. Theal, *Records,* XXV.

23 G. M. Theal, *Records,* XXVIII.

24 G. M. Theal, *Records,* XXIII.

25 G. M. Theal, *Records,* XXIV.

CHAPTER 11

MILITARY EXPENDITURE AT THE CAPE
AND AT ST. HELENA

After the second and permanent British occupation in 1806, there was a great revival in the demand for frontier products. The presence of 4,000–5,000 troops and a large squadron, involving large military and naval expenditure, offered a good market for farm produce (1, p. 352). Meat, butter, tallow, candles, sheep's tail fat, and soap, products mostly originating in the interior and frontier districts, were all in good demand. It is also safe to assume that, as during the first British occupation, there was a good demand for skins of wild animals, ivory, ostrich feathers (2, p. 204), and ostrich eggs. Meat was in short supply, and livestock prices as well as prices of other animal products were high. In 1811, for instance, the Griquas were getting as much as 20 rix-dollars for an ox (2, p. 364). The price realized by the Bokkeveld farmers was 30 rix-dollars (over £4) per draft ox, while near Tulbagh the price of a draft ox was as high as 35 rix-dollars (2, p. 134).

As may be seen from Table 7, the number of troops at the Cape continued to be high up to about the second half of 1817. Unfortunately, no figures are available as to the strength of the squadron that was stationed at the Cape, but it was known to have been very large, at least during the Napoleonic Wars.

Although the number of livestock in the colony was now gradually increasing, the demand exceeded the supply. Thus, in 1812, the government entered into a contract for the supply of 3,000 barrels (1,008,000 pounds) of salted meat from Algoa Bay at what was considered at that time the very low price of 4¾d. per pound (3, p. 356). But this price far exceeded what van Reenen considered a very high price in 1803, namely, 3 stuivers (or 3d.) per pound (4, p. 280).

The existence of a cattle shortage in the colony is also demonstrated by the fact that in 1812 the Commission of Circuit was apprehensive lest the salting of meat at Algoa Bay might affect not only the fresh meat supply of Capetown but also the supply of draft oxen. The commission therefore recommended that the Governor should rather "grant places to the graziers on the old liberal footing" in the reconquered Zuurveld in order to extend cattle breeding in the colony (5, p. 89–90).

TABLE 7.—NUMBER OF BRITISH TROOPS AT THE CAPE OF GOOD HOPE,
SPECIFIED DATES 1810–26*

Date		Number	Source
October	1810	3,775	VII, p. 414
August	1811	3,869	VIII, p. 138
September	1811	4,897	VIII, p. 150
January	1813	4,568	IX, p. 135
August	1813	4,726	IX, p. 230
April	1814	5,000	IX, p. 497
August	1814	4,987	X, p. 160
July	1815	4,072	X, p. 323
February	1816	5,363	XI, p. 78
January	1817	4,526	XI, p. 261
September	1817	3,447	XI, p. 389
October	1817	2,744	XI, p. 400
October	1818	2,603	XII, p. 51
January	1819	2,725	XII, p. 131
June	1821	3,210	XIV, p. 35
March	1822	2,584	XIV, p. 322
May	1823	2,531	XVI, p. 32
September	1825	2,459	XXIII, p. 160
January	1826	2,431	XXV, p. 365

* Data from G. M. Theal, *Records of the Cape Colony*, 36 vols. (Govt. of the Cape Colony, 1897–1905), indicated volumes.

Cattle and sheep numbers in the Cape Colony are shown in Table 8. The figures for sheep for the years 1806, 1811, 1816, and 1821 do not include the numbers of Merino or Spanish sheep and are thus lower than the figures given in Table 4.

As may be seen from Table 8, the number of livestock in the colony was gradually increasing so that the shortage of cattle was probably becoming less acute. In fact, the Commission of Inquiry upon the Trade of the Cape of Good Hope stated in its report of 1828 that the number of cattle in the colony had more than trebled between 1806 and 1824 (6, p. 269), though the figures given below indicate an increase of only 70 per cent over this period. However, the fact that 4,000–5,000 troops were still

TABLE 8.—NUMBERS OF CATTLE, SHEEP, AND GOATS IN THE COLONY OF THE CAPE OF GOOD HOPE, 1806–24*

Year	Draft oxen	Breeding cattle	Wethers	Breeding sheep	Goats
1806	69,487	138,958	16,821	1,223,330	256,664
1807	69,060	130,601	25,285	1,450,889	261,880
1808	63,596	130,808	15,424	1,581,218	296,375
1809	85,378	148,186	17,461	...	342,353
1810	87,762	144,831	17,177	1,944,430	356,020
1811	92,943	171,500	29,682	2,077,933	355,452
1812	84,264	158,541	27,801	1,793,830	323,472
1813	88,992	166,728	33,738	1,783,449	307,341
1814	74,417	135,674	16,675	1,211,151	197,756
1815	90,375	167,627	21,484	1,556,059	249,850
1816	93,888	166,850	30,167	1,526,621	216,968
1817	99,016	172,269	24,395	1,580,341	222,889
1818	103,968	181,692	28,763	1,595,350	333,706
1819	99,489	233,433	26,554	...	275,193
1820	111,228	232,048	22,747	1,919,502	287,066
1821	116,002	253,435	134,619	1,708,772	307,837
1822	109,395	237,276	19,894	2,063,102	310,988
1823	112,553	240,475	27,006	1,076,659	349,378
1824	115,415	236,925	34,545	2,157,757	369,967

* Data from G. M. Theal, *Records of the Cape Colony*, 36 vols. (Government of the Cape Colony, 1897–1905), VI, pp. 75, 248, 442; VII, p. 239; VIII, p. 233; IX, pp. 48, 299; X, p. 228; XI, pp. 51, 238, 439; XII, pp. 129, 415; XIII, p. 350; XIV, p. 247; XV, p. 199; XVI, p. 489; XIX, p. 387.

stationed at the Cape up to about 1816–17 would suggest that the market for livestock was still good.

ST. HELENA AS AN EXPORT MARKET

The Cape was also fortunate in that a new market was opened up at St. Helena in 1815 for livestock, butter, soap, and other Cape produce to supply the troops and ships guarding Napoleon. Although no figures are available as to the size of the garrison at St. Helena and the number of ships stationed there, it may be assumed that they were of considerable strength, especially in view of the fact that the troops and ships were not so much to guard Napoleon as to forestall any attempt to rescue him.

Brooke, in pointing out that St. Helena could never feed its population of under 4,000 inhabitants, states that the arrival of Napoleon "occasioned a sudden increase of that population to double its previous numbers" (*7*, pp. 388–91). This estimate did not include the large squadron stationed at St. Helena.

Historians have accepted the view that from 1815 to 1821 St. Helena constituted a very important market for Cape produce, and that the disappearance of that market after the death of Napoleon was responsible to a large extent for the depression that set in at the Cape in 1821 (*8*, p. 327; *9*, p. 163). On the other hand, some doubt has been expressed by Schumann about the part the St. Helena market actually played in the economy of the Cape. Unfortunately the absence of comparative export figures to St. Helena prior to 1821 does not lend support to either contention. Schumann argues that the decrease of the trade with St. Helena could only have played a minor part in intensifying the depression after 1821, since the fall in exports to St. Helena between 1820 and 1822 (from £30,844 to £15,440) was more than compensated for by the rise in exports to Great Britain from £105,604 in 1820 to £132,922 in 1822. He would thus attribute the 1821–26 depression in the Cape to several other causes, such as the "normal reaction after the relative prosperity" of 1806 to 1814–15; the failure of the wheat crops of 1821 and 1822, followed by bad floods in 1823; and, finally, to the fact that during 1821 and 1822 economic conditions in England, the Cape's principal market, were not favorable (*10*, pp. 67–74).

We are unable to accept Schumann's views for the following reasons. In the first place, the period of prosperity in the Cape did not end in 1814–15, but in 1821–22, that is, about five years after the depression had set in in England. As to the harvest theory, it is not always easy to say, on general reasoning, whether a bad wheat harvest is good or bad for trade. The Cape, in fact, was also known to have suffered from good harvests. Moreover, there is an abundance of historic evidence to show that the St. Helena market did play a very important part in the economy of the Cape between 1815 and 1821. Nor are there good reasons to believe that the increase in exports to Great Britain in 1822 was sufficient to compensate for the loss of the St. Helena market.

Grant, a contemporary of that period, writing on the state of the colonial currency and foreign exchange at the Cape of Good Hope, says that "the six years ending with 1819–20 was perhaps the most prosperous period the Colony ever experienced" (*10*, p. 53). He further states that "from 1815 to 1819, both years included, there cannot be a doubt that the commerce and circumstances of the Colony generally were in a state of the highest prosperity" (*11*, p. 59).

Bird, a well-informed and keen student of the conditions of the colony at that time, regarded "the captivity and the detention of Napoleon Buonaparte, at the island of St. Helena, in 1815" (*12*, p. 3) among the historically important events that have contributed to the development and prosperity of the Cape. In his opinion, "the immediate and continued necessity of supplying that island with flour, cattle, wine and other articles for the use of the navy, the army, and the captive, with his train of followers, operated with immense power on the Cape, and has been the hot-bed of its productions; forcing, by a continued demand, the utmost powers of its agriculture, in order to produce corn (wheat, barley and oats) for Saint Helena, as well as for its own increasing population" (*12*, p. 3). The following products exported from the Cape to St. Helena are mentioned by Bird: oats, whale oil, wheat, flour, barley, dried fruits, hay, horned cattle, sheep, poultry, butter, soap, wine, and a few horses (*12*, p. 119).

The report of the Commissioners of Inquiry upon the Trade of the Cape of Good Hope, the Navigation of the Coast, and the Improvement of the Harbours of that Colony mentions that the largest tonnage of vessels that entered Table Bay and Simon's Bay in any one year between 1819 and 1823 was 88,778 tons, exclusive of British and foreign ships of war, transports, chartered store ships, and coasters. It goes on to state that "in consequence of the reduction which took place in the establishment of the island of St. Helena in the year 1820, the tonnage of vessels entering Table Bay in 1821 was reduced to 54,319 tons, and that of Simon's Bay, whence a considerable portion of the supplies for St. Helena were shipped, was reduced from 21,000 to 13,000 tons" (*6*, p. 234). It also states that the "exportations to St. Helena appear to have been very considerable

during the continuance of the large naval and military establishments, but they have also declined since the year 1820, and
are now nearly limited to a supply of wine purchased on account
of the East India Company" (*6*, p. 239).

Furthermore, a very considerable portion of the exports to
St. Helena was not recorded, while another part was in the category of "invisible exports," such as money spent on refreshments both by ships' crews and by passengers while staying at
the Cape. It has been estimated, for instance, that in the 1820's
the average amount spent by a British ship at the Cape for refreshments, including those of passengers, was about £600 (*6*,
p. 244).

The following quotation from Bird, who was the comptrol-
ler of customs at Capetown and Simonstown at that time, is of
particular interest. Apparently referring to the year 1821, Bird
says (*12*, pp. 123–24):

A judgment may be formed of the importance of the detention of Buonaparte
to the Cape interest, by inspecting the customhouse valuation of the colonial and other exports to St. Helena, exclusive of presents, ships' stores,
stock for the passage, stock really for sale at St. Helena, shipped as stores,
all of which will be under-estimated at one-eighth more. The colonial and
other produce at the customs forms the sum of . . .

	347,697	Rix-dollars
to which ⅛ (unentered)	43,462	"
and supplies to the navy		
entered also at the		
customs	165,544	"
	556,703	Rix-dollars

The whole of this payment was made to the Cape in Spanish dollars or in
bills on England, and the continuation of this description of commerce, would
have been most important in its effects. Produced from the soil, worked by
the hands of man, it is in its nature the most beneficial of all possible exports.

In other words, even in the year 1821, according to Bird,
the value of Cape exports to that island (at the rate of exchange
of 1*s*. 8*d*. per rix-dollar) was still about £45,000 (*12*, p. 123).
The figure of £30,844, quoted by Schumann as being the value
of Cape exports to St. Helena in 1820, probably does not include
supplies to the navy nor all the other important items mentioned
by Bird. In fact, the same objection applies to the figures quoted

by Theal, which give the value of exports from the Cape to St. Helena as follows (in rix-dollars) (*13*, p. 496):

Year	Value
1820	330,421
1821	253,994
1822	184,742
1823	117,336
1824	100,842
1825	...
1826	131,560

As will be seen from Table 9, there was a large and sudden increase in the number of merchant ships and men-of-war and transports arriving at Simonstown in 1815, which continued large until 1822, when it dropped suddenly. The increase in shipping thus coincided with the arrival of Napoleon at St. Helena in 1815 and the opening of a market there for Cape produce, while the death of Napoleon in 1821 coincided with the fall in shipping and the consequent loss of that market. This cannot be regarded as a mere coincidence, for, as we have seen earlier, a considerable portion of the supplies to St. Helena was shipped from Simonstown.

TABLE 9.—NUMBER OF SHIPS ARRIVING AT SIMON'S BAY, 1814–22*

Year	Merchant ships	Men-of-war and transports
1814	26	26
1815	42	46
1816	41	43
1817	37	50
1818	43	34
1819	54	55
1820	32	53
1821	41	31
1822	28	19

* Data from G. M. Theal, *Records of the Cape Colony*, 36 vols. (Govt. of the Cape Colony, 1897–1905), XV, p. 254.

The loss of the St. Helena market must therefore be regarded as a major factor in the depression that set in at the Cape after 1821. What was the effect of this depression on the frontier areas? Ordinarily, the consequences of this sudden change on the frontier economy, based as it was on the sale of animals and animal products, would have been very serious indeed, had it not been for the influx of 4,000 British settlers in 1820 who, until they were able to produce their own food, were an important market not only for meat and other animal products, but also for draft oxen, breeding cattle, and sheep. It was for these reasons that the crisis was confined to Capetown and to products of arable farming, especially wine farming. It probably had very little effect on the frontier economy.

In fact, this is essentially the view expressed by Bird on the state of the Cape in 1822. "The recent death of Napoleon," says Bird, "caused a considerable convulsion, of which the effects would, in case of abundant harvests, have been more fatal to the agriculture of the colony, had not a large full-grown population dropped suddenly upon the Cape some months previous to Buonaparte's death, prepared to replace, by increased home consumption of its produce, the loss of the market of St. Helena" (*12*, p. 3).

THE EXPANSION MOVEMENT, 1821–26

Between 1821 and 1826 there was once more a disparity between the economic conditions prevailing at the Cape and those prevailing at the frontier. At the Cape, we have it from Bird that in 1822 "the distress of trade has lowered the purchase price of land and houses; and those of fixed certain incomes have found rather an improvement than reduction in their means of living; but the number of these is small compared to the real sufferers" (*12*, p. 129). Every means was used to maintain Capetown's declining trade, including the discouragement of direct trade between Port Elizabeth and Mauritius, in order to bestow on Capetown the profits on the resale of goods from Mauritius (*14*, p. 208).

Prosperity also vanished from the arable farmers of the western Cape. "The abolition of the slave trade, which enhanced so greatly the price of slave labour, by which the vine is exclusively cultivated," and the loss of the favorable position which Cape wine had held on the English market "have contributed to weigh heavily on the wine farmers, and greatly to impair their general prosperity" (*15*, p. 321). The wheat farmer was not much better off (*15*, p. 322).

The favorable position of the frontier grazier stood out in contrast with the deplorable conditions of the arable farmers at the Cape. "The great supply of sheep consumed in Cape Town and its neighbourhood" was still from the frontier areas, "for the farmers on the Cape side of the mountains do not breed a sufficiency for their own families, buying their supply chiefly from the numerous flocks driven down by the Hottentots for the butchers of Cape Town" (*12*, pp. 96–97). In 1822 a Cape sheep sold for about 7*s.*, while the price of an ox fit for slaughter, "weighing from 400 to 500 lbs. of meat," was still about £3, and the value of a draft ox was about £3.3*s.* (*12*, p. 99). The price of butter was relatively high in 1822 and 1823, and a considerable export trade was developing in hides and skins at prices which continued to be high until 1825–26. This was also the time when horns began to be exported from the Cape (*12*, p. 119). Ivory, gum, and ostrich feathers found a good market in Europe, while small numbers of sheep and cattle and some quantities of butter and soap were exported to Mauritius and St. Helena (*15*, p. 418).

To sum up, between 1806 and 1821 the expansion movement to the northeast was more in the nature of a diversion from the east where Kaffir depredations and Hottentot labor difficulties presented serious problems. This was also a time when the older arable districts of the colony were making the best of an increased demand and high prices for wine and grain. From 1821 to 1826, however, there was a deterioration in the economic conditions of the older arable districts, and it is very likely that people from the older settled districts migrated to the frontier. As in the early part of the eighteenth century, the relative profitableness of arable and pastoral farming once again came into play in influencing the expansion movement. For this movement was not merely the result of an increase in the frontier population, with the sons of the frontier farmers trying to secure 3,000-morgen farms. The plight of the older arable areas rather suggests that the sons of the wine farmers and wheat growers had good reasons for migrating to the frontier. To this must also be added the fact that, as in the eighteenth century, it was comparatively easy to establish oneself as a stock farmer (see chap. 4, above). It was also in this period that the frontier of the colony was carried to the Orange River.

CITATIONS

1 G. M. Theal, *Records of the Cape Colony*, 36 vols. (Govt. of the Cape Colony, 1897–1905), XXVIII.

2 W. J. Burchell, *Travels in the Interior of Southern Africa*, 2 vols. (London, 1822), I.

3 G. M. Theal, *Records*, VIII.

4 D. G. van Reenen, *Die Journal van Dirk Gysbert van Reenen, 1803* (Van Riebeeck Society Publication, No. 18).

5 G. M. Theal, *Records*, IX.

6 G. M. Theal, *Records*, XXXV.

7 T. M. Brooke, *History of the Island of St. Helena* (2d ed., London, 1824).

8 G. M. Theal, *History of South Africa Since 1795*, 5 vols. (London, 1927), I.

9 E. A. Walker, *A History of South Africa* (2d ed., London, 1940).

10 C. G. W. Schumann, *Structural Changes and Business Cycles in South Africa, 1806–1936* (London, 1938).

11 P. Warden Grant, *Considerations on the State of the Colonial Currency and Foreign Exchange at the Cape of Good Hope* (Capetown, 1825).

12 W. W. Bird, *State of the Cape of Good Hope in 1822* (London, 1823).

13 G. M. Theal, *Records*, XXVII.

14 G. M. Theal, *Records*, XVI.

15 George Thompson, *Travels and Adventures in Southern Africa* (London, 1827).

CHAPTER 12

THE CENTER OF GRAVITY SHIFTS
TO THE EAST

DISTANCE AND DIFFICULT ROADS AS LIMITING FACTORS
OF EXPANSION

For a long time Capetown was the sole market, not only for the wheat and wine of the western districts, but also for the animal products as well as the products of hunting and collecting of the interior and frontier regions. Capetown was also the sole distributive center for all imported goods required by the colonists.

However, while it is true that the Cape market was the *raison d'être* of the expansion of the colony, it must also be borne in mind that the farther the colonists advanced into the interior, the more they lengthened their lines of communication with Capetown. Very frequently such natural obstacles as mountains, ravines (*kloofs*), and rivers tended to grow more numerous with distance, thus rendering more and more difficult the exchange of the colonists' products for merchandise that could only be obtained at the Cape.

Distance and difficulty of transportation to the Cape became the limiting factor on production for the market. In the absence of navigable rivers or waterways, bulky commodities had to be transported by ox wagon. For instance, the production of grain for the market had to be given up at a distance of about 70 miles from Capetown (*1*, p. 62). On the other hand, the production of an article of comparatively high value per weight, like candles (which are liable to breakage when carried over mountains and *kloofs*) was determined more by the nature of the roads than by distance (*2*, p. 332). Again, the fact that soap could be transported with far greater ease than either candles or tallow determined its manufacture on the distant farms of the interior. In other words, distance, weight, and nature of the roads, by limiting the range of articles which could be carried to the market, not only became dominating factors in the process of production for the market, but also imposed certain limits on the expansion movement itself.

With regard to livestock, however, the position was much more favorable. Sheep and cattle could walk hundreds of miles to the Cape. There was no need for the farmer to "stir out of his own house," as the butcher's agent (*slagters knegt*) went about the country buying up sheep and cattle for the Cape market (*3*, pp. 247–48). In the outlying frontier areas where the *slagters knegt* would not make his appearance (*4*, p. 212), sheep farming, exclusively for the production of fat and the manufacture of soap, was the only alternative to rearing sheep for the market (*5*, pp. 112–13). The production of butter for the market was the alternative to selling cattle. However, beyond a certain point, expansion into the interior, with soap and butter as the only basis of production, had its definite limits. Beyond a certain point, soap and butter would prove insufficient, and further expansion into the interior could take place only if soap and butter were taken to market together with articles of higher value per unit of weight, such as ivory, ostrich feathers, and skins of wild animals—articles which could be obtained by hunting or trading with the native tribes. But here was also the point where the realm of the pure grazier ended and the realm of the hunter or trader began. The graziers who combined stock farming with hunting and trading formed the vanguard of the expansion movement.

The view that there was very little economic intercourse between the frontier and the Cape market is obviously erroneous. According to this view, the frontier farmers, having turned into nomads or Robinson Crusoes, wandered away to the remotest parts of the interior where, in a life of complete self-sufficiency, the problems of production for a distant market were nonexistent. The journeys to Capetown in wagons would likewise seem to be not for the purpose of buying and selling, but mere pilgrimages undertaken by rural inhabitants curious to see the wonders of the capital. Nor is it sufficient to admit that the farmers had to obtain ammunition and some other articles in Capetown, without at the same time realizing that they had also to get their wherewithal for the purchase of both ammunition and other articles, which could not be had in Capetown just for the taking.

The notion of the frontier farmer's self-sufficiency has no historical foundation. Moreover, it betrays a lack of understanding of the fundamentals of the frontier economy. This notion has tended to obscure the fact that the Boers not only needed guns, powder, and iron for wagons, but also the wagons themselves, which did not last very long. All these articles were absolutely indispensable to the frontier graziers and had to be purchased from outside. Moreover, such little luxuries as tea, coffee, sugar, and brandy, and some clothing, which were found on the most remote frontier farms, could be obtained only in exchange for products which had to be taken from the frontier areas to Capetown. In fact, throughout the eighteenth century and the early part of the nineteenth the internal commerce of the Cape, apart from live animals, consisted mostly of what the colonists could bring in their ox wagons to Capetown and what they could take back. Beyond the limits of arable farming, products like butter, soap, ivory, and ostrich feathers represented the only means of acquiring iron for the wagons, guns and gunpowder, cloth, linen, rice, tea, sugar, coffee, etc. These visits to Capetown were not very frequent, and the articles taken back to the interior had to be sufficient to last until the next visit (6, p. 120). The fact that such a visit to the capital was often combined with sightseeing and matrimonial affairs detracts in no way from our argument. On the contrary, it adds to the number of the grazier's transactions with the outside world and helps to dispel the myth of self-sufficiency.

COASTAL TRADING

From the end of the eighteenth century the economy of the Cape gravitated toward the cattle wealth, products of hunting, and labor resources of the eastern areas. However, with Capetown as the sole outlet, the range of products that could be sent to the market was limited by distance and the nature of the roads. The need for coastal shipping between the eastern part of the colony and Capetown was felt at the end of the eighteenth century, but it was not before the 1820's that coastal trading became a powerful factor in the development of the eastern areas. This fact had a direct bearing on the expansion movement, for not until the establishment of coastal trading between Algoa Bay and Capetown was "going by wagon" from the eastern and northeastern districts to the Cape rendered unnecessary.

The slow development of coastal shipping was in part due to the fact that freight was very expensive. Van Reenen, Barrow, and others spoke of the great advantages of coastal shipping, and as late as 1812 the Commission of Circuit stressed the great need of encouraging vessels in every bay as the "only means of giving any life to inward trade, which would also promote agriculture and encrease the different products of the Colony" (7, p. 89). But the observations made by a writer who traveled to the Cape eight years later, in 1820, are of particular interest, (8, pp. 37–38):

> It would be of incalculable advantage to all this side of the country if a greater number of coasting vessels were embarked in the traffic, as at present there is a good deal of monopoly in this way, and freight is enormously high. . . . It will startle a stranger to be informed that the carriage of goods from Algoa Bay to the Cape, a voyage performed in from three days to as many weeks, but generally in a week or ten days, is as expensive as shipping goods from the Cape to England. There is, no doubt, danger in the navigation; but as colonisation takes place, we may confidently look forward, if not to a removal of the obstacles, at least to a more thorough knowledge of the coast, and a greater expertness, which will considerably diminish that danger.

As may be seen from the above quotation, a number of coasting vessels had already been engaged in the coastal traffic by or before 1820. Furthermore, in spite of its high cost, sea transport, for some commodities at least, was apparently less expensive in those days than land transport by ox wagon. Although very little information is available about the beginnings of coastal trading between the eastern parts of the colony and the Cape, there is reason to believe that some coastal trade had already existed as far back as the beginning of the second decade of the nineteenth century. For instance, in 1812 salted meat was sent under government contract from Algoa Bay by boat to Capetown. This is perhaps the earliest recorded coastal-trading venture between the eastern frontier and the Cape. The shipments of salted meat from Algoa Bay to Capetown continued in 1813, and it is possible that the vessels arriving at Algoa Bay brought merchandise from Capetown. Moreover, there is reason to believe that a few coasting vessels were carrying on some traffic at an earlier date.

The following information contained in a little-known pamphlet by Chase (9) throws interesting light on the development of coastal trading in the early part of the nineteenth century. Chase reports that previous to 1811 the vessels visiting Algoa Bay were mostly government schooners. They visited the bay about once a month, and the trade "consisted of a few kegs of butter and a small number of bags of salt." Referring to the government contract in 1812 for the supply of salted meat from Algoa Bay, Chase says (9): "The tenders for the first contract were advertised for 28th December, 1811, and it was entered into March, 1812, for 3000 barrels of salted beef, the contractors and their people to be exempted from commando service, with liberty to cut wood for casks in the Government forests." Previous to the promulgation of the government invitation, a Mr. Korsten, the contractor, undertook a contract to furnish salted beef for Mauritius and elsewhere. Korsten also put up a large trading establishment, which continued under his personal management up to the year 1820. Chase continues (9):

Some idea of the extent and nature of the business carried on at this commercial outpost and entrepôt may be conceived when it is stated that it was usual to find twenty farmers' wagons resorting to it almost daily, the farmers bringing their produce in exchange for Cape Town and foreign articles (thus saving the tedious and expensive annual visit to Cape Town), that frequently no less than forty oxen were slaughtered daily and salted, chiefly by experienced Europeans introduced by Mr. Korsten. The military officers and messes on the frontier were supplied with all their important essentials, as were the civil servants of George, Uitenhage and Graaff Reinet.

As mentioned earlier, it was not before the early 1820's that coastal trading between Port Elizabeth (on Algoa Bay) and Capetown assumed larger proportions. The immediate need for more coastal shipping in the 1820's arose as a result of a large number of British settlers who had to be supplied with groceries and other merchandise from Capetown by coasters (6, p. 121).

Freight appeared to be still expensive even in 1828, though apparently less expensive than in the second decade of the nineteenth century. In 1828 the Commission of Inquiry upon the

Trade of the Cape of Good Hope, the Navigation of the Coast, and the Improvement of the Harbours of that Colony stated that although the coasting trade had increased, "the expense of freight from Port Elizabeth, the River Knysna and Mossel Bay, from the most remote of which the ordinary length of passage does not exceed 7 days, is stated to be equal to the expenses of freight from the northern ports of Europe to England" (*10*, p. 250). In other words, in 1828 the expense of freight from Port Elizabeth to Capetown compared only with that from the northern ports of Europe to England, instead of, as in 1820, with the expense of shipping goods from the Cape to England. A gradual reduction in freight rates may therefore be assumed to have taken place in the 1820's, and further reductions were probably made in subsequent years.

THE GROWTH OF THE TOWNS

The development of coastal shipping, accompanied as it was by a reduction in freight rates, and the subsequent establishment of a harbor at Port Elizabeth, not only resulted in an increased exchange of goods between the frontier and the outside world, but also led to a further expansion of the frontier itself. For with the development of shipping, the eastern coast of the colony became a new and more advanced starting point than Capetown for new frontiers and for further expansion into the interior of Africa.

The growth of older towns and markets and the emergence of new ones in the eastern and northeastern parts of the colony were chiefly the result of this new development. Indeed, as long as the farmer in the interior could not obtain his necessary domestic and farming requirements locally, he was "obliged to have recourse to Cape Town for that purpose . . . [and to] put up with the long and troublesome carriage," preferring to bring his goods there "in order from their proceeds to supply himself with such articles as he may stand in need of" (*11*, pp. 97–98). With the development of coastal shipping, however, merchandise was brought by coasters to Algoa Bay and forwarded from there to the local markets, while at the same time the farmer's produce could be brought for sale to these markets and forwarded from there to Algoa Bay for shipment to Capetown or elsewhere.

Now it was quite possible, of course, for local traders to transport by land the farmer's goods to Capetown and to bring back merchandise for the farmer's needs. This, in fact, is what some traders in Graaff Reinet were still doing in the 1810's. However, this could not have made any material difference as far as the distance and difficulties of transport to Capetown were concerned, and consequently could not have influenced to any extent the character of production for the market. In fact, it is doubtful whether the function of transporting goods by ox wagon to and from Capetown, in itself the most expensive item in the marketing operation, could be performed more efficiently by the trader than by the farmer. There is, therefore, reason to assume that the development of local markets in these areas went hand in hand with the development of coastal shipping.

Let us now examine the historical evidence concerning the growth of some of the villages and towns in the eastern and northeastern parts of the colony. Graaff Reinet was founded in the 1780's, but at the close of the century it had a population consisting of only 12 families. The village itself "consisted of an assemblage of mud huts at some distance from each other, in two lines, forming a kind of street" (12, pp. 64–65). The European inhabitants were mostly mechanics, "and such as hold some petty employment under the landdrost. . . . Neither milk, nor butter, nor cheese, nor vegetables of any kind are to be had on any terms. There is neither butcher, nor chandler, nor grocer, nor baker. Everyone must provide for himself as well as he can" (12, p. 65). Such were the conditions in Graaff Reinet in the late 1790's.

Burchell's description of Graaff Reinet in 1812 was as follows (5, p. 145):

Seven years before this, the number of houses was between 15 and 20; but at this date there were 72; of which, indeed, some were not yet completed; besides eight more already planned. I saw at this time, three smiths' shops, a waggon makers', and several shops or houses at which a variety of European goods might be bought. There were also a town butcher and baker and *pagter*, or retailer of wine and brandy; who were appointed by licence from the landdrost.

Burchell does not state whether the merchandise was brought to Graaff Reinet by wagons directly from Capetown or from

Capetown via Algoa Bay. The latter possibility cannot be excluded, especially in view of the available evidence on coastal trading in 1812.

By 1823 the coasting trade was already well established, and Thompson, who visited Graaff Reinet in that year, found that the town had about 300 houses, almost all of which were "neat and commodious brick edifices," that many were even elegant, and that the total population of Graaff Reinet amounted to about 1,800 (*13*, p. 43).

Thompson's observations with regard to the trade of Graaff Reinet in 1823 are of particular interest (*13*, pp. 43–44):

Formerly, a considerable trade was carried on between this place and Cape Town, by means of waggons, which crossed the Great Karroo (or arid desert) in the winter or spring, and returned before the summer heats had destroyed the vegetation and dried up the springs and rivers. By this road the Cape butchers still procure a large proportion of the sheep and cattle which are wanted for the use of Cape Town and the shipping in Table Bay. But of late years most of the merchandise required by Graaff Reinet, which forms a sort of emporium for a large extent of country, is brought by coasters to Algoa Bay, and forwarded by waggons from that port. This reduces the land-carriage to about one-third of the distance through the Karroo.

The development of Graaff Reinet as a trading center may also be seen from the fact that the number of licenses granted to keep a retail shop increased from 20 in 1815 to 57 in 1820 and to 119 in 1824 (*14*). Steedman, who visited the town in the early 1830's, reports that it "consisted of between three and four hundred well-built houses." Furthermore (*15*, p. 124):

A considerable trade is carried on with the farmers residing in the interior districts, who bring down their produce, consisting of ostrich-feathers, ox-hides, soap, tallow, etc., for barter with the inhabitants, these supplying them with British manufactured goods, purchased at Graham's Town, and conveyed across the country in waggons; thus avoiding a tedious journey of a month across the arid Karroo to Cape Town, whither they formerly resorted for their annual supplies—a practice now altogether discontinued.

A similar development is found in the case of other villages and towns. In the early 1820's, Grahamstown, established in 1812 as the headquarters of the troops, was another important trading center. In 1822 groceries and other provisions were sent by boat from Capetown to Port Elizabeth and from there to Grahamstown. In return, Capetown received, in addition to money derived from soldiers' pay, "aloes, butter, soap, tobacco, hides, skins, ostrich feathers and ivory," which were taken to Port Elizabeth and from there shipped to the Cape (*6*, p. 121). Thompson, who visited Grahamstown in 1823, wrote (*13*, pp. 25–26): "I found this town much increased in size and population since I was there in January, 1821. At that time it contained only about eighty houses; now there are upwards of 300." In January 1826 "the population of Graham's Town amounted to about 2,500 souls, the great majority of whom were English" (*13*, p. 26). In the late 1820's Grahamstown had already grown from a military post to a comparatively large place with about 3,000 inhabitants including soldiers (*16*, p. 45).

The same applies to Port Elizabeth. In 1820, when the settlers arrived, Port Elizabeth contained only three thatched houses, "erected for the government officers, and a few huts inhabited by Hottentots and free blacks" (*13*, p. 11). Another traveler, writing in 1820, says (*8*, p. 126):

A few houses have been built at Algoa Bay, the inhabitants of which are occupied chiefly in salting butter, and drying fish, for the Cape market, for which the situation is sufficiently well adapted. This butter is sent down in considerable quantities from the district of Graaff Reinet, which lies far in the interior, at the back of the new settlement, and is the great grazing country of the colony.

Since 1820 Port Elizabeth "has, in consequence of the great increase of the coasting trade, risen rapidly in importance" (*13*, p. 11). In 1823 the town had many houses and stores and about 500 inhabitants (*13*, pp. 11–12).

It may be of further interest to note that at the end of 1821 a vessel of 50 tons was built at Capetown for coasting trade to the Kowie and back. Butter, salted provisions, and leather were sent from the Kowie to Capetown and Mauritius (*17*, p. 189), and, in 1822, vessels from Capetown on the way to Mauritius or elsewhere to the east filled up with butter at Port Elizabeth for the Mauritius market (*6*, p. 121). In 1821 there was great building activity in Port Elizabeth, Grahamstown, Bathurst, and Fredricksburg, and the town of Salem had a market every week (*17*, p. 189–90).

To the northeast the village of Cradock, which in 1823 contained about twenty houses and "a couple of small retail shops" (*13*, p. 35), had, in the early 1830's, from 40 to 50 houses with about 350 inhabitants (*15*, p. 184). Further north, Colesberg, 12 miles from the Orange River, in the early 1830's was becoming a new trading center for the surrounding farmers, with traders from Graaff Reinet attending this northern market (*15*, p. 169).

We thus see the close connection between the establishment of coastal shipping in the east and the development of trading centers and local markets for the products of the eastern and northeastern frontier districts. In the 1820's the need for going by wagon to Capetown from these distant parts of the colony was disappearing rapidly and Capetown lost its position as the commercial Mecca of the eastern and northeastern districts of the colony.

CITATIONS

1 J. W. D. Moodie, *Ten Years in South Africa*, 2 vols. (London, 1835), II.

2 John Barrow, *Travels into the Interior of South Africa*, 2 vols. (2d ed., London, 1806), II.

3 Andrew Sparrman, *A Voyage to the Cape of Good Hope from the Year 1772 to 1776* (London, 1785), I.

4 O. F. Mentzel, *A Geographical and Topographical Description of the Cape of Good Hope*, 3 vols. (Van Riebeeck Society Publication, No. 25), III.

5 W. J. Burchell, *Travels in the Interior of South Africa*, 2 vols. (London, 1824), II.

6 W. W. Bird, *State of the Cape of Good Hope in 1822* (London, 1823).

7 G. M. Theal, *Records of the Cape Colony*, 36 vols. (Govt. of the Cape Colony, 1897–1905), IV.

8 Anonymous, *Notes on the Cape of Good Hope Made During an Excursion in the Colony in the Year 1820* (London, 1821).

9 J. C. Chase, *Old Times and Odd Corners, The Founder of the Eastern Province Commerce and His Frontier Home* (Port Elizabeth, 1868).

10 G. M. Theal, *Records*, XXXV.

11 Report of Commission of Circuit in 1813, quoted in G. M. Theal, *Records*, X.

12 John Barrow, *Travels into the Interior of South Africa*, I.

13 George Thompson, *Travels and Adventures in Southern Africa* (London, 1827).

14 *Register of Licences, Miscellaneous, 1809–1826*, No. 8077, Cape Archives.

15 Andrew Steedman, *Wanderings and Adventures in the Interior of Southern Africa*, 2 vols. (London, 1835), I.

16 C. Rose, *Four Years in Southern Africa* (London, 1829).

17 G. M. Theal, *Records*, XIV.

CHAPTER 13

THE ITINERANT TRADER

Another important development of the early part of the nineteenth century was the emergence in the interior and frontier
districts of the itinerant trader or smous,[1] as he was then commonly called. In this chapter we shall consider the part played
by the smous in the expansion movement and the economy of the
frontier from the early part of the nineteenth century.

An early reference to traders who "ride round with goods
and dispose of them among the inhabitants" is found in the report of the Commission of Circuit of 1813 (*1*, p. 98). The commission referred to the fact that these traders provided "for the
convenience of the farmer by supplying his wants without his
being reduced to the necessity of making long and expensive
journeys from the far distant districts to Cape Town." At that
time the smouses did not have to take out any trading licenses,
much to the resentment of the Graaff Reinet shopkeepers, under
whose pressure the commission recommended that "if the country shopkeepers are to continue to be obliged to take out licences
as customary, those pedlars should in future be put on the same
footing."

The smous is known to have played an important part in the
frontier economy during the time of the Great Trek (in the
1830's).[2] It was usual for him to come to the remote farms with
two or three wagonloads of wares containing articles of clothing,
groceries, and most other things required by the colonists. He also
took orders to deliver goods to the farmers, usually letting them
know beforehand when he would come again and what road he

---

[1] The Dutch word *smous* was common in Holland in the eighteenth century and
meant a German Jew. It usually referred to a German Jewish peddler. Etymologi-
cally the word is supposed to be an adaptation of the Jewish *schmuoss*, Hebrew
shmuoth, tales, news, the reference being to the persuasive eloquence of peddlers.

[2] "*Die smous was 'n hele faktor in die lewe op die grens, en menigeen van hulle
het saam getrek, tot die Vrijstaat, en daarvandaan teruggekeer om nuwe negosieware
to haal, en dan weer op die trek-spoor te volg*" (*2*, p. 217).

would follow. The smous was thus a welcome visitor on the South African farm, and his arrival was a great event, for he also brought the mail and news from the outside world (*2*, p. 217).

There are several references to smouses by nineteenth-century travelers, and those of Steedman and Harris are of particular interest. Steedman, who traveled in the northeastern parts of the colony in the early 1830's, reports that he was mistaken by a farmer's wife for a trader, "or smouse, as they usually denominate the class of men who go about the country selling goods to the farmers and taking sheep in exchange,—as the boors have seldom many rix dollars, and make their principal payments out of the produce of their farms" (*3*, p. 146). During his halt near the Orange River, Steedman was also mistaken for a trader by the natives, who, on learning from the Hottentot servants that he was not a trader, "appeared very much disappointed." Steedman was urged by the Griquas on the Orange River to barter guns, powder, and shot for cattle (*3*, p. 163).

Harris, who traveled in the interior of South Africa in the late 1830's, reports as follows (*4*, p. 53):

Traders, or *smouches*, as they are called by the colonists, constantly visit Litakoo and its neighbourhood, and often proceed to a considerable distance beyond it into the interior, for the purpose of thus collecting ivory and peltries for the Cape market; availing themselves of the opportunity of supplying the farmers and missionaries lying in their outward route, with the portable luxuries of life. The profession of a gentleman being quite unknown in the Colony, we were ourselves constantly taxed with being itinerant pedlars, the tea and snuff-loving vrouws never failing to rush out as we passed their houses to inquire what we had in the waggon. It must, however, be observed, that the field of traffic is extremely limited, and that fortunes are rarely made, unless by those, who, baffling the vigilance of the frontier field cornets, contrive to smuggle gunpowder across the boundary; or by the adventurous man who is the first to visit the chief of some new tribe among the northern nations, and can thus make his own market, and establish his own price-current.

The fact that profits in the late thirties were small may suggest that competition among these traders must have been very keen. On the other hand, the smous trade seems to have been more profitable in the early thirties, as may be seen in the following extract from a letter[3] written in 1831 by a Mr. Crout, an

---

[3] For this information I am indebted to Mrs. Colin Gill (Una Long), who discovered the letters of W. E. Crout in Graaff Reinet.

employee of the Grahamstown trader John Norton, to his parents in England:

In a few weeks I am going to trade among the Dutch farmers with all sorts of goods, about 3 months every year, for cattle and sheep and then sell the fat cattle and sheep to the butchers. If I have good luck I shall make about £80 in 3 months that I go up the country. I shall go about 400 miles from Graham's Town. I have been up one journey for Mr. J. Norton and I have made a good profit, about a £100. I was only gone 3 months . . . Mr. J. Norton is going to let me have about £300 worth of goods on a good long credit. I am going up with waggons.

The above quotation is of interest in more than one respect. It shows that a regular trade, about three months in every year, was carried on from Grahamstown with merchandise taken in wagons to farms about 400 miles distant, to be exchanged for cattle and sheep. But what is of particular interest is the fact that the smous trade was carried on not only by peddlers but also by traders who had their business in fixed trading centers (see also below).

THE SMOUS AND THE BUTCHER

When the monopoly of the cattle trade held by the privileged butchers in Capetown was broken is a matter of some speculation. In 1826 a government commission recommended "the abolition of the privileges of the licenced butchers, who conduct by their agents the trade in cattle from the country" (5, p. 66). "The establishment of fairs in the interior," the commissioners argued, "will give encouragement to this trade, and to the breeding of superior stock, and will gradually supersede a system which has never held out that encouragement to the farmer" (5, p. 67). The commissioners, therefore, recommended that "freedom of internal trade may be extended to the villages in the interior of the Colony, where the restrictive system has been adopted, and without any apparent reason or benefit" (5, p. 67). For some years, however, the butchers' monopoly appears to have remained unshaken, and the first cattle fairs held at Somerset and Grahamstown had very little success (6, p. 256), probably because both the farmers and the privileged butchers preferred private sale to competition in the open market.

The first important change in the cattle trade was brought about not by government measures but by effective competition of the smouses. As may be seen from a later report of the same commission in 1828, the monopoly of the privileged butchers was affected by the change that had taken place in the manner of conducting the cattle trade (*6*, p. 256):

. . . cattle are now purchased of the farmers in the country by licenced hawkers and pedlars in exchange for dry goods, and instead of the cattle being driven, as formerly, directly to Cape Town, they are grazed at intermediate places, or on farms situated near the high roads. The cattle driven to Cape Town and other markets by these dealers, some of whom are English settlers, are likely to arrive in better condition, and upon the whole, we are of opinion that although the price of goods sold by the itinerant merchants, as well as by those who have fixed establishments at the smaller ports on the coast, is enhanced to the farmer, and that of his produce is diminished by the trade of barter, which has succeeded in a great measure to the system of payment by means of privileged and accredited bills, yet he is relieved from the expense and loss of time and of stock occasioned by the journeys he formerly made for the purchase of his supplies.

It is thus clear that in the late 1820's the smouses had already consolidated their position to such a degree as to be able to compete successfully with the all-powerful Capetown butchers. Such a development was to the benefit of both stock farmers and meat consumers. As was observed by the same commission (*6*, p. 256):

The effect which the regulations have had in limiting competition in the trade to those alone who are able to find the securities, and in confining the sale of cattle to those who are privileged by their license to kill them, has had a direct tendency to raise the price of meat to the general consumer, and to augment unduly the profits of the trade to the few who enjoyed the privilege, which sufficiently accounts for the privileged butchers being amongst the most opulent individuals of Cape Town.

We cannot dwell here upon the interesting question as to the effect these developments in the cattle trade had had on the butchers' monopoly in the meat market, but the serious competition of the smous in the cattle market already foreshadowed an all-round deterioration of a position which the Cape butchers had held unchallenged for over a century.

WHEN DID THE SMOUS APPEAR IN THE CAPE OF GOOD HOPE?

We spoke earlier of the emergence of the smous in the early part of the nineteenth century. It would, however, be more appropriate to speak of the *re-emergence* of the smous, for in the early part of the eighteenth century the *togtganger*, the smous's more adventurous brother, in search of cattle and ivory, had already opened up the trade with the Kaffirs (7, chap. III). It was the road of the *togtgangers*, i.e., hunters and traders, that Ensign Beutler followed into the abode of the Kaffirs in 1752 (*8*, p. 16). While the *togtgangers* probably traded mostly with the native tribes, there were also peddlers or hawkers who traded with the colonists. Thus, in 1772, a government commission brought to light the fact that "for some time back some persons have made it their business to wander about everywhere in the interior, from one district to another, with goods and merchandise, conveyed on waggons, carts, horses or pack oxen" (*8*, pp. 24–25). Presumably these traders were bartering their merchandise with the colonists for cattle, native cattle in particular, a trade which in those days the government was determined to stop. This is also confirmed by the circumstance that in 1774 the governor and council resolved that "henceforth no one shall proceed with any goods or merchandise conveyed on waggons, carts, horses, or pack oxen, into the interior, or ride about with the same for sale to the inhabitants, whether for cattle or any other article, either in the Cape District or in those of Stellenbosch, Drakenstein, or Swellendam" (*9*, pp. 24–25). The above quotation shows that in the second half of the eighteenth century these peddlers or hawkers were carrying on their trade not only among the natives, but also among the European farmers within the colony. In fact, the prohibition was intended as a measure of combating cattle bartering not only between the peddlers and the natives, but also between the frontier farmers and the natives, for it was found that various inhabitants were in possession of the Kaffir breed of cattle which they sold to the smouses (*9*, p. 24).

As has been shown earlier, most of the prohibitions intended to restrict the cattle trade between the colonists and the native tribes had very little effect. To what extent the prohibition of 1774 succeeded in eliminating these peddlers or hawkers from the cattle trade or even in restricting their movements is not known. In any case, the persons strategically best suited for carrying on the trade with the border tribes were not so much the traders as the frontier farmers themselves. As shown earlier, not only had the frontier farmers been combining stock farming with cattle trading, but many persons in Capetown had kept loan farms at the frontier for the sole purpose of being better able to carry on the cattle trade with the native tribes. It was not before the end of the eighteenth century or the beginning of the nineteenth century, after the abolition of many trade restrictions, that the differentiated services of the country trader could re-emerge.

The foregoing discussion demonstrates that the smous trade was intimately connected with the development of the Cape Colony at an early stage, a fact which has long been overlooked. It is necessary to stress this fact here because the subject has received very little attention in historical literature, and what has been written so far is apt to give the impression that the smouses appeared on the South African scene only about the time of the *Voortrekkers* (*10*, pp. 202–03). Indeed, peddlers and hawkers had already carried on their traveling trade with the farmers in the early 1770's.

As we have seen earlier, the re-emergence of the smous was an important factor in the economy of the interior and frontier districts as early, at least, as the beginning of the 1810's. In those days merchandise was probably brought by these peddlers all the way from Capetown in wagons, though some peddlers might have obtained their wares in Graaff Reinet, Mossel Bay, Uitenhage, Tulbagh, or Algoa Bay. It was only after the establishment of coastal trading that the carrying of goods in wagons from Capetown to the frontier districts became unnecessary even for the smous. Graaff Reinet, Grahamstown, and Port Elizabeth were fast becoming new centers of trade and, consequently, new points of departure for supplying the most distant frontier farmers with all their requirements. Not only were these farmers spared the trouble of making long journeys to Capetown, but the fact that the smouses brought clothing, groceries, and other wares, literally up to the farmers' doorsteps, and even accepted orders from the farmers to deliver goods on the following visit, made it unnecessary to go even to Grahamstown, Graaff Reinet, or Colesberg, except on rare occasions. More than that, the colonists could now advance further inland without making it more difficult for them to obtain their requirements or to dispose of their produce, for the market was now following them on their wanderings in the smous's wagon. In short, the moving frontier had found its counterpart in the moving market. The colonists had at last freed themselves from a fixed market place and could now advance without a halt into the interior of the African continent.

CITATIONS

1 G. M. Theal, *Records of the Cape Colony*, 36 vols. (Govt. of the Cape Colony, 1897–1905), X.

2 Lourens Christian de Klerk quoted in G. S. Preller, *Voortrekkermense*, 3 vols. (Capetown, 1920–25), I.

3 Andrew Steedman, *Wanderings and Adventures in the Interior of Southern Africa*, 2 vols. (London, 1835), I.

4 W. C. Harris, *The Wild Sports of Southern Africa* (3d ed., London, 1841).

5 *Report of the Commissioners of Inquiry upon the Finances of the Cape of Good Hope* (Capetown, 1827).

6 G. M. Theal, *Records*, XXXV.

7 P. J. van der Merwe, *Trek: Studies oor die Mobiliteit van die Pioners-bevolking aan die Kaap* (Capetown, 1943).

8 G. M. Theal, *Belangrijke Historische Dokumenten Over Zuid Afrika*, 3 vols. (Govt. of South Africa, 1911), II.

9 D. Moodie, *The Record: or a Series of Official Papers Relative to the Condition and Treatment of the Native Tribes of South Africa* (Capetown, 1838–41), Pt. III.

10 P. J. van der Merwe, *Die Trekboer in die Geskiedenis van die Kaap-kolonie (1657–1842)* (Capetown, 1938).

CHAPTER 14

THE FRONTIER ECONOMY, 1826–36, AND THE GREAT TREK

THE MARKET FOR CAPE OF GOOD HOPE PRODUCTS

The prosperity of the frontier areas during the 1820's and 1830's continued to depend largely upon the demand for meat and other animal products and for the high-valued products of hunting. As in former days, this demand came mostly from the urban population of the colony, the troops stationed at the Cape of Good Hope, and the passing ships and their passengers and crews on shore.

With the development of a considerable export of animal products to England, the colony was also affected by the collapse of the boom that had followed the Napoleonic Wars, a collapse that had particularly severe effects in England in 1825. From about that year until well into 1827 the colony of the Cape of Good Hope was in the throes of a severe depression.

The plight of Capetown and the western districts was described at the end of 1826 in a petition from the inhabitants of the Cape of Good Hope to the British Parliament. The petitioners complained that "property of every sort has fallen greatly in value, trade is languishing, and the production of the soil seems no longer to reward the labour, or even to replace the capital sunk in its cultivation." Wine had fallen "below a remunerating price to the growers," grain farmers were in great distress, "whilst the minor articles of colonial produce have fallen to about one half of their usual price" (*1*, p. 370).

But 1826 and 1827 appear to have been lean years also for the stock farmers in the frontier areas. In his evidence before the Council in Capetown at the end of 1826, a farmer from Graaff Reinet complained that there were more cattle than were wanted. He had brought cattle to Capetown from Graaff Reinet, but could find no purchaser for them. The farmers in the Graaff Reinet district had an abundance of cattle, most of them in a lean condition on account of the drought, and "can get no price for them." In former times, the Graaff Reinet stock farmers "used to get wheat from the corn farmers," but the latter preferred now to sell their grain "to the troops on the frontier for money than to barter for cattle" (*2*, p. 477–78).

Apparently the corn farmers could now obtain sufficient slaughter sheep and cattle from areas nearer Capetown, to judge from the words of Moodie, who lived in the Cape in the 1820's (*3*, p. 143):

Where the bulk of the population are producers, the consumption cannot keep pace with production. This is already beginning to be felt by the farmers of the interior in the diminished request for sheep and cattle, from the great increase of stock in the parts of the colony near Cape Town. Of late years, indeed, there has been some call for fat cattle, which are salted for exportation to the Mauritius: but what are the sheep-farmers of the interior to do when their flocks have increased beyond demand? They must improve their wools, or they will in time sink to a level with the Kaffres.

The above quotation contains two significant observations: first, that there was a decline in the demand for faraway stock because of a greater supply near Capetown; second, that there was a better demand for cattle than for sheep, especially for export as salted meat. The increasing importance of beef is also confirmed by the fact that in the twenties, while salted beef was both exported to Mauritius and supplied to ships touching Port Elizabeth, "on their way to India, and eventually for the West India Islands," the Cape sheep, owing to "the long and slender form of its legs" was not considered well adapted for "sea stock" (*4*, pp. 269, 270). It apparently did not make a good "leg of mutton."

The demand for meat from the frontier areas declined not only in consequence of the greatly reduced garrison at the Cape—between 1828 and 1834 the number of troops stationed in the colony was only about 1,500 (*5*, p. 85)—but probably also because the British settlers in Albany were now in a position to produce their own meat requirements.

Unfortunately, the *opgaaf* livestock figures from about the middle of the twenties are no guide to the real supply position of slaughter stock, since the continual droughts compelled a large number of graziers to seek grazing for their flocks and herds outside the boundaries of the colony. But there is reason to believe that livestock numbers were steadily increasing.

The year 1826 was also unfortunate in that it marked the first failure of the Kaffir trade on the eastern frontier. Apart from the illicit and lucrative cattle trade with the Kaffirs, in which both Boer and English colonists participated (*6*, p. 159), the most important article of trade with the native tribes on the eastern frontier was ivory. The failure of this trade in 1826 had two causes: the ivory hoards of the natives were all but exhausted, "while at the same time, the taste of the Kaffirs, satiated with the old and cheap description of bead, became extraordinarily capricious, and required for its indulgence a more expensive kind, the shape, colour and size of which varied with almost every succeeding Fair" (*7*, p. 259). This dissatisfaction of the Kaffirs with the terms of trade was evidently the consequence of an excessive supply of beads, a sort of inflation of the means of payment in a primitive community.

The following figures show the amounts and value of ivory purchased by the traders at Fort Willshire in 1824–25 and in the three subsequent years:

Year	Quantity (*lb.*)	Value (£)
1824–25	94,836	19,317
1826	22,933	11,599
1827	9,545	7,538
1828	2,224	7,525

In 1827, general economic conditions in the colony were showing signs of recovery, but the frontier areas suffered from locusts and drought, the latter preventing the Capetown butchers from coming to take cattle from Graaff Reinet through the Karroo (*8*, p. 134). This was probably the immediate reason for the complaints made in that year by the landdrost and heemraaden of Graaff Reinet to the colonial secretary (*9*, p. 208) about the

... state of poverty and distress to which the inhabitants of this district are reduced, and their utter inability to meet the taxes proposed by His Majesty's Commissioners. ... Every species of trade and traffick is completely at a stand; the flocks in the possession of the farmers, far from being a source of revenue, are a burden to the proprietors, as they have no market whatever for their produce, the most trifling loan is not be procured on any terms, and money seems to have totally disappeared, so that we look with terror to the period when the several contributions shall be called for.

TABLE 10.—AVERAGE VALUE OF SELECTED PRODUCTS EXPORTED FROM
THE CAPE OF GOOD HOPE, 1822–37*

(Pence per pound, except as otherwise indicated)

Year	Butter	Candles (tallow)	Soap	Tallow	Wax (berry)	Wool	Tail oil[a]	Horns (d/horn)	Hides (s/hide)	Goat Skins (s/skin)	Sheep Skins (s/skin)	Cattle (£/head)	Sheep (s/head)
1822	13.0	12.0	3.8	...	4.6	4.2	...	3.9	16.3	2.6	1.1	...	10.0
1823	12.2	5.1	11.5	...	7.2	19.0	...	...	14.7	2.8	1.3	...	9.6
1824	8.3	...	...	...	2.9	17.0	...	4.7	16.2	2.7	1.3	5.7	6.2
1825	6.1	10.7	4.9	...	4.0	13.6	...	5.6	15.8	3.1	1.3	4.5	7.9
1826	7.0	...	...	...	9.3	2.4	...	6.0	10.5	2.5	1.0	3.3	8.2
1827	7.0	...	1.1	4.7	...	11.2	...	7.7	7.2	1.7	8.2	3.9	7.5
1828	9.0	7.6	8.3	3.8	...	7.5	...	8.3	8.1	1.7	10.2	4.3	8.1
1829	11.3	7.9	4.7	7.3	...	8.0	...	5.3	8.5	1.8	11.8	4.0	9.0
1830	13.5	8.7	4.8	4.9	...	11.5	...	6.8	10.2	1.7	1.0	4.2	9.0
1831	6.5	6.8	4.8	5.0	...	12.4	...	8.0	13.7	1.5	1.1	2.7	7.2
1832[b]	4.0	6.7	4.1	3.9	...	11.9	6.1	8.8	14.8	1.6	10.8	3.1	7.8
1833	4.2	6.4	3.8	3.8	...	10.6	2.7	8.7	14.8	1.7	11.4	4.7	6.0
1834	7.8	6.4	5.0	4.2	...	7.4	1.1	4.7	13.4	1.4	11.3	5.0	7.1
1835	7.9	7.7	...	4.6	...	8.2	...	6.1	8.9	1.5	10.9	...	...
1836	9.6	8.6	...	3.7	...	5.1	...	8.7	17.2	1.3	15.9	...	...
1837	9.8	7.4	...	5.1	...	6.8	...	5.6	11.8	2.0	12.0	...	...

* Calculated from quantities and values of products exported from the Cape in each of the years 1822–37 as given in Colonial Secretary's Office, *Cape of Good Hope Blue Book* (Capetown, various years), unless otherwise stated.

[a] Sheep's tail oil, pence per gallon.

[b] George Greig, compiler, *South African Directory and Almanac*, 1834 (Capetown).

Although these complaints should not be taken literally, there is no doubt that producers of animal products were suffering from lack of markets and low prices. As may be seen from Table 10 (and Appendix Table III), nearly every pastoral commodity underwent a serious price decline in 1826 and 1827, as compared with the previous years. The export values of these commodities reflect not only lower prices, but also a considerable decline in the quantities exported.

It is true that with the growth of population in the twenties and thirties, especially after the influx of British settlers, the local demand for fresh meat gradually increased; but it was probably increasing at a slower rate than the livestock population. Moreover, with the small number of troops stationed at the Cape between 1826 and 1834 the demand for meat from this quarter was smaller than in former days. On the other hand, salted meat exports were steadily gaining in importance, with an annual average value amounting to £5,160 during the 1831–35 period (5, p. 43). However, the most important foreign demand for meat still appears to have come from passing ships, especially after 1827.

TABLE 11.—NUMBER AND TONNAGE OF VESSELS, AND NUMBER OF MEN EMPLOYED IN NAVIGATION AT CAPE OF GOOD HOPE PORTS, 1825–27 AND 1829–35*

	Inwards			Outwards		
	Vessels			Vessels		
Year	Number	Tons	Men	Number	Tons	Men
1825	135	46,569	3,530	...	...	...
1826	151	46,895	...	...	...	...
1827	166	58,712	4,525	162	59,403	4,330
1829	251	73,216	5,062	244	70,092	4,882
1830	253	76,004	5,139	245	71,239	4,765
1831	231	68,258	...	...	...	...
1832	281	82,928	...	...	...	...
1833	353	109,231	...	...	...	...
1834	358	107,655	...	...	...	...
1835	486	134,875	...	...	...	...

* Data for 1825–27 and 1831–35 from Colonial Secretary's Office, *Cape of Good Hope Blue Book*, various years; for 1829 and 1830 from George Greig, compiler, *South African Almanack and Directory*, 1831 (Capetown), p. 97, and *ibid.*, 1832 (Capetown), p. 55, respectively.

As may be seen from Table 11, shipping increased considerably after 1827; the number of ships from 1829 far exceeded the peak years of shipping at the Cape in the eighteenth century. Most of the ships with their crews and passengers stayed several weeks at the Cape, thus adding to the demand for fresh meat and other animal products. Table 12 shows a similar trend for Port Elizabeth.[1]

TABLE 12.—NUMBER AND TONNAGE OF VESSELS, AND VALUE OF IMPORTS AND EXPORTS AT PORT ELIZABETH, SELECTED YEARS, 1821–35*

Year	Inward vessels		Outward vessels		Imports (£)	Exports (£)
	Number	Tons	Number	Tons		
1821	6	1,000	5	962	...	1,500
1825	23	1,870	22	1,100	13,090	5,200
1830	50	7,306	47	6,902	18,454	24,438
1835	73	11,080	63	9,476	39,755	33,299

* Data from J. C. Chase, *Cape of Good Hope and the Eastern Province of Algoa Bay* (London, 1843), p. 202.

The other important products for which there was both a local and foreign demand were hides and skins, tallow, butter, horns, ivory, and ostrich feathers (see chaps. 6 and 7 above). As pointed out earlier, the development of an export market in these products played an important part in the expansion movement of the 1820's and 1830's. It was largely to these products that the eastern frontier areas owed their prosperity during this period. As observed by a writer in the early thirties (*12*, p. 446), "while hides, horns, and tallow maintain their present prices, the occupation of a grazier indeed will be found far from unprofitable." Although on a number of farms tallow was still being converted into soap not only for domestic use but also for the local market (*13*, p. 68), Cape soap was steadily losing ground in competition not only with imported soap but also with soap manufactured

[1] No information is available on how much ships' passengers and crews spent in Cape ports in any of the years under review. However, the figures for the year 1842 may give some idea as to the magnitude of spending. In that year the total number of ships, both inwards and outwards, that put in to all Cape ports amounted to 865 (see *10*) and the amounts spent on provisions and supplies, including the amount spent by Indian visitors, totaled £120,000, or £140 per ship (*11*, p. 199).

in Capetown and Grahamstown. Capetown had its first soap factory in 1834, Grahamstown in 1837 (*14*).

THE NORTHEAST AND TRANSORANGIA

It was pointed out in chapter 12 that the expansion to the northeast during the period 1821–26 was due mainly to a diversion of the expansion movement from the eastern frontier areas, though very likely there was also an exodus from the older arable districts of the colony. But the advance to the northeast posed new problems for the colonists. Here was a region subject to periodic droughts, which might last for two or three years in succession. Ordinarily, the numbers of sheep and cattle that could be maintained in this region would be determined by the carrying capacity of the land in the driest years, i.e., when it is naturally very low. In such a case farms would have to be stocked very much below the carrying capacity of the land in "normal" years. Another, and better, alternative was to stock the farms up to their maximum carrying capacity in "normal" years and to remove flocks and herds to the higher-rainfall areas of Transorangia in drought years. This was the alternative actually chosen by the graziers.

By storing water and building dams, colonists can increase the carrying capacity of the land in such regions without having to resort to pastures in other regions. But this is true only from a purely technical point of view, without any consideration of whether such capital investments as water storing and dam building would require are economically justifiable. True, the technique of water storing was less developed in those days, but what matters is that under extensive forms of stock raising such technical improvements are economically out of the question. Indeed, bearing in mind the great scarcity of labor and capital and the abundance of good pasture land to be had for the taking in Transorangia, it would have been contrary to common sense to go in for expensive improvements south of the Orange.

Thus the trekking to Transorangia began, not with the intention of abandoning the farms south of the Orange, but merely to escape occasionally the ravages of the drought. The permanent abode of the graziers was still within the borders of the colony; Transorangia was simply the means by which the semiarid regions south of the Orange could be more fully utilized. What the Karroo was in the seasonal migrations from the summer veld to the winter veld in the eighteenth century, Transorangia now became in the periodic migrations from the drought-stricken areas south of the Orange. Crossing the Orange with his flocks and herds had thus become an integral part of the northeastern grazier's system.

A question arises: If the Transorangia region was so much superior, why did the graziers bother about returning to the arid areas of the colony? Did they return from Transorangia because they were reluctant to sever their relations with the colony? As far as economic relations with the colony were concerned, Transorangia was no longer so remote from the market as to make the exchange of the graziers' products for those of the colony more difficult. Nor could allegiance to the government adequately explain the eagerness of the graziers who owned no land in the colony to return to the areas south of the Orange whenever the drought was broken.

In our opinion, the answer to this question is to be found elsewhere. What seems to have escaped the attention of investigators is the fact that the arid districts south of the Orange have certain qualities of their own which make them excellent grazing lands. Not only is the vegetation there more palatable and nutritious than in the more humid parts of Transorangia, but the animals in the arid regions are also less subject to certain diseases. The Karroo bushes provide excellent fodder, while the Karroo grasses contain more phosphorus than in the grassveld. The fact that the Karroo shrubs have the capacity of carrying stock throughout the winter and that all the plants there have a high calcium content is another advantage (15, pp. 343–58, 362).

The view has been advanced by van der Merwe that overpopulation was the main cause of the migration from the northern frontier (15, pp. 326–27). Overpopulation is a relative term, and in this particular instance may only mean that landless colonists found it difficult to obtain free land in the colony (15, p. 329). However, landlessness in those days had very little to do with what is usually understood by this word today. In the 1830's it was a more serious matter to be a sheepless, goatless, or cattleless Boer than to be a landless one. The particular case of 225 graziers who owned no land in the colony (*"ons is almal veeboere, maar ons besit geen grond in die Kolonie nie,"* cited in *15*) only proves that as long as one owned livestock one could farm either in the colony or in Transorangia without actually owning the land. When the northern districts of the colony suffered from drought, these graziers usually went across the Orange with their livestock (*"Gedurende droogtes, wat van tyd tot tyd in die Kolonie heers, het ons gereeld oor die grense getrek om ons vee aan die lewe te hou,"* cited in *15*). They would probably have had to trek to Transorangia even if they had owned land in the colony. It was rainlessness rather than landlessness that mattered.

The periodic migrations of colonists led to permanent settlements in Transorangia, and this process went on with very little interruption before, during, and after the Great Trek (*15*, pp. 343–48, 362). The foundation for such an expansion was laid in the first quarter of the century, in the re-emergence of the smous and his moving market at the frontier and beyond; the development of coastal shipping; and the consequent growth of new centers of trade. Colesberg, for instance, became such a northeastern center of trade for the surrounding farms in the early thirties, and its stores continued for a long time "to supply all the inhabitants of the extensive district bearing the same name, and that of 'Hantam,' and the Boers settled on the other side of the Orange River in all directions, with their necessary provisions, in hardware and other merchandise" (*13*, p. 89).

Nor was it always necessary to go even to Colesberg. Thus Boschoff, who visited Transorangia in 1838, says of the farmers who had settled in Kok's country (*16*, p. 157):

They do not trouble themselves about politics; and as they can readily sell or exchange their slaughter oxen at a rate of Rds. 50 per head, cows at Rds. 20, and wether sheep at Rds. 4 or 4½ without trouble of going any distance to market to dispose them, and as the traders not only purchase their cattle, but supply them at their own doors with everything they require, they seem to be content.

In other words, before the Great Trek the landless Boers, especially if they wished to become graziers, could find farms in the northeast and across the Orange.

FARM LABOR PROBLEMS IN THE EASTERN AREAS

Next to Kaffir depredations, the most vexatious problem in the eastern frontier areas was that of labor. Indeed, the triple question of the Hottentots, the slaves, and the Kaffirs was essentially a labor question. Of these three, the Hottentot emancipation was the most serious. Macmillan, referring to the resentment over the Hottentot legislation, says (*17*, pp. 167–68): "In a more confined country there might well have been a general rebellion. In the wide spaces of South Africa an obvious alternative suggested itself, and some hundreds of the malcontents resolved rather to leave the Colony altogether, and to found new states of their own, *where they should be free to pursue a 'colour policy' more in harmony with their own tradition and prejudices.*" The economic problem of the Hottentot legislation was probably at the root of the Boers' resentment. For this legislation involved the colonists in considerable difficulties in handling free labor.

At the end of 1826, Bathurst ordered that the employment of slave labor on all grants of land within the district of Albany be prohibited, "and that such prohibition may extend throughout the whole of the territory which is bounded by the District of Albany in the South, by the Great Fish River and by Baviaan's River in the East, by the ancient boundary of the Colony in the North, and in the West by a line, which drawn at the distance of 30 miles from the ancient frontier, shall extend from the District of Albany to a point which shall intersect the Sea Cow River, thirty miles south of the place where the River flows across the frontier." This line was to be considered "as the fixed and permanent limit, beyond which no class of colonists shall ever be permitted to acquire lands, unless upon condition that they shall not be cultivated by slave labour" (*1*, pp. 63–65).

How acute the farm labor problem was in the eastern frontier areas may be seen from the lively arguments that arose in 1826 around the question of slave labor. When it was proposed that only free laborers should be employed in the frontier districts, the inspector of government lands and woods declared that if the restrictions were to be applied to loan farms the effect would be to dispossess the farmers of their loan places. "Where can they get free labour to replace that which they derived from their slaves?" (*1*, p. 27).

The following arguments put forward by the inspector of government lands and woods are of particular interest (*1*, pp. 28–29):

There is another consideration connected with the carrying of this order into effect, namely, the very considerable extent of land that is illegally occupied in the frontier districts, particularly in Graaff Reinet and Worcester. It will in the first place prevent the illegal occupiers from applying for legal titles, which is so desirable they should do, yet which, with great difficulty and much management, is only slowly progressing, and to force this object, or to dispossess the occupiers is not practicable, the extent of the evil is become too great to use coercion: they will therefore retain the occupancy as it were in defiance.

He further went on to ask, "Will it not have the effect of obliging a great number of farmers to remove into the interior districts in search of land that shall not be subject to the said order?" If all applications for new land were granted and accepted on terms of that restricted clause, he said, most of the land would remain waste, "for the quantity of free labour that would be required for it does not exist in the Colony." Free labor consisted mostly of Hottentots and did not amount to anything like 8,000 males for the whole colony (*1*, p. 29).

The importance of slave labor in the eastern frontier districts is reflected in Table 13.

TABLE 13.—POPULATION OF THE CAPE OF GOOD HOPE BY DISTRICTS, 1828*

District	Whites, total[a]	Slaves		Free blacks	
		Male	Female	Male	Female
Capetown	5,805	3,338	2,884	1,611	1,658
Cape district ...	3,703	2,514	1,327	1,262	1,014
Stellenbosch ...	5,850	5,019	3,170	1,124	895
Worcester	5,506	2,265	2,042	2,520	2,346
Swellendam ...	6,844	1,678	1,408	2,117	2,044
George	3,741	938	866	1,106	1,102
Uitenhage	3,397	582	504	1,619	1,461
Albany	4,200	49	47	906	784
Somerset	5,370	735	611	1,910	1,883
Graaff Reinet...	7,939	1,265	1,001	2,389	2,207
Total	55,355	18,383	13,860	16,564	15,394

* Data from George Greig, compiler, *South African Almanack and Directory*, 1830 (Capetown), p. 137.

[a] Exclusive of King's troops.

As may be seen from the above table, in the four eastern districts (Uitenhage, Albany, Somerset, and Graaff Reinet) there were 2,631 males and 2,163 female slaves, or a total of 4,794. But after 1828 the number of slaves increased considerably (*18*):

District	1830–31	1833–34
Uitenhage	1,251	1,298
Albany	126	144
Somerset	1,393	1,441
Graaff Reinet	2,704	2,449
Total	5,474	5,332

The frontiersmen were not exclusively cattle and sheep farmers; they also raised grain and tobacco and had vineyards, and for the cultivation of these crops slave labor was employed even at the frontier. Indeed, the labor requirements of the farmers of these districts were far greater than their purely pastoral pursuits would suggest. In 1831, for instance, the total number of acres under crops in the district of Graaff Reinet was 3,637, of which 1,880 acres were under wheat and 1,209 under vines and gardens (*19*, p. 204). Nor was their pastoral economy as labor-extensive in every respect as it is usually described. As we have shown earlier, the eastern districts were the chief producers of butter, tallow, soap, and sheep's tail fat in the 1830's. All these articles required a considerable amount of labor for their production.

Moreover, the leaders of the Trek, who were wealthy farmers, were known to possess a number of slaves, while some of them had interests in Capetown, Grahamstown, and other places where the slave question was of great practical importance at that time. It is reasonable to assume, therefore, that while the slave question probably played a very unimportant part with the mass of the poor farmers who joined the Trek, the economic aspects of slave emancipation greatly affected the wealthy frontier farmers and the leaders of the Trek movement, particularly in the years 1834–36.

To understand the consequences of slave emancipation on the economy of the frontier, we must distinguish clearly between the property aspects and the labor aspects of the slave problem. The grievances in connection with the depreciation of slave property[2] and the manner of compensating the owners for the slaves they had possessed are all property aspects; property losses were incurred by all those who possessed slaves in the colony, regardless of their occupations. The labor aspects, on the other hand—i.e., the scarcity of labor and the difficulty of managing whatever labor force was available—were the concern only of those who employed laborers. The whole question of whether all the slaves in the eastern frontier areas were owned by the trekkers or not is relevant only to the property aspects of the slave problem—in particular, to slave owners in towns like Graaff Reinet who hired out their slaves to farmers (*2*, p. 479). What is often forgotten is that the emancipation of slaves was of direct concern to employers of labor even if they did not own the slaves themselves.

The great attention that has been devoted to the property aspect of the slave problem of that period, to the almost complete exclusion of its labor aspects, was bound to confuse the issue and to draw historical research along false lines. For it can hardly be overemphasized that it was not so much the loss of slaves as a form of property as their loss as a source of labor that undermined the foundations of the farm economy of the eastern frontier.

There is also an essential difference between the graziers *pur sang* and the stock farmers whose main occupation, though mostly pastoral, did not exclude arable farming for home or local consumption. The graziers of the eastern districts belonged to the latter category. As to the graziers of the northern districts, owing to the arid nature of the country, they could not go in for agricultural crops. Chase states (*11*, p. 75) that "the scarcity of water in this division [Colesberg] condemns it to a chiefly pastoral existence, for nothing cultivable by art can be raised without irrigation, and the opportunity of effecting this is somewhat rare; the consequence is that it is dependent upon the other districts for its bread corn."

The labor aspect of the slave problem was also stressed by the *Voortrekker* Pretorius, who stated in his narrative (*20*, p. 230) that "the chief incentive to the emigration was the dissatisfaction

---

[2] As far back as 1826 slave property in Graaff Reinet declined to about half its former value, largely owing to the fact that "the farmers were alarmed at the new regulations" (*2*, pp. 478–79).

felt at the emancipation of the slaves, upon whose labour the colonists were dependent in their agricultural and other pursuits, and for whom the compensation made to their masters and owners was ruinously insufficient." Pretorius' order of importance is correct. Leaving the colony was no remedy against the loss of slave property unless the slaves were taken along; but it did solve the colonists' difficult labor problems, for outside the colony there was no restrictive labor policy. The emancipation of the Hottentots in 1828 was bad enough; the emancipation of the slaves in 1833 was the *coup de grâce*.

TRADING AND HUNTING ON THE EASTERN FRONTIER

In the twenties and thirties the Boers were probably losing their trade with the native tribes, a trade which, as will be remembered, had always played a very important part in the frontier economy of the Cape. It is true that in this period trade with the eastern native tribes assumed proportions undreamed of before, but it was largely carried on by professional traders from among the British settlers who were more expert in trade than in farming. (After 1830 a number of traders had even settled in Kaffraria.) What chance did the Boers of the eastern frontier have to compete against professional traders? Gradually the functions of the trader and farmer became more differentiated. Only in the interior could farming and bartering with the natives still be successfully combined.

The interior offered yet other advantages. Whereas on the eastern frontier game was becoming all too scarce, the interior abounded with it; and the Zulu tribesmen had plenty of cattle, skins, and ivory. In a word, the untapped resources of African labor, cattle, and game were awaiting exploitation by enterprising Boers.

WOOL FARMING: A COMPARISON WITH AUSTRALIA

The 1820's and 1830's were the years when thousands of settlers flocked to Australia to grow wool. In the Cape, too, many western wine and wheat farmers fell back on wool to escape the emancipation crises, while in the eastern areas a large number of British settlers became wool farmers. It is therefore surprising that only a comparatively small number of eastern frontier Boers went in for wooled sheep.

There are several plausible, though not very convincing, explanations of why the African fat-tailed sheep was more suitable than the Merino breed in the eastern frontier areas. The African fat-tailed sheep has a greater resistance to diseases than the Merino and is better able to subsist than any other breed on the scanty pasturage of arid and semiarid regions. Two other supposed obstacles to Merino breeding were the presence of thorny shrubs which occasioned some loss of wool, and the "want of running streams," which made it difficult to wash the fleece and clean it of sand and dust before shearing (*4*, p. 270). Other alleged difficulties were poisonous plants, the complications that arose from the Kaffir wars, and the perils presented by Bushmen, wild dogs, jackals, and leopards. These enemies of the Merino sheep are by no means friends of the fat-tailed sheep; the point is that, sheep for sheep, the pecuniary losses would be greater to the breeder of Merinos.

Yet, when all this is said in excuse of the sheep breeder in South Africa, the question still remains why Australia, under similar climatic conditions, was able to forge ahead. The answer is that in the 1820's and 1830's there was a much greater supply of labor and capital in Australia than in the Cape. On the other hand, the Cape always had the choice of breeding sheep for meat and fat instead of for wool. Australia had no such choice. Tallow production, a very inferior alternative, became important in Australia only in the early forties when the price of wool was very low.

Australia's plentiful labor supply was perhaps the most decisive factor. The supply of capital followed the supply of labor. In 1821, out of Australia's total white population of around 35,000, about 30,000 were convicts. Between 1816 and 1820 alone, 11,250 convicts were brought from England to Australia, so many that the governor found difficulty in assigning them all to private employers. "At the end of 1819 nearly 30 percent of the convicts were in Government service, and the provision of public works for their employment involved the colonial authorities in considerable expense" (*21*, pp. 45–46). By 1821 the growing of fine wool was prepared by the work of Macarthur and by the discovery of fine grazing areas west of the Blue Mountains in New South Wales, and also in Tasmania. The number of convicts sent from England to Australia between 1822 and 1831 was about 30,000, while the number of convicts sent to Australia in the next decade, 1832–41, was probably between 40,000 and 45,000 (*21*, pp. 47–49). With labor and land cheap and plentiful, what an opportunity of gaining wealth in wool farming for free settlers with capital! Burton says (*21*, pp. 47–48):

Feeble as the labour of the convicts was, it was sufficient for the work of shepherds, and though the stream of convicts increased through the 'twenties, the demand for labourers was so insistent that they were readily absorbed in pastoral employment. This employment was provided by a growing stream of free settlers flocking to Australia to grow wool, and by the growth of capital investment from Great Britain in companies such as the Australian Agricultural Company.

While these developments were taking place in Australia, the Cape continued steadily to increase its native flocks and herds, producing meat, fat, hides and skins, and other animal products for its own population, for passing ships, and for export. It was not until the late twenties, when the demand for Cape mutton fell off, that a keener interest was taken by the eastern frontier farmers in wooled sheep. But where was the necessary capital to come from for expanding wool production in the Cape? Without an adequate supply of labor the Cape did not seem to hold out much hope of gain to investors.

The different circumstances of Australia and the Cape as far as labor and capital were concerned were well appreciated by Moodie (*3*, p. 141):

We find that the wools of Australia, a similar climate, have, under the management of men of intelligence and capital, attained a great degree of fineness: and this fact, which should be an argument for the practicability of improvement in the wools of the Cape, has been unfairly urged against it, without considering the different circumstances of the two colonies.

Australia has had immense advantages over the Cape in this respect. Men of large capital have settled there as sheep-farmers, who have imported the best breeds from Europe, and have had an almost unlimited command of cheap labour.

Some writers contend that the presence of the African fat-tailed sheep was one of the main obstacles to the development of Merino breeding in the Cape (*22*, p. 175), but this seems an oversimplification. As pointed out earlier, the breeding of the African fat-tailed sheep was the result of conscious choice rather than of indifference or backwardness. Up to the middle 1820's sheep breeding for meat, fat, and skins proved more advantageous than sheep breeding for wool. When wool farming became relatively more profitable, the frontier farmers were not uneager to go in for Merinos. In 1834 the Graaff Reinet farmers, for instance, intended to purchase Merino sheep with the slave compensation money. They were of the opinion that the country they inhabited was "not calculated to support the large troops of African sheep" which they possessed, and that it "would sustain sufficient wool sheep to enable them to live comfortably" (*23*, pp. 63–64). Clearly it was the absence of capital rather than the presence of the African fat-tailed sheep that proved an obstacle to the development of wool farming.

We have endeavored to give an outline of the economic situation at the Cape and the frontier areas as they appeared to exist on the eve of the Great Trek. Little attention has been given to noneconomic factors, not because they had no influence on the Great Trek, but because they have been dealt with by other writers, usually to the neglect of the economic factors.

However important the immediate political factors leading up to the Great Trek might have been, they did not take effect in an economic vacuum. For one thing, the political crisis, in part at least, was engendered by dissatisfaction with economic conditions on the eastern frontier. For another, the trekkers would not necessarily have left the colony had they not believed it possible to reproduce the economic life of the eastern frontier areas, based as it was on native labor, trading with the native tribes, and hunting, beyond the borders of the colony. It is not sufficient to know merely why the trekkers wanted to leave the colony; it is also important to know how such a venture was economically feasible.

The *Voortrekkers* did not venture into unknown lands. Nor were they aware of the dangers which they would have to face. As pointed out by Boyce, "aware of the vast extent of unoccupied and unclaimed country to the north-east of the Orange River, in the direction of Delagoa Bay and Port Natal, they never anticipated any hostile collision with the native tribes" (*16*, p. 145). Above all it was the economic developments preceding the Great Trek that made a mass exodus into the interior economically possible.

The territory from the eastern frontier to Delagoa Bay and Port Natal had already been explored by trading expeditions, and a number of traders from the colony had already settled around Port Natal in the early thirties (*24*, p. 209). Furthermore, the smouses who followed the *Voortrekkers* into the interior (*25*, p. 217) supplied them with many household articles and probably also with ammunition (a most indispensable article in the wilds) in exchange for sheep, cattle, etc. The itinerant traders thus kept open the lines of communication of the *Voortrekkers* with the colony.

Boschoff, who traveled from the colony across the Drakensberg range to Natal in April 1838, speaks of a Griqua farmer who had built a neat little cottage, at a distance of about an hour and a half by horse wagon from the Orange River, "expressly for the accommodation of travellers and strangers." "A day seldom passes," says Boschoff, "without visitors, either traders or Boers, with both of whom he appears to be on the best and most friendly terms. . . . The main road runs across his place, and every day such visitors pass his door either backward or forward" (*16*, pp. 155–56). What is more, communication and trade with the outer world was now possible through Port Natal and Delagoa Bay, a circumstance which made the trekkers even less dependent upon the markets of the colony.

Several British traders from the colony had visited Port Natal in the early thirties, and Mr. Collins, the trader, upon his return from Natal in 1834, gave "the most flattering description of his adopted country, in respect of its fertility, the friendly disposition of the natives and the capabilities of the place for colonisation and trade" (*26*, p. 34). Natal, in fact, soon became the dreamland not only of the frontier farmers who had heard of its fertility, but also of the trader, mariner, and explorer (*24*, p. 210).

While Natal was the destination of many *Voortrekkers*, others intended "to proceed far into the interior, with a view of settling in the neighbourhood of Delagoa Bay, but at some distance from the coast where a considerable extent of fertile country previously explored by one Louis Treckard was known to be vacant" (*16,* p. 145). As in the case of Port Natal, access to Delagoa Bay was thought important by the trekkers for obtaining gunpowder, clothes, and other articles.[3]

In short, there was no need to live within the boundaries of the colony in order to exchange the produce of the land for manufactured articles. The colony's market was coming to them in the smous's wagon, and what is more, the Promised Land in the northeast had its own markets.

CITATIONS

1 G. M. Theal, *Records of the Cape Colony,* 36 vols. (Govt. of the Cape Colony, 1897–1905), XXVII.

2 G. M. Theal, *Records,* XXIX.

3 J. W. D. Moodie, *Ten Years in South Africa,* 2 vols. (London, 1835), I.

4 G. M. Theal, *Records,* XXXV.

5 G. M. Theal, *History of South Africa Since 1795,* 5 vols. (5th ed., London, 1927), II.

6 G. M. Theal, *Records,* XXX.

7 George Greig, compiler, *South African Almanack and Directory* (Capetown), 1830.

8 G. M. Theal, *Records,* XXIV.

9 Cape Ordinance 512, quoted by P. J. van der Merwe, *Die Trekboer in die Geskiedenis van die Kaapkolonie (1657–1842)* (Capetown, 1938).

10 Colonial Secretary's Office, *Cape of Good Hope Blue Book* (Capetown), 1842.

11 J. C. Chase, *The Cape of Good Hope and the Eastern Province of Algoa Bay* (London, 1843).

12 Stephen Kay, *Travels and Researches in Caffraria* (London, 1833), II.

13 George Nicholson, *The Cape and Its Colonists, with Hints to Settlers in 1848* (London, 1848).

14 Colonial Secretary's Office, *Cape of Good Hope Blue Book* (Capetown), 1834 and 1837.

15 P. J. van der Merwe, *Die Noordwaartse Beweging van die Boere voor die Groot Trek (1770–1842)* (Amsterdam, 1937).

16 William B. Boyce, *Notes on South African Affairs from 1834 to 1838,*

---

[3] "*Want seij seggen dat seij een streak veldt will soeken soo naa aan die Portigese cantoor dat seij die ken bereijken om hum kruijt, kleedern en soo voort van daar te hebben, seij will voor eers na Vaal revier van daar seij een reijs doon om te spekuleeren*" (G. D. Joubert to W. C. V. Rynveld, quoted in *15,* p. 370). This has very little to do with the question whether the Boers had confidence in the smous or whether their dependence on the Cape market continued. The important point is that the Boers could only break away from the Cape and its markets if a new outlet for their products could be found elsewhere.

with Reference to the Civil, Political and Religious Condition of the Colonists and Aborigines (Grahamstown, 1838).

17 W. M. Macmillan, *Bantu, Boer and Briton* (London, 1929).

18 George Greig, compiler, *South African Almanack and Directory* (Capetown), 1832; *South African Directory and Almanac* (Capetown), 1835.

19 Colonial Secretary's Office, *Cape of Good Hope Blue Book* (Capetown), 1831.

20 "Narrative of Willem Jurgen Pretorius, 1834–39," in John Bird, *The Annals of Natal* (Pietermaritzburg, 1888), I.

21 H. Butron, *The Peopling of Australia* (Melbourne, 1933).

22 H. B. Thom, *Die Geskeidenis van die Skaapboerdery in Zuid-Afrika* (Amsterdam, 1936).

23 Andrew Smith, *The Diary of Dr. Andrew Smith* (Van Riebeeck Society Publication, No. 20).

24 Andrew Steedman, *Wanderings and Adventures in the Interior of Southern Africa*, 2 vols. (London, 1835), II.

25 Lourens Christian de Klerk quoted in G. S. Preller, *Voortrekkermense*, 3 vols. (Capetown, 1920–25), I.

26 J. C. Chase, *Natal Papers* (Capetown, 1843).

CHAPTER 15

SUMMARY AND CONCLUSIONS

Frontier expansion has in the past been explained in terms of a self-sufficient economy whose dynamics of expansion were supposed to have been determined by the natural increase of the frontier inhabitants. Great emphasis was, therefore, laid on the "extraordinary fecundity" of the frontier population and on their ever-growing need for new land. Great play has also been made of the so-called wanderlust of the frontier farmers who were supposed to be trekking in all directions out of sheer joy of wandering. Barter with native tribes was regarded as part of a self-sufficient economy, instead of a manifestation of a full-fledged exchange economy.

We have demonstrated the basic fallacies of such an approach. We have also shown that the dynamics of the expansion movement sprang from entirely different sources. Not only was the economy of the frontier an exchange economy, linked directly with either local or foreign markets, or with both, but the *raison d'être* of the expansion movement itself was largely this market demand for the products of the frontier.

In this respect the South African frontier was not unique and bears comparison with frontier expansion in America, Argentina, Australasia, Brazil, and Canada. The settlement of Brazil in the sixteenth century began with the production of crops for export, with sugar as the principal crop. The development of a successful export industry gave rise to local centers of consumption and to local markets, which in turn led to further expansion of the frontier. A good example is the development of the Brazilian cattle industry, which was based not only on the demand for leather but also on the demand of the sugar industry for fresh and jerked meat and draft oxen. It was this demand for cattle that was largely responsible for the occupation of the interior regions of Brazil long before gold and diamonds were discovered there at the end of the seventeenth century. The Indians in Brazil, as the Hottentots in the Cape, proved more useful in cattle raising than in crop production. Similarly Argentina's expansion until late in the nineteenth century proceeded only in response to the foreign demand for its cow and horse hides, tallow, jerked beef, unwashed wool, and sheepskins.

In North America, the exploitation of the fur and timber resources and the development of the northeast fisheries were closely linked up with export markets in Europe and the West Indies. In fact, the West Indian market for American fish, lumber, livestock, grain, and other agricultural produce, which played such an important part in American economic development and frontier expansion, was itself another outpost of Europe: it owed its development to Europe's demand for the tropical products that could be grown in the West Indies. The development of Virginia, Maryland, and other southern colonies in North America was along similar lines: Europe's demand for tobacco and other products, the influx of a large amount of capital for investment in plantations, in slave labor, and in shipping and other transport facilities. Here again the export industries gave rise to local markets which became new points of departure for further expansion.

In Australia, the first chapter of real economic development and expansion opened with wool farming. It was the ready market for wool in England and the abundance of convict labor in Australia which attracted capital for investment in the wool industry. There followed a stream of free settlers (accompanied by an influx of capital) eager to take up wool farming in the semiarid rolling grasslands.

Even more spectacular were the effects on frontier expansion of discoveries of precious metals and precious stones. In Brazil, the gold and diamond rushes of the eighteenth century were responsible for the mass movement into the interior. In Australasia, the gold rushes in New South Wales and Victoria in 1851 and the Otago gold rush in New Zealand in the sixties were followed by great waves of fortune seekers. They all gave rise to a rapid development of local markets with a high purchasing power for the products of local agricultural and pastoral industries.

In general, the frontier economy was not based solely on

agriculture and stock raising. It was also combined with trading with the native tribes (in Brazil, North America, and South Africa), fishing, trapping, hunting, lumbering, and some processing. Examples of the latter are the production of jerked beef for local and foreign markets (Brazil, Argentina, and North America); tallow and butter production almost everywhere; sheep's tail fat and soap in the Cape of Good Hope; and producing wood tar, collecting rosin, sawing timber, and producing bear's fat in North America. These nonagricultural pursuits often constituted most valuable sources of revenue, performing in a sense the same function that "cash crops" had for the early settlers.

These nonagricultural opportunities were not unknown and their value as a source of ready cash entered into the calculations of the frontier settlers before they embarked on new ventures. To appreciate the importance of a source of ready cash to every frontier settler it must be realized that the frontier farmer—even on the edge of the pioneer settlement—was dependent upon certain indispensable articles, such as guns, gunpowder, iron rods for the forge, salt, tea or coffee, some utensils, and some clothing for himself and his family. These articles could be obtained only from the outside world in exchange for frontier products which had to be of high value in relation to their bulk. This is why the frontiersman's economy had to be a market-bound economy, even if he went to live in the wilds for extra-economic reasons. Regarded purely as a means of procuring the indispensable articles from the trading centers, the "cash crop" or its expectation at the frontier of settlement was probably of decisive importance to any settler, however self-sufficient, and the important part played by such a "cash crop" in frontier expansion was out of all proportion to the value of "subsistence crops" of such a frontier economy. What the trade in peltries with the Indians was to the American settler, the barter of ivory and skins of wild animals with the native tribes was to the Cape frontiersman.

As in the Americas and in Australasia, the impelling force of expansion in South Africa came largely from the world outside the frontier—from Capetown and later from other trading centers. The Cape, by the very nature of its establishment as a provisioning station for passing ships, was a surplus producer depending on foreign demand. The provisions demanded may be divided into two categories: products of arable farming such as wheat, wine, vegetables, and fruit, which came from a comparatively small area in the neighborhood of Capetown, and meat and slaughter stock which came from the interior. In addition there was also a market for a great variety of such products of the interior regions as ivory, karosses, ostrich feathers and eggs, sheep's tail fat, soap, and berry wax.

Owing to their perishability, fruit and vegetables could come only from the immediate vicinity of Capetown. Wine production, too, was confined to areas near Capetown, while commercial grain growing was unprofitable at a distance greater than 60 or 70 miles from Capetown, owing to the high cost of road transport. On top of all this was the circumstance that recurring overproduction and low prices often rendered the position of even the established wheat and wine farmers very precarious. Moreover, as far as the passing ships were concerned, grain could be obtained elsewhere at lower prices. It is therefore obvious that arable farming could not serve as a basis of expansion into the interior.

It was the cattle trade, the meat trade, and the trade in other animal products that together constituted the most important single factor in the expansion of the colony from the days of van Riebeeck to the Great Trek. It was the production of and trade in animal products that must form the most important clue to South African economic development during the first 200 years of its history.

For a period of about 200 years before the steam engine had revolutionized transportation and brought the meat-producing areas of the world relatively nearer to the consuming centers, South Africa was fortunate in having her foreign market for fresh meat and butter literally at her very doorstep. The crews and passengers of the passing ships that rounded the Cape on their way to the East and on their way back to Europe all clamored for fresh meat, live animals, and other fresh provisions. The export market for all these products was thus not many months' journey away but literally at the Cape harbors. What is more, the native races not only provided the sheep and cattle—they either had to be induced or coerced to part with them—but they also proved good shepherds and herdsmen for their European masters. This, indeed, was a position for which there is hardly any parallel in colonial history.

Another circumstance which had a direct bearing on the expansion movement was the fact that in the eighteenth century the pastoral economy of the frontier graziers was based mainly on sheep ranching, the Cape sheep and goats having proved particularly well adapted to the scanty pasturage of the arid and semi-arid regions of the interior. Without sheep and goats, the utilization of the arid or Karoid areas of the interior would have hardly been possible. Furthermore, owing to the fact that Cape mutton was of excellent quality, while Cape beef was tough and tasteless, sheep ranching had a further advantage over cattle ranching.

From the early part of the eighteenth century, one of the reasons which impelled people in the settled areas of the Cape to take up stock farming in the interior was the unfavorable position of arable farming relative to that of pastoral farming. Whereas for a long time the Cape had been in an unrivaled position as a provisioning station for fresh meat, its position as a supplier of grain, wine, and other arable produce was more often than not rather precarious. The Cape experienced its first crisis in arable farming in the 1690's when Batavia refused to continue paying high grain prices. Later, in 1707, the overproduction of grain and wine at the Cape compelled the Dutch East India Company to restrict the issue of freehold land, and new settlers or the sons of older colonists could start on their own only by obtaining a "loan farm" in the interior and by becoming graziers. This, no doubt, encouraged stock farming, which led to an expansion of the colony, but it was the greater lucrativeness of stock farming that was the power behind the expansion movement. The loan farm system merely sanctioned what had been taking place already. A more stringent policy in the giving out of loan farms in the interior would, perhaps, have retarded the movement to the interior, but it could not have made arable farming more profitable. Nor can the loan farm system be blamed for having impeded the development of more intensive agriculture. Under conditions where extensive areas of land can be had for the asking, or taking, labor is bound to be scarce for the simple reason that anyone who possesses a few animals can set up on his own. Besides, there is no virtue in farming more intensively, i.e., in apply-ing larger amounts of capital and labor per unit of land, if the returns on the expended capital and labor are inadequate. Under such conditions the problem is rather how to utilize large areas of land with relatively little labor and capital. This can best be solved by means of ranching, a form of land use which can utilize a relatively large area of land with a relatively small amount of labor and capital.

As to the various phases of the expansion movement, it is to be noted that on the whole the migration from the arable areas of the colony during the 1717–43 period appears to have been not so much the result of high prices of slaughter stock as of the relatively low prices of the products of arable farming. The 1740's marked the turning point from depression to prosperity in the economic life of the colony. French ships and English warships, particularly the latter, and transports, entering Table Bay for the purpose of provisioning, brought with them great prosperity not only to Capetown but also to the frontier areas. In general, the demand of the passing ships was primarily for fresh meat, live animals, and other animal products, with the probable consequence that the stockbreeders, including the meat trade, rather than the arable farmer reaped the greater benefit.

Fresh meat and live animals were perhaps the most important products sold to ships; but butter, fat, ostrich eggs, preserved meat, as well as ivory, skins of wild animals, and ostrich feathers also played an important part in the Cape trade with passing ships. The sale of meat to foreign ships, as distinguished from ships belonging to the Dutch East India Company or other Dutch ships, constituted the most remunerative part of the meat trade, so that at the frontier the prosperity of the graziers and the expansion movement were to a certain extent linked up with the number of foreign ships putting into Cape harbors.

The third phase of the expansion movement, however, was the most important one. It began in the late 1750's and continued almost without interruption for a period of about 35 years. This period coincided with an increase in foreign shipping, a develop-ment which assumed large dimensions in the 1770's and 1780's.

Thus from the 1740's the chief cause of expansion was Cape-town's demand for meat and livestock—for its own population, for the Company's needs, and for the passing ships and their crews and passengers while on shore. From that time until the end of the century the part played by foreign ships was important not merely in adding to the total demand for meat, but also on account of the fact that the meat and live animals sold to foreigners were disposed of at much higher prices than to the Dutch East India Company.

One of the means of satisfying the ever-increasing demand for meat and live animals was a continual opening up of new grazing areas in the interior; but the demand was at times increasing so rapidly that it could be satisfied only by exploiting the livestock resources of the native tribes of the interior. To a very large extent the great rapidity with which the expansion took place can be attributed to this circumstance.

We have also dealt at length with the part played, in the frontier economy and in the expansion movement, by draft oxen, butter, soap, sheep's tail fat, tallow, ostrich feathers and ostrich eggs, ivory, karosses, skins, and berry wax. Unlike livestock, which could walk to market, all the other articles had to be carried by ox wagon over long distances and difficult roads. As the capacity of the ox wagon was limited, preference was naturally given to articles with the highest value per unit of weight and volume. While soap, butter, dry hides, and berry wax, for instance, made up the bulk of the products taken to market, the value of the load was enhanced by the addition of ivory, ostrich feathers, skins of wild animals, and other high-priced products. The products of hunting thus became complementary to the products of the pastoral economy, with hunting and stockbreeding as interrelated pursuits. This, as well as the fact that the grazier at the frontier relied to a large extent upon game for his meat in order to save his tame animals for the market, could not fail to give the expansion movement an additional impetus; for hunting required even larger areas than ranching.

Consideration of the frontier economy led to a more detailed study of the development of the early soap industry in the Cape. The prevailing view has been to regard soap as an article which was produced on the farms primarily for home use and as having very little significance from the point of view of an exchange economy. Our investigation shows not only that large quantities of soap produced in the frontier areas were sold in the trading centers of the colony, but that some quantities were also exported abroad. Indeed, the income derived from the sale of farm soap played an important part in the economy of the frontier farmers, and the development of soap production in the interior regions was closely connected with the expansion of the frontier. The link was formed by the fat-tailed sheep, whose significance lies in the fact that not only is it an animal eminently suited to utilize the fleeting vegetation of the arid and semiarid regions, but it is also able to convert that vegetation into fat. However, owing to certain difficulties connected with its transportation, fat was not in itself an easily marketable commodity. It became so only when converted into soap, which was made possible with the use of the *kanna-bosch* (*Salsola aphylla*) as a source of alkali. It was thus the combination of these two circumstances (the fat-tailed sheep and the *kanna-bosch*) that contributed greatly to the opening up of the arid regions of the Cape.

The first depression in the frontier districts occurred in the early 1790's with the decline in the number of ships putting into Table Bay and the reduction of the garrison. But this depression did not last long, for with the coming of the British in 1795, the 5,000 troops and the large fleet stationed at the Cape provided a very good market for all products coming from the frontier areas. This was followed, however, by another short depression under the Batavian rule during which the market for Cape produce was determined by the limited spending power of the government and the small number of regular troops stationed at the Cape. On the eastern frontier, the Kaffir war of 1799 was disastrous to the farmers of Graaff Reinet, while the Hottentot and Kaffir depredations that followed it were so ruinous that most of the colonists had hardly anything to take to market. The rising of the Hottentot farm servants against their masters was the most serious calamity that had befallen the frontier farmers. It was also the first great reverse in the eastward expansion movement. The devastation made itself felt in a meat shortage which affected Capetown, the army and navy, and the passing ships. This was also one of the chief reasons why the government was bound to keep the peace at the frontier by all available means. However, it was only after the second British occupation, in 1806, that the government began to pursue a more active policy in an attempt to solve the difficult farm-labor problem.

The scarcity of farm labor was also to a considerable extent responsible for diverting the expansion movement from the eastern districts to the northeastern borders. For, while in the east Kaffir depredations and cattle stealing continued and many Hottentot herdsmen deserted either to Bethelsdorp or across the border, in the northeast the little Bushmen were receiving ever-greater praise for their services. But one of the chief attractions of the northeast was trading and trafficking with the tribes of the northern border. Indeed, in view of the great demand for meat and other animal products after the second British occupation, the cattle resources of the Griquas and Bechuanas beyond the Orange River offered excellent opportunities for cattle trading. This was the beginning of the fourth phase of the expansion movement. As in the eighteenth century, the northward expansion in the early part of the nineteenth century was initiated by a combination of trading and livestock farming, the only difference being that the northern tribes bartered their cattle mainly for firearms and gunpowder instead of for beads and trinkets.

From 1815 to 1821 the demand for Cape meat, live animals, butter, soap, and other frontier products was kept up by the troops and ships guarding Napoleon at St. Helena. We have demonstrated the important part played by the St. Helena market in the economy of the Cape between 1815 and 1821. The loss of this market was a major factor in the depression that set in at the Cape after 1821. The effect of this depression on the frontier economy, however, was mitigated by the influx of 4,000 settlers in 1820 who, before being able to produce their own food, constituted an important market not only for meat and other animal products, but also for draft oxen, breeding cattle, and breeding sheep.

Between 1806 and 1821 the high prices for animal products, occasioned both by an increased demand and a short supply, was one of the main factors behind the movement to the northeast, the other causes being unsettled labor conditions and Kaffir depredations in the east. The older arable districts of the colony, too, were making the best of an increased demand and high prices for wine and grain, so that probably few people from these districts migrated to the frontier during this period. The expansion to the northeast during that period was, on the whole, more in the nature of a diversion from the eastern area, where Kaffir depredations and Hottentot labor difficulties represented serious problems. But from 1821 to 1826 the relative prosperity of the graziers, as compared to the depressed state of arable farming, must have also attracted immigrants from the older districts. It was in this latter period that the frontier of the colony was carried to the Orange River.

The fifth phase of the expansion movement coincides with the shift in the center of gravity from Capetown to the east. Capetown had for a long time been the sole market for the animal products as well as for the products of hunting and collecting of the interior and frontier regions. Capetown had also been the sole distributive center for all imported goods, including firearms and gunpowder, required by the colonists. While it is true that the Cape market was the main economic reason for the expansion of the colony, it is also true that the farther the colonists advanced into the interior the more they lengthened their lines of communication with the trading center. The range of goods which could be carried by ox wagon to the market was limited by distance, by the nature of the roads, and by the nature and weight of the commodity itself. These factors, therefore, were bound to impose certain limits on the expansion movement itself, for beyond a certain point expansion into the interior, with soap and butter as the basis of production, had its definite limits. Beyond these limits expansion could take place only if soap, butter, etc., were taken to market together with articles of higher value per unit of weight, such as ivory, ostrich feathers, and skins of wild animals—articles which could be obtained by hunting or trading with the native tribes. The marketing of live animals was the only important exception, for sheep and cattle could walk hundreds of miles to the Cape.

As has been emphasized throughout this study, the idea that the distant frontier graziers could sever their economic connection with the Cape has no historical foundation. It obscures the fact that firearms, gunpowder, and iron for the wagons, and the wagons themselves, articles which had to be purchased from outside, were absolutely indispensable to the frontier graziers. These as well as clothing, tea, coffee, sugar, and brandy could only be obtained in exchange for products which had to be taken from the frontier areas to Capetown.

It was only with the establishment of coastal trading that going by wagons from the eastern and northeastern districts to the Cape was rendered unnecessary. Some coastal trading was probably carried on between Algoa Bay and Capetown throughout the second decade of the nineteenth century, but it was not before the early 1820's that coastal trading assumed larger proportions. The gradual reduction in freight rates and the establishment of a harbor at Port Elizabeth not only resulted in an increased exchange of goods between the frontier and the outside world, but also led to a further expansion of the frontier itself.

Hand in hand with the development of coastal trading, towns and villages grew up in the eastern and northeastern parts of the colony. Merchandise was now brought by coasters to Port Elizabeth and other ports for forwarding to the local markets; and the farmer could bring his produce to the local markets for forwarding to Port Elizabeth and eventual shipment to Capetown and elsewhere. The need for going in wagons to Capetown from these distant parts of the colony was disappearing rapidly and Capetown lost its position as the commercial Mecca of the eastern and northeastern districts.

Of the greatest significance, however, is the fact that the newly opened-up trading centers and local markets of the eastern and northeastern frontier districts now constituted a more advanced point of departure than Capetown for new frontiers, and for further and further expansion into the interior of Africa.

An important part was played by the smous (itinerant trader) in the early development of the Cape. Peddlers and hawkers had already carried on their traveling trade with the farmers in the early 1770's. After that time the differentiated function of the country hawkers and peddlers appears to have been restricted, and it was not before the end of the eighteenth or the beginning of the nineteenth century that the smous trade could re-emerge. In the early part of the nineteenth century merchandise was probably brought by these peddlers all the way from Capetown in wagons, though some might have obtained their wares in Graaff Reinet, Mossel Bay, Uitenhage, Tulbagh, or Algoa Bay.

It was only after the establishment of coastal trading that

the smous trade in the eastern and northeastern frontier districts began to play a decisive part in the expansion movement. By the late twenties the smouses had already consolidated their position to such a degree that they were able to compete successfully with the all-powerful Cape butchers.

With the development of coastal shipping, Grahamstown, Graaff Reinet, and Port Elizabeth were fast becoming new centers of trade, and consequently new centers of departure for supplying the most distant frontier farmers with all their requirements. But it was in the moving market of the smous that the moving frontier had found its counterpart. The colonists had at last freed themselves from a fixed market place and could now advance without a halt into the interior of the African continent, for the market in the smous's wagon was now following them on their wanderings.

Between 1825 and 1827 the Cape was passing through a severe depression. The demand for meat declined not only in consequence of the greatly reduced garrison at the Cape, but probably also owing to the fact that the British settlers in Albany were now in a position to produce their own meat. In general, stock farmers were suffering from lack of markets and low prices. The year 1826 was also unfortunate in that it marked the first failure of the Kaffir trade on the eastern frontier.

However, with the growth of population in the 1820's and 1830's the local demand for meat was gradually increasing, and there was also an increasing demand for beef, especially for export as salted meat. But the most important foreign demand for meat would appear to have come from passing ships, which from 1827 were putting into Cape ports in ever-increasing numbers. In fact, the number of ships from 1829 onward far exceeded the peak years of shipping at the Cape in the eighteenth century.

The other important frontier products for which there was both a local and foreign demand were hides and skins, tallow, soap, butter, horns, ivory, and ostrich feathers. The development of an export market in these products played an important part in the expansion movement of the 1820's and 1830's. One article, soap, was slowly but steadily losing ground in competition not only with imported soap but also with soap manufactured in Capetown and Grahamstown. All this, together with the growing demand for beef, after the establishment of coastal shipping, tended to encourage expansion in regions of higher rainfall which are more suited to cattle raising.

Many economic problems confronted the colonists in the eastern and northeastern frontier areas of the Cape in the 1820's and 1830's. The northeast was a region subject to periodical droughts. Ordinarily, the numbers of livestock that the land in this region could carry would be determined by its carrying capacity in the driest years. The solution was to remove the livestock to the pastures of Transorangia in drought years, an alternative which was actually chosen by the graziers for the maximum utilization of the pasturage of arid regions. Transorangia thus became the means through which the semiarid regions south of the Orange could be more permanently utilized. What the Karroo was in the eighteenth-century seasonal migrations from the summer veld to the winter veld, Transorangia became in the periodic migrations from the drought-stricken areas south of the Orange in the 1820's and 1830's. Crossing the Orange with his herds and flocks was thus an integral part of the grazier's system of land utilization in the northeastern parts of the colony, which could be better utilized only in conjunction with the better-watered areas of Transorangia. These migrations eventually led to permanent settlement beyond the Orange. But the economic foundation for such an expansion was laid in the first quarter of the century, in the development of coastal shipping, in the growth of new trading centers, and in the development of the smous trade.

In the eastern frontier areas the most vexatious problem of this period, next to Kaffir depredations, was that of labor. The farmers in the eastern frontier areas were not exclusively stock farmers, and their labor requirements were far greater than their purely pastoral pursuits would suggest. This combination of agriculture with stock raising imposed certain limitations upon the eastern frontier farmers in the choice of new land for settlement when they decided to quit the colony. The new country had to be suitable for both stock raising and agriculture. This in part helps to explain why the majority of the *Voortrekkers* did not settle immediately north of the Orange River, a region which could not have the same attraction for them as it had for the pure graziers of the northeastern areas.

A distinction was made between the *property* and *labor* aspects of the slave problem. The depreciation of slave property and the problems of compensation were all property aspects of the slave problem, while the ease or difficulty of handling such labor was the concern of all those who engaged slave labor, irrespective of whether they owned the slaves or not. Slave labor was employed in most agricultural operations in the eastern frontier areas; and even if the eastern frontier farmers did not own the slaves, they were able to hire them from the owners residing in the towns and villages. With the emancipation of the slaves, this source of labor suddenly disappeared. It was thus not so much the loss of slaves as a form of property, as it was their loss as a source of labor that undermined the foundations of the farm economy of the eastern frontier. As to the property aspect of the slave problem, it is known that the leaders of the Trek, who were wealthy farmers, possessed a number of slaves. It is, therefore, reasonable to conclude that while the property aspect of the slave problem probably played a very unimportant part with the mass of the poor farmers who joined the Trek, it undoubtedly played some considerable part with the wealthy frontier farmers. On the whole, however, the farm-labor problem, which had always been very acute in the eastern frontier areas, was the decisive factor. The emancipation of the Hottentots in 1828 was bad enough. The emancipation of the slaves in 1833 was the *coup de grâce*.

Although the British settlers possessed no slaves, the confusion created at the frontier by the emancipation of the Hottentots and the freeing of the slaves could not but have affected them greatly had it not been for the fact that a large number of settlers had become artisans and traders, while others had gone in for wool farming. To the Boer farmers, however, this was no solution at all. Lack of capital had always been the main obstacle to taking up wool farming. As to the trade with the native tribes, the Boers of the eastern frontier had very little chance to compete against professional traders from among the 1820 settlers. On the eastern frontier the functions of the trader and farmer had become more differentiated. Only in the northeast could farming and bartering with the natives still be successfully carried on together.

In conclusion, the popular belief that the *Voortrekkers* ventured into unknown land was shown to be untenable. The territory from the eastern frontier to Delagoa Bay and Port Natal had already been explored by trading expeditions, while the itinerant traders kept open the lines of communication of the *Voortrekkers* with the colony. What is more, communication and trade with the outer world were now possible through Port Natal and Delagoa Bay, and made the trekkers even less dependent upon the markets of the colony. Historical events cannot be viewed in isolation, for it was largely the economic development preceding the Great Trek that made mass migration into the interior at all possible.

APPENDIX TABLES

TABLE I.—PRICES OF SELECTED COMMODITIES IN CAPETOWN, BEFORE
(1797) AND AFTER (1798) BRITISH OCCUPATION*

Commodity	Unit	1797			1798		
		Rd.	Sch.	St.	Rd.	Sch.	St.
Ox, draft	Head	12	0	0	14	0	0
Ox, fat	Head	10	0	0	20	0	0
Sheep	Head	1	4	0	2	3	0
Beef	4 lbs.	0	1	0	0	2	0
Mutton	5 lbs.	0	1	0	0	2	0
Butter, fresh	Lb.	0	2	0	0	6	0
Butter, salt	Lb.	0	1	0	0	3	0
Soap	Lb.	0	1	2	0	2	0
Candles	100 lbs.	14	0	0	25 to 28	0	0
Hides	Each	1	6	0	1	6	0
Sheep skins	Each	0	0	2	0	0	2

* Data from G. M. Theal, *Records of the Cape Colony*, 36 vols. (Govt. of the Cape Colony, 1897–1905), II, pp. 237–38.

TABLE II.—LIVESTOCK PRICES IN THE CAPE OF GOOD HOPE BY DISTRICTS, 1827*

(Sterling prices per head except as noted)

District	Draft oxen			Slaughter oxen			Milch cows			Sheep, goats[a]		
	£	s.	d.	£	s.	d.	£	s.	d.	£	s.	d.
Cape	2	1	3	2	5	0	1	17	6	3	15	0
Graaff Reinet...	1	5	8	..	..	..		10	1	2	10	10
Uitenhage	1	7	0	1	13	9		15	0	..	..	..
Albany	1	13	0	1	17	6		15	0	3	7	6
Somerset	1	17	6	2	5	0		15	0	1	10	0

* Data from G. M. Theal, *Records of the Cape Colony*, 36 vols. (Govt. of the Cape Colony, 1897–1905, XXXIV, p. 488.
[a] Price per score, for wethers.

TABLE III.—VALUE OF EXPORTS OF SELECTED PRODUCTS FROM THE CAPE OF GOOD HOPE, INDICATED YEARS 1813–35*

(Pounds sterling)

Commodity	1813ᵃ	1815ᵃ	1816ᵃ	1817ᵃ	1822ᵇ	1823ᵇ	1825ᵇ	1826ᶜ	1827ᵇ	1829	1831	1832	1833ᶜ	1834ᶜ	1835ᶜ
Beef, pork, salted	...	4,054	...	...	3,955	1,393	1,390	102	887	4,875	5,410	7,632	3,504	1,164	2,234
Ivory	3	59	282	1,091	4,675	4,258	16,586	7,796	4,308	3,759	2,731	2,515	777	1,400	715
Ostrich feathers	6	50	185	222	15,095	12,554	6,471	2,784	1,258	1,840	1,154	1,156	2,248	2,156	1,492
Hides, cattle, raw	541	796	1,036	1,103											
Goatskins, raw	14	594	569	508	22,595	20,043	34,324	30,187	33,780	46,229	48,034	52,215	39,519	32,517ᵈ	46,580ᵉ
Kidskins, undressed	...	49	49												
Sheepskins, undressed	905	538	1,076	1,121											
Wool	293	484	584	240	2,038	1,751	1,853	545	2,228	1,220	1,895	3,358	3,238	6,527	10,335
Butter	...	...	...	...	3,400	3,626	3,000	2,441	3,342	5,545	8,140	7,018	4,609	3,558	3,763
Horns	...	...	...	...	479	1,797	1,456	1,681	2,502	6,621	6,143	6,129	2,318	4,572ᵈ	3,303ᵉ
Soap	...	...	...	...	493	72	18	...	12	24	30	218	227	58	...
Live sheep	...	...	...	...	1,198	956	414	992	561	1,429	702	1,187	481	304	...
Other live animalsᶠ	...	...	...	...	916	3,574	256	434	547	1,782	327	496	366	55	...
Suet	...	...	...	...	119	73	...	...	...	...	...	...	...	...	...
Candles, tallow	...	...	...	...	...	...	156	...	76	383	436	413	775	518	918
Tallow	...	...	...	...	...	...	...	...	735	408	8,697	10,742	7,481	5,435	3,232
Tail fatᵍ	...	...	...	...	...	...	...	...	...	...	...	375	258	...	...

*Exports from all ports except as otherwise noted. Data for 1813 and 1815–17 from G. M. Theal, *Records of the Cape Colony*, 36 vols. (Govt. of the Cape Colony, 1897–1905), XI, p. 293; for 1822–26, 1829, and 1833–35, from *Cape of Good Hope Blue Book and Statistical Register* (Capetown, 1822–40), various issues; for 1827, Theal, *op. cit.*, XXX, pp. 92–99; for 1831 and 1832, from *South African Almanack and Directory, 1832* (Capetown), pp. 53–54, and *South African Directory and Almanac, 1834*, pp. 145–46, respectively.

ᵃ Presumably from all ports.
ᵇ From Table Bay and Simon's Bay.
ᶜ From Table Bay only.
ᵈ The total export value of hides, horns, and skins from all ports in 1834 amounted to £83,435. See J. C. Chase, *The Natal Papers* (Capetown, 1843), p. 198.
ᵉ Chase, *op. cit.*, p. 201.
ᶠ Slaughter stock.
ᵍ Sheep's tail fat and oil.

<small>TABLE IV.—NUMBER OF LIVESTOCK IN THE CAFE OF GOOD HOPE, 1828–34*</small>

Year	Cattle	Sheep	Goats
1828........................	357,531	2,181,952	517,930
1829........................	322,021	1,839,402	444,162
1830........................	311,938	1,905,728	465,613
1831........................	315,355	1,687,614	608,906
1832........................	...	...	...
1833........................	343,644	2,940,860	620,802
1834........................	312,564	1,919,773	1,628,862

* Data from *Cape of Good Hope Blue Book and Statistical Register* (Capetown), various years.

INDEX

Aereboe, Friedrich, 73, 93
Agar-Hamilton, J. A. I., 20–21, 26
Algoa Bay, *see* Port Elizabeth
American frontier, 172, 173, 174
Animal husbandry in arid areas, 70–79
Animal numbers, 75–79
Animal products, 155; *see also under specific commodities*
Arable farming, 41, 175; economic position, 27–36, 45, 132–33
Argentina, 71, 172, 174
Australia, 71, 165–67, 172, 173, 174

Bandeiras, 5
Bantu tribes, 11, 12, 24, 25, 97–106; *see also* Xosa
Barrow, John, 17, 26, 36–39 *passim*, 49, 57, 60, 61, 69, 74, 78, 83, 85, 91, 93, 110, 111, 124, 138, 144
Batavian Republic, 12, 111, 115
Beef: exports, salted, 62, 153, 156; quality, 54, 60, 77
Beriquas, *see* Griquas
Berry wax, 90–92
Beutler, Ensign, 149
Beyers, Coenraad, 39
Bird, John, 171
Bird, W. W., 49, 57, 69, 93, 129, 130, 132, 134, 144
Boschoff, ———, 160, 169
Botha, C. G., 40, 57
Botha, F., 85
Boundary changes of Cape Colony, 56
Boyce, W. B., 169, 170
Brazil, 172, 173, 174
British occupation: 1795–1803, 12, 109; 1806, 13, 115
British settlers, 132, 139, 143, 153
Brooke, T. M., 128, 134
Burchell, W. J., 69, 83–84, 86, 91, 93, 134, 141, 144
Burton, H., 167, 171
Bushmen, 11, 120, 121
Butchers' monopoly, 147–48
Butter, 58–60, 133, 155, 189, 190

Canada, 172
Candles: export, 155, 190; manufacture, 79–80, 91–92; prices, 189
Canna bush, 82–85 *passim*

Capetown, 135–44 *passim*; boarding houses, 9–10; British troops, 12, 46, 153; commodity prices, 32, 58–59, 63, 88, 189; depression, 132, 152; food consumption, 110; freighting by wagons, 34, 150, 182; market for farm products, 9, 16, 41, 48, 53, 58–65 *passim*, 79, 80, 85, 86, 92, 99, 104, 108, 109, 133, 148, 177–78, 181; meat shortage, 113, 126, 179; shipping, 62, 150, 182; ship provisioning, 46, 174–75, 177; soap making, 84, 158, 183; supply center, 108, 109, 181
Cattle, 37, 72, 108, 109; drought losses, 117; in European-native trade, 11, 16, 25, 94–107, 121, 123; and expansion movement, 42, 136; exports, 133, 135; numbers, 75, 76, 77, 126–27, 152–53, 191; for passing ships, 49, 53; prices, 110, 189; and smouses, 147–50 *passim*; stealing, 11, 25, 95, 96, 102, 121–22, 180; trade monopoly, 147–48; *see also* Beef
Chase, J. C., 69, 139, 144, 170, 171
Chavonnes, ———, 39, 47, 57
Climate, 70, 71
Coastal shipping and trading, 61, 137–40, 160, 182–83; *see also* Growth of towns
Colesberg, 144, 160
Collins, Richard, 101, 107
Collins, trader, 169
Colonial wars, 45–46, 53
Commission of Circuit, 138, 145
Cory, G. E., 19, 26
Cradock, 143–44
Crout, W. E., 146–47

Da Gama, Vasco, 6
De Kiewiet, C. W., 21, 26
De Klerk, L. C., 151, 171
Delagoa Bay, 168–70
De Mist, J. A., 12–13, 31, 39, 69
Depressions at Cape, 111–12, 131–33, 152–56
Diaz, Bartholomeu, 4, 6
Dispersion, *see* Expansion movement
Draft animals, demand for, 34–35
Dutch East India Company: as colonizing agency, 7–8; conflict with colonists, 16–18; control of cattle trade, 42–43; and meat trade, 54

193

also Cattle (European-native trade) *and under individual commodities*

Transorangia, 119; periodic migrations, 158–60

Treckard, Louis, 170

Troops: demand for provisions, 42, 48, 110, 125; effect on meat prices, 43, 46; numbers, 110, 111, 126–27; reduction (1828–1834), 153, 156; at St. Helena, 127

Van der Merwe, P. J., 35, 40, 65, 69, 93, 107, 151, 159, 170

Van der Stel, Simon, 7

Van der Stel, W. A., 8

Van der Walt, A. J. H., 17, 18, 26, 35, 39, 47, 57, 93, 107

Van Imhoff, ———, 28, 39, 47, 57

Van Reenen, D. G., 25, 26, 31, 39, 61–62, 69, 92, 110, 111–12, 124, 125, 134, 138

Van Riebeeck, Jan, 6

Voortrekkers, 15, 168, 169

Walker, E. A., 6n, 15, 20, 26, 39, 57, 107, 124, 134

Ward, A. W., 47

Wax bush, 90–92

Wheat, 27–34 *passim*, 132, 133

Wine, 28–34 *passim*, 132, 133

Wool farming, 8, 165–70

Xosa, 11, 14, 102, 103, 104, 116

Zuurveld, 14, 116

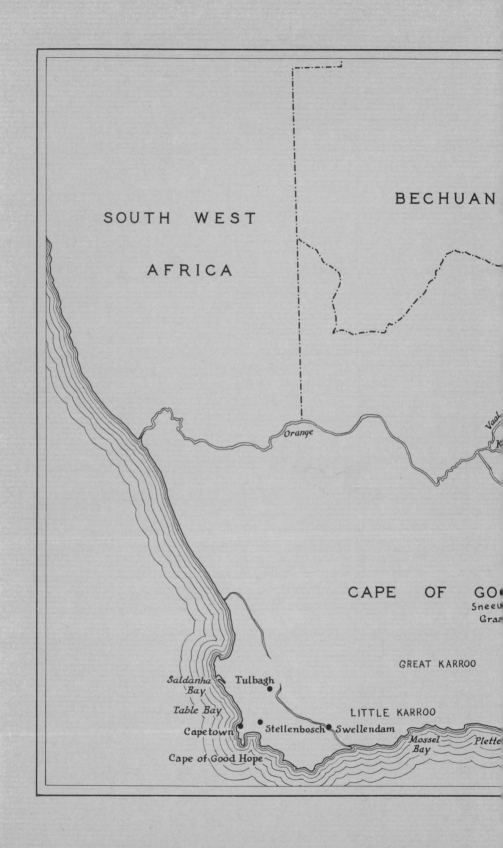